THE SOCIOLOGY
OF
RELIGION

An Explanation of the Unity
and Diversity in Religion

THE SOCIOLOGY OF RELIGION

An Explanation of the Unity and Diversity in Religion

Harold Fallding

University of Waterloo

McGRAW-HILL RYERSON LIMITED

Toronto • Montreal • London • New York
Sydney • Johannesburg • Mexico • Panama
Düsseldorf • Singapore • New Delhi
Kuala Lumpur • São Paulo

251655

ISBN   0-07-077640-7

Library of Congress Catalogue Card Number 73-10793

1 2 3 4 5 6 7 8 9 10 AP74 3 2 1 0 9 8 7 6 5 4

Printed and bound in Canada

CONTENTS

FIGURES

Preface

For a number of years now I have traversed the subject matter of this book in courses given to sociology students. I have been on a quest for understanding, for the intellectual problems raised by excursions into religion are quite formidable. Any understanding I may eventually have reached can be very largely attributed to the students, for they were always keen. I have, in addition, engaged in research on the sociology of religion, as I had opportunity. I find it necessary to hold research and the study of principles together, so that research can be significant and kept from turning into an exercise in method or an adjunct to someone's policy. To those who have assisted me in research, as much as to those who attended my lectures, I am indebted for many things I have learned.

It would never have been possible, however, to express my thoughts in finished form without a sabbatical year in which to bring this book to completion. I am grateful to the University of Waterloo for the liberality which enabled me to spend 1971-72 in Cambridge, and to the Canada Council for the Leave Fellowship that made the plan feasible. Throughout that year, my wife and I were both Associates of Clare Hall in the University of Cambridge, and we lived with our family in the leafy, sequestered quiet of Grantchester Meadows. The resources of the University Library were made available to me. Professor John Barnes and others connected with the Social and Political Science Committee showed a lively interest in what I was doing. The President of Clare Hall, Professor A. B. Pippard, drew us into the stimulating circle there. Not least of the benefits resulting from the association with Clare Hall, was the introduction to Mrs. Diane Pledger. It was she who typed the drafts and final manuscript of the book. It would scarcely have been possible to find better conditions for work.

No doubt the same question will be asked concerning this book that has been asked of other books. For whom was the book written? The answer is that it is intended for anyone who cares to benefit from the sociological approach adopted. The fact that it grew out of courses for sociology students does not mean that others beside them cannot use it. People in a variety of vocations have an occupational interest in the study of religion, many more a general educational interest. However, the book does maintain a strictly scientific approach. From time to time I have found myself under pressure to write something which people can apply directly in their various occupations, it being urged usually that this would be more relevant. But that is something I could not undertake to do.

There is, after all, a dash of egoism in the vogue to have everything relevant. For it assumes that the person speaking is in command of the most important perspective. But, as often as not, there is a larger perspective from which it can be asked how relevant is he. This more global perspective is precisely what the scientific approach can supply. The science of sociology has a greater contribution to make than to be relevant in any limited sense. It can satisfy intellectual curiosity about the nature of society itself, and so increase wisdom and understanding. In doing that, it supplies something that can find an application in any action the person undertakes, by making it more circumspect.

Cambridge   HAROLD FALLDING

June, 1972.

Introduction

To stand back and look at religion can be difficult. Yet it is possible to achieve a degree of objectivity. Whether they are for it or against it, many people are helpless victims of feeling when religion comes up for discussion. But that need not always be so. It is possible for the same person to *think* about religion with detachment and to *feel* about it passionately. I cannot believe that the way for a person to think with detachment is to extinguish feeling. What he needs is the same distance on himself as he has on others. For some people this self-transparency comes relatively easily, but for most people it could probably be improved with training. At any rate, the scientific study of religion that this book engages in assumes that stance to be possible.

To many people, the very idea of thinking about religion implies an intention to destroy it. Religion seems so hot a thing and thought a thing so cold. Some of them welcome the burial as much as some others fear it. Yet I would discourage the first as much as I would encourage the second. There is nothing necessarily destructive of religion in thinking about it. It is possible, on the contrary, that there may be some enhancement—although it would be mainly in the direction of an added sophistication. A person who thinks about religion may be neither more nor less religious because of it, but he should be more sophisticated about his position.

There is, to balance this expectation, another one which hopes that a vindication of religion will come from reflection on it. Since it is so prone to be knocked by detractors, how nice it would be to see some giant of the intellect spring to its defence. If, perhaps, he could prove it to be functional that would be ammunition in its cause. Yet it does not seem to me that the scientific study of religion can supply a defence any more than it can a burial. The most it can do in this direction is to show that we have to accept the fact of religion, since it occurs. But perhaps that is a defence in a way, though all unintended, since prejudice against religion may blind some people to its very existence.

The real benefit from the approach to religion I am attempting is, indeed, this kind of acceptance. The aim of science is explanation, and in so far as we have anything explained we are reconciled to it. So far as religion is concerned, there has certainly seemed to be much that needed explaining. Is it not one of the persistent conundrums of mankind? The root of the puzzle, of course, is the mixture of unity and diversity it presents. In that they are religious at all, different peoples are profoundly alike. But in that their religions differ they walk apart. The two popular ways of solving this puzzle seem to have been equally unsatisfactory. They suppressed recognition of one or other aspect. Either there was truth in one religion only, so that the radical difference of the others allowed their existence to be neglected, or there was truth in all of them, so that the differences between them could be neglected.

But the realism of the scientific approach demands that we suppress recognition of nothing. It is possible by this approach to recognize both the unity and diversity in religion and be reconciled to both. I believe that it is recent developments in the science of sociology in particular that enable us to see a necessity in religious phenomena that reconciles us to them. What was called "the comparative study of religion" was really a contribution to the sociology of it, in that it studied it as a social and cultural phenomenon. But its descriptive materials have to be grafted onto the materials and concepts of the systematic discipline for the problem of explanation to be fruitfully formulated. In this book I exploit what sociology now has to offer in this regard. From this foundation, the book will argue that the unity in religion can be traced to a concern for unity in experience, and its diversity to a concern for assurance under diverse conditions of life and knowledge.

Basically, the approach is a marriage of the approaches of Durkheim and Weber, but the book does illustrate the convergence on a similar understanding of religion on the part of a number of authors beside. For admission, there is no requirement that an author be a sociologist officially or professionally, yet his thought is made relevant by being sociological. Thinkers qualified in fields like literature, history, anthropology, philosophy and theology may make a contribution here. It would be an inverted perception, however, that saw this to make it an inter-disciplinary discussion. What is nearer the truth is that these scholars have turned sociologist because the sociological approach suits their problem. In this they simply illustrate how society has become the intellectual preoccupation of the age, just as the living organism became the intellectual preoccupation of a previous age. One net result of this body of modern thought about religion has been a radical relativization of it. "Religions pass, religion remains," might summarize the point of view attained. An examination of these authors thus yields both a guiding definition of religion and a means for organizing data on it in a comparative and developmental way.

The material of the book is divided into two parts. The four chapters of Part I are devoted to the unity found in religion, the four chapters of Part II to the diversity. In Chapter 1 we follow leads provided by Durkheim and Swanson to develop a sociological definition of religion. It is an inclusive definition which allows us to give recognition to the religious character of many phenomena besides those associated with churchgoing. At the same time, it enables us to see just how much religion is inherent in things that some would call religious surrogates—for instance, drug experience. Next, in Chapter 2, we turn to the question which, as we note, many modern minds have felt compelled to pursue vigorously. Is man orienting to a reality in religion or is he the victim of illusion? In my judgment, the disagreement in the answer reached is largely due to the different evaluation placed on the role of ideals. There is a point of view from which both sides can be seen to be testifying to a reality behind religion. It is a reality of ideals. Moreover, the thought reviewed shows a convergence on the definition of the religious object proposed in Chapter 1. There it is proposed that religion is man's response to the reality of the objectively existing ideal society. Chapters 3 and 4 show how men employ religion's five distinct vehicles of expression—doctrine, fellowship, ritual, ethic and experience—to affirm this reality.

In Part II three quite different sources of variation in religious phenomena are recognized. Each of them can account for a different part of the diversity shown by religion. The first is particularly interesting in its polarity, so a separate chapter is given to each end of the continuum. This source of variation is the growth in general acceptance of the religion. At one pole religion, as the sectarian protest of an alienated group, has virtually no general acceptance. This phase of growth is considered in Chapter 5. At the other pole, religion has earned acceptance and has won respectability—which is the phase of growth considered in Chapter 6. The second source of variation is the evolution of the vision of life's possibilities and the assurance of realizing them. Chapter 7 is devoted to this. The third source of variation is the extent to which religion is exposed to and incorporates in itself the advances of reason. The effects of this process, which is called "secularization," are considered in Chapter 8. Finally, the book concludes with a speculative Postscript. On the basis of the general understanding arising from the data and principles in the book, a comment is made on some aspects of religion's probable future.

Part One
UNITY

The Unity in Religion Explained by a Concern for Unity in Experience

Chapter 1

Religious Surrogates and Religion with and without the Capital

In *The Sociological Interpretation of Religion* Roland Robertson draws attention to the divergence in the way students of religion choose to define it.[1] Inclusive and exclusive definitions are both encountered. The inclusive view sees religion as a pervasive force in social life and is, for example, ready to include all the "isms" under it. Communism, fascism, humanism, nationalism, secularism and psychoanalysis as a way of life—these are religion no less than Christianity and Judaism. The exclusive view keeps the term "religion" for activities intentionally oriented to the supernatural or spiritual, and thereby employs it in its more colloquial and conventional sense.

The Inclusive View of Religion

To me the significant fact is that some sociologists are straining to stretch a concept here—although I would not necessarily want it stretched with complete abandon. But I believe it is possible to define religion in a way which is inclusive in a sense yet does not forfeit the essential reference to the supernatural or spiritual. It is important to appreciate by what strategy I would move towards inclusiveness. Rather than wanting to wash out the supernatural so that conventional religion is equated with the natural character of other things, I am suggesting that certain things not commonly recognized as supernatural have that character in the way conventional religion has. It all turns on a particular understanding of the supernatural or spiritual. I think the Durkheimian notion of the sacred is still the best lead we have on that, although it needs qualification and some further elaboration. In the course of this chapter I shall explain what I have in mind. First, however, I should illustrate this awareness that religion must be something more inclusive than conventional churchgoing and its correlates. I propose that we look at the following, since these are often invoked as evidence: (1) the totalitarian ideologies of nazism and communism; (2) psychoanalysis; (3) the psychedelic experience; and (4) certain revealing aspects of everyday activity. The distinction between a pervasive religiosity and a namable religious system—like Presbyterianism or Buddhism—has become popularly recognized. Since it is common to call the former "religion without the capital" and the latter "religion with the capital," I am adopting this usage.

The Totalitarian Ideologies

In his *Sociology of Religion* Glenn M. Vernon quotes a comment on communism from the *Christian Century* of October 22, 1952.[2] It runs:

> *Years ago observers of the growth of international communism began to see it as a secular religion, so closely approximating in its purposes the social concepts of Christianity that Archbishop Temple called it a "Christian heresy." The parallel between the development of the Christian institution and apparatus and the Communist institution and apparatus have often been pointed out. Think of almost any element supposedly distinctive in the Christian church—its inspired revelators, its inerrant dogma, its heresy trials and excommunications, its saints, its martyrs, its hagiology, its demonology, its pope, its hierarchy, its consecrated priesthood, its missionaries, its initiatory vows, its sacred shrines and ikons, its reliance on an apocalyptic future to compensate for a grim present—and communism, less than seventy years after the death of Karl Marx, already shows a counterpart.[3]*

As the author says, this is an observation of a kind commonly made. In 1937 Berdyaev had contended that communism's intense antagonism to Christianity was attributable to the fact that it was *de facto* a rival religion.[4] Hannah Arendt's analysis of communism is also informative and she treats it, together with nazism, as two species of the same genus, both of them movements inspired by totalitarian ideologies.[5] The term ideology has been used very variously, and we have to remember that Arendt's meaning is a special one. Ideologies, with this meaning, are a specifically modern phenomenon. They are world views which claim to have scientific validation and to hold the key to nature's entire unfolding. Given this clue, one can know the course of all that is going to happen in history by logical deduction, so there is no need to test belief against experience. They are totalitarian by virtue of their competence to pronounce on the entirety of things.

It is characteristic of their scientific modernity that the entirety they envision is nature and the development they envision that of all mankind within it. Neither movement could confine itself to the country of its origin because mankind was its cause.

They were never political movements merely. Also, the nature they envision is quite definitely a Darwinian nature of struggle, with survival guaranteed for the fittest and elimination for the remainder. In the case of nazism it is assumed that the fittest race will triumph, in the case of communism the fittest class. Terror rather than tyranny becomes the political technique, this being the appropriate means for cooperating with nature in its grand enterprise. Everyone has to be socialized to be either an executioner or victim, or each in turn, according to what nature may demand at any stage. Arendt suggests that meaning for anyone's life depends on his keeping in this current by being expendable in whatever way required.

Now I shall return to an examination of how much actual religion is implied by the resemblances to it in these movements. But for the moment I think we would probably be willing to accept the parallels as suggestive.

Psychoanalysis

In the case of psychoanalysis, however, the correspondence with religion is not so straightforward. As soon as we introduce it we hesitate: in what ways it is like religion or a substitute for it, is really not clear. Presumably, it is seen to have an affinity with religion on account of its offering a remedy for the sick mind. For Freud himself, and for other practitioners in the tradition, it is self-sufficient and needs no supplementation by religion.[6] Others, like Fromm in *The Sane Society*, aver that religion and psychotherapy each has something to offer the other—which, of course, immediately draws attention to their distinctness.[7] And, presumably, the outcome of that mutual instruction could only be a religion-indebted therapy and/or a therapeutically enlightened religion. There does not seem to be any intention in this enterprise of reducing either one to the other or of superseding both in an amalgam.

Fromm opts for the religion-indebted therapy. Edwin A. Burtt, who also advocates the interchange, opts for both.[8] Since he has this breadth of sympathy, it is worth looking closely at the outcome he would hope to see. In his study of the history and comparison of religions, *Man Seeks the Divine*, he directs his concluding comments to the question.[9] He thinks psychoanalytic therapy can bring five quite disparate benefits to religion. It can (1) correct the unhealthy dependence of followers on the religious founders; (2) supply a contemporary and more adequate terminology; (3) free believers from loyalty to specific and fixed sets of dogmas; (4) eliminate censoriousness from those who give counsel; and (5) remove prejudice by giving followers of different ideals insight into their choice. But psychotherapy must accept two facts concerning religion. (1) Religion does not accept the modest goal of simply doctoring the sick in order to get them back on the rails of culture: it presents a notion of ideal health which brings the culture under criticism. (2) A belief in divine reality is presupposed by the very nature of psychotherapy, since it is as much by personality maturation as by anything else that we seek to have divine reality disclosed.

Yet Burtt leaves us wondering why psychotherapy and religion have to accept anything from one another unless they choose. Since the Freud-like, Fromm-like and Burtt-like attitudes to therapy can all exist (and presumably others besides), it is apparent that its religious character is pretty equivocal. We could bracket with psychoanalysis every other brand of psychotherapy and recognize them for techniques for the limited goal of achieving a sufficient degree of mental health. They need then have no specifically religious character at all, any more than surgery has. One of the possibilities of this practice's assuming a religious character would be for someone to divinize the end sought. This, of course, is possible but not necessary. But if that is done we would then have a case of what I choose to call "cultism." In what sense that kind of behaviour is a religious expression is something we have to come to in due course. Yet we might take note of the fact that we are already countenancing the possibility that something can assume a religious character not because of what it is in itself but because of the importance it is given. Perhaps there is still another possibility involving psychoanalysis that ought to be recognized. In the opening paragraph mention was made of "psychoanalysis as a way of life." This could mean the cultism I am referring to. But if it is ever the case that psychoanalysis supplies a person with a whole totalitarian world view, and becomes his way of life in that sense, then it would be classifiable with the other totalitarian ideologies.

Before leaving this subject I would draw attention to what is possibly the focal subterfuge for the whole area. How justified is anyone in assuming that the mental health sought by the psychotherapist is the same thing as the salvation of soul sought through religion? To me, at any rate, it seems extremely likely that the correspondence between these two things is nothing more than that of an analogy. And that could still be so, even though in some of the twice-born—like the Bunyan and Tolstoy described by William James—the experience of salvation is *accompanied by* the integration of a formerly divided self.

The Psychedelic Experience

What amount of religion is there in the psychedelic experience? Savage epitomized the prevailing wonderment when he asked whether this betokened "Instant Grace, Instant Insanity or Instant Analysis."[10] Aldous Huxley and Timothy Leary, for two, have insisted that it was a religious experience and much too liberating to reject.[11] In *The Doors of Perception* in 1954 Huxley opined that mankind might come to adopt it as a surrogate for religion.[12] Yet it is but fair to remember that he did not himself equate the experience with, as he put it, "the realization of the end and ultimate purpose of human life: Enlightenment, the Beatific Vision."[13] He said:

> *All I am suggesting is that the mescalin experience is what the Catholic theologians call 'a gratuitous grace,' not necessary to salvation but potentially helpful and to be accepted thankfully, if made available. To be shaken out of the ruts of ordinary perception, to be shown for a few timeless hours the outer and the inner world, not as they appear to an animal obsessed with survival or to a human being obsessed with words and notions, but as they are apprehended, directly and unconditionally, by Mind at Large—this is an experience of inestimable value to everyone and especially to the intellectual.*[14]

A sober appraisal of psychedelic experience is presented by R. E. L. Masters and Jean Houston in their book *The Varieties of Psychedelic Experience.*[15] They state:

> *The materials here presented are based upon first-hand observation of 206 drug sessions and upon interviews with another 214 persons who have been volunteer subjects, psychotherapy patients, or who have obtained and taken the drugs on their own. Our own work, covering a combined total of more than fifteen years, has been very largely with two of the psychedelic drugs: LSD-25 and peyote.*[16]

It is instructive to notice what a variety of possibilities they find in drug experience. They emphatically aver that "an authentic religious experience may occur within the context of the psychedelic drug-state,"[17] yet they consider that the vast majority of experiences examined by them were not of this kind. They had to apply their own criteria for identifying cases that were, of course; for much of the difficulty springs from the fact that many subjects are disposed to call their experiences religious, often for no better reason than that they are exotic in comparison with everyday life.

For an experience to be accepted as genuinely religious Masters and Houston require three things: (1) There has to be an encounter with the Other Reality—a Presence which may be variously described, for example, as God, Spirit, Ground of Being, Mysterium, Noumenon, Essence, and Ultimate or Fundamental Reality. (2) There has to be an accompanying transformation of the self. (3) In most cases, at any rate, entry into this experience will come as entry into a fourth—and deepest—level of psychedelic experience: it will be the end of a progression through three antecedent levels. Masters and Houston call this fourth level "integral." Most of the psychedelic journeys of which they have knowledge terminate at some level above it. Forty-five per cent of their subjects claimed religious experience, but the authors reject a large number of these claims.

The most superficial level, called sensory, simply furnishes rich imagery, to which the subject attaches no meaning. The next, deeper, level, called recollective-analytic, is one where the subject may recover material from the unconscious and gain insight: it is the level on which psychotherapists typically range. The third level, called symbolic, is one where the self can be reorganized and reoriented, usually through the subject participating in mythic and ritualistic dramas. Although at this level the subject will typically draw his symbols from the religious traditions, the authors do not consider that the experience rates as a religious one. It is a level for religious language. They point out, as I have done above, that there can be analogues of religious experience in psychological reorganization.

Mystical experience is given separate treatment as a special kind of experience: the authors do not consider it religious *per se*. They accept Stace's distinction between extrovertive and introvertive mysticism.[18] Their consideration of the former is confined to cosmological mysticism, which is the commonly reported ecstatic vision of the inner life of the natural universe, and they say that almost one half of their LSD subjects experienced this. But they do not classify it as a religious experience since it is a privileged view which leaves the person uninvolved. Incidentally, this makes one case of the limited preternatural experience which Zaehner believed it impossible for drug-induced experience ever to exceed.[19] The evidence collected by Masters and Houston shows such experience to be far commoner than religious experience, but these authors diverge from Zaehner in believing that it is also possible for religious experience to occur.

Introvertive mystical experience they do consider religious. Out of 206 subjects there were six who achieved it. The authors accord it a place among religious experiences which is like the place given to the second blessing in the Pentecostalist traditions. It is not the life-reorienting experience of a conversion, but the "fullness of being filled with God," to employ a phrase actually used by one of their subjects and common to both mystical and Pentecostalist traditions. The transformation consequent on this experience is not so much a reorganization of the self as a suffusion of all aspects of practical life with deeper significance. It is not baptism but the transfiguration. All six of the subjects having it were over forty, of superior intelligence, well-adjusted and creative, and had actively sought it or at least made a study of it for some years before coming under the drug.

Finally, before leaving this book, we should note that in the course of it Masters and Houston draw attention to a cult-like development amongst certain drug advocates. Again we see the phenomenon of a practice being made to seem religious because of the importance given to it rather than because of what it is in itself. They refer to a tendency on the part of some to give religious status to drug experiences that are consciousness-expanding but stop short of religion.[20]

And yet—it is possible to view at least some *spontaneous* drug-taking in a different light. It can be seen as supplying the lunatic fringe of a pervasive movement of youth protest which has many other sides to it. Distinguishable within it is the activist arm of the New Left and an arm more directly concerned with values and the exploration of sensory, artistic, occult, mystical and sexual experience, and the cultivation of companionship, idleness and love—can we call it Hippieism? Their common focus of protest, according to Roszak, is their resistance to the tyranny of technocracy.[21] Alienated by this system, appalled by its dehumanization, they may throw obstructions into its machinery by the political technique of direct confrontation or may simply withdraw. The great attraction of the passivity of Zen, as eulogized by the movement's spokesmen Ginsberg, Kerouac and Watts, is that it brings one back to nature and plunges one in its current.[22] Here, for all its apparent archaism, are the germs of an ideology, and the same sound in a more strident note comes out in Leary.[23] For it is a far cry from Huxley to Leary. Leary explicitly champions something which he is compelled to call a *politics* of ecstasy, a *politics* of the nervous system. Roszak depicts his stance in the following way:

> *Leary has begun of late to assimilate the psychedelics to a bizarre form of psychic Darwinism which admits the tripper to a "new race" still in the process of evolution. LSD, he claims, is "the sacrament that will put you in touch with the ancient two million year old wisdom inside you"; it frees one "to go on to the next stage, which is the evolutionary timelessness, the ancient reincarnation thing that we always carry inside." After this fashion, the "politics of ecstasy" become the wave of the future, moving in mysterious ways to achieve the social revolution. When Leary is criticised, as he often is, for preaching a form of a-political quietism, his critics overlook the fact that his pitch to the young actually makes ambitious political claims.[24]*

If Roszak is right what Leary has come at length to preach is a totalitarian ideology which differs from nazism and communism only in the way that they differ from each other, namely, in the conquering élite. In the Darwinian struggle neither the superior race nor the superior class will triumph, but the beautiful people with the most uninhibited natures, including the most expanded minds. If, then, we are prepared to see drug-taking swallowed up in that greater movement, the question shifts: it is not whether through the use of drugs a religious experience is achieved but whether the totalitarian movement of which mind-expanding of all degrees is a part, has a religious character. The answer depends on what we decide about totalitarian ideologies in general.

Revealing Aspects of Everyday Activity

Now let us turn to the evidence of religion in everyday activity. I shall use some reflections of Eliade, Berger and Goffman to point up particular features of this, while Luckmann's work will illustrate it in a more general way.[25] I would also like to refer to some earlier work of my own in this connection and, finally, to make a brief reference to Simmel.[26]

Eliade is of interest because, as a historian of religions, he notes that the widespread profession of irreligion seems to be a peculiarly modern phenomenon. But in *The Sacred and the Profane* he shows himself distrustful of this, not being willing to believe that modern man can be as irreligious as he makes out.[27] What Eliade suggests has happened is a kind of lateral displacement of the modern's religiosity. He has slipped away from adherence to traditional religion only to re-enact its forms in his everyday secular life. Moderns, he suggests, may be found with quite a stock of camouflaged myths and degenerated rituals. They have countless mythical motives in their plays, novels and films, and rituals in New Year festivities, housewarmings, the "celebration" of marriages, births, promotions—and so on. The various ordeals by which one is admitted to more mature responsibilities in the course of a career are the modern's initiations. Through them he dies to an old life and is reborn to a greater one. Eliade does not really pursue the implications of such a state of affairs. He does not say whether moderns are making a religion that is more meaningful to them than the traditional ones, whether they have exchanged true religion for a counterfeit, or whether something else is transpiring. But he does at least suggest a persistence of the religious propensity that can make a man religious in spite of himself.

In 1969 Peter Berger wrote *A Rumor of Angels* to suggest that moderns might rediscover the supernatural by noting that some prototypical human gestures assume that life is lived in a larger context than the empirical world. Such gestures constitute signals of transcendence since they show our natural life to be the foreground of a larger life. They betray an ordinary, everyday awareness that we are, in the words of Enid Welsford, "uneasy in this world" because we are "at home elsewhere."[28] It could be claimed, then, that everyone, by virtue of being human, is a supernaturalist, whether or not he endorses theological propositions. Berger does not give a systematic or exhaustive treatment of these signals of transcendence, but asks us to consider five in illustration of his argument.

The first that he deals with is our propensity for order. Whenever we act to put our experience in order—when, for example, a parent assures an anxious child that everything is all right—it is on the assumption that this stance is vindicated by the nature of things. It really rests on a faith that reality is in order. But this exceeds what we have proof of in the visible world. The second signal of transcendence is the way in which, in play, we hold time in suspension. Since in play we create a fictional world with its own time, we are escaping from the tyranny of inexorably passing real time. By the clock it may be 11 A.M., but to that we are indifferent, Berger says. In the game we are playing it is the third round, the fourth act, the second kiss. If we actually realize joy we have escaped into eternity. (Berger does not make explicit to me why, but seems to suggest it is because joy is a state of complete engrossment in which the sense of passing time drops completely away.) The third signal is the way in which we redeem the intolerableness of any present situation by hope. We refuse to accept the intolerable present as final but set it in the context of a larger picture which is as yet completely hypothetical, but which would give it an acceptable meaning. The fourth signal is the way in which our moral sense, when categorically outraged by atrocities, believes they will be visited with damnation. Confronted with atrocities like the murder of children or the attempted extermination of the Jews we feel that nothing can extenuate or relativize the guilt, nor will human punishment be its only nemesis. The evil-doer has brought damnation on himself, having separated himself from a moral order that transcends the human community. The fifth signal is humour. Human situations strike us as humorous when they can be placed simultaneously in two independent series of events and so wear an aspect of incongruity. The fundamental discrepancy, from which all others are derived, is that between man and the universe. There is something in man—a kind of infinitude—which keeps him out of step with finite nature. So the comic reflects the imprisonment of the human spirit in the world.

Goffman does not write with any such intention of reinstating the supernatural in modern consciousness. I allude to his observations because they are so acute, and because of what they suggest. One thing that has arrested his attention is the way in which interaction is pervaded by ritual; but ritual, we generally assume, belongs to religion. Social interaction is no purely utilitarian affair, according to Goffman's vision of it, but is overlaid by another dimension. One of his most interesting commentaries on the fact is a paper entitled "On Face-Work." In it he reflects on the cooperation we engage in to save face for one another whenever we come into interaction. We are as concerned to save face for ourself as for the other, this double duty being imposed on both of us by social expectation anyway. No one must be allowed to drop out because of his feelings being hurt: the continuance of the operation is too precious. So a great respect and deference for everyone's feelings has to be ritually enacted. But it is the *sacred* self that this ritual, and these feelings, are all about, Goffman says. The "face" that has to be saved is the social self, the imposed image of something socially valuable that the person is supposed to have and which is sacred just because it is socially valuable. What would hurt his feelings is any implication, however oblique, that he is not entirely as serviceable as he is supposed to be. Goffman is saying that in the presence of another person, whose cooperation is indispensable to us, we are in the presence of the sacred. The ritual is indeed religious, a kind of worship. Not that we deify a concrete, fallible individual. He has worth because in society he is more than himself, if I may put it that way, and respecting his feelings is insisting that he continue to be so.

Luckmann thinks we do no violence to language if we call all culture-making and all socialization religion. He writes:

> The organism—in isolation nothing but a separate pole of "meaningless" subjective processes—becomes a Self by embarking with others upon the construction of an "objective" and moral universe of meaning. Thereby the organism transcends its biological nature.
>
> It is in keeping with an elementary sense of the concept of religion to call the transcendence of biological nature by the human organism a religious phenomenon. As we have tried to show, this phenomenon rests upon the functional relation of Self and society. We may, therefore, regard the social processes that lead to the formation of Self as fundamentally religious.[29]

Religion, thus understood, can have various social forms and the institutional specialization expressed in standardized doctrine and church organization is only one. It can happen, too, where that form has been in existence, that social change may cause the official doctrine to seem hollow. This is really what modern secularization has amounted to. The individual is then left to construct his own personal identity and his individual system of ultimate significance, selecting syncretistically from the variety of competing philosophies being peddled to him.

> Syndicated advice columns, "inspirational" literature ranging from tracts on positive thinking to Playboy magazine, Reader's Digest versions of popular psychology, the lyrics of popular hits, and so forth, articulate what are, in effect, elements of models of "ultimate" significance. The

models are, of course, non-obligatory and must compete on what is, basically, an open market.[30]

This retreat into the private sphere for finding life's meaning is the big religious advance and transformation of our time in Luckmann's view. We would be misled, he thinks, if we viewed it as an interregnum between one official religion and another. This *invisible* religion is precisely a new religious form and the end of official religion. For all the fact that it allows so much scope to private judgment, Luckmann is able to discern dominant themes in it for society as a whole. It takes such varied hues simply because individualism is at the heart of what is everywhere held sacred: the autonomy of the individual and his entitlement to self-realization and self-expression. Two things essential for this are given prominence: (1) scope for social mobility and (2) making a private matter of sexual morality. Accompanying it also is a new familism. This is different from the old familism of the time when kinship was important in the social fabric. The family assumes importance as the individual's private domain, with whose assistance especially he forges his world-and-life-view. Although he does not call it this, what Luckmann describes is suggestive of an ultra-Protestantism where the individual's salvation and his own exclusive authority to prescribe for it are made all.

In a paper circulated in 1964 and published eventually in 1967 in the *Sociological Quarterly,* I proposed a way of viewing the supernatural that has some resemblances to Berger's notion, especially to the idea that the appeal to order is tantamount to supernatural faith.[31] I stressed the person's awareness of a *cosmic* unity and wholeness.

For the sacred has to be regarded as supernatural or extra-ordinary at least in one sense. (Possibly it is the only sense, yet one sense would suffice to make it true.) Insofar as a wholeness is ascribed to the totality it is, like any whole, greater and other than the sum of its parts. God (if we may summarize all names of the object of worship under that term) is more than nature, society, and history: as the principle of unity in them He is their ground and creator. He is more than these, although never detachable from them. In the religious view, the ordinary events of the world make a meaningless tale told by an idiot, even in their complete sum, unless God is added to this again. However diversely or elliptically they approach it or dimly apprehend it, it is the principle of unity in the cosmos that all men are affirming in religion. Yet the character of this transcendent being stands revealed by the unity of any union men may experi-ence—wholly within nature, society, and history. Smaller wholes are epiphanies of the great and ultimate (and strictly speaking only) one: segments of it can be epiphanies also. For, as both Durkheim and Eliade have shown, single objects of the world—a rock, a tree—may seem to be invested with the being of the whole of it, when they are viewed in the aspect of their total immersion in it. At the same time the unity of God, to use Simmel's words, "documents itself in symbol and approximation in the organism and the social group." Christianity considers the integrity of a character, and the unity of the following it inspires, the supreme epiphany.[32]

I would take this presumed unity in all that envelops him to be the person's intellectual and emotional ground for belief. It gives rise, for example, to myth and dogma on the one hand and to mystical states on the other. But his actual experience of transcendence starts with his immediate involvements. In this same paper I say:

Yet, even while we acknowledge this, we may insist that anyone's experience of transcendence will originate in simple personal relationships, where the "we" is felt to have transcendence and constraint over the "I." Men discern, with differing degrees of real insight, that they belong to ever more inclusive (though ever more absent) fraternities which repeat the moral stringency that is to be plumbed in relationships like sonship and parenthood, marriage, partnership, and so on. The exhilarated unison of the ceremonial assembly scarcely supplies the original experience of transcendence. This is better viewed (as Durkheim in fact saw it) as an enacted symbol of the moral immensity. Insofar as that immensity is felt to excercise some constriction on immediate experience at any point, the transcendence of the sacred stands revealed: insofar as immediate experience loses its separateness by dissolving into this all-inclusive context, its immanence is revealed. It seems necessary to preserve transcendence, immanence, and revelation as properties of the sacred.[33]

In *The Sociological Task* in 1968 I aimed to find the appropriate anchorage for this notion of the supernatural in a systematic sociology. Naming it sacralization to oppose it dialectically to secularization, I suggested that sacralization is the full flowering of the process of institutionalization in that it is the attempt to infuse order and unity not into one department of life only, but into the whole of it.

It has not been customary to view sacralization as the full flowering of the process of institutionalization, yet this is how it should, I believe, be regarded. Institutionalization is essentially a two-sided process of keeping up a valued practice and building it into a whole. The practice is cut down to size even as steps are taken to perpetuate it, and it is thus legitimated. The religious quest is simply this same operation in its most inclusive reach. A people's postulation of a supernatural is an action of exactly the same kind as their pursuit of a political union or an integrated family. The supernatural they postulate is simply the wholeness in their total involvement with life, just as government is the wholeness in their political life and family unity the wholeness in their domestic life. . . . . That men repeatedly push through to the supernatural in their pursuit of meaning, and take it for their only guarantor of meaning, is simply a fact for sociology to receive. Some of the most sensitive nerves in the social organism can only be dissected when religion is accepted in this capacity. It is a pity so few moderns can take the relaxed attitude to religion that would let them accord it its proper character as a social fact. No doubt every religion has a theology, but not all questions concerning the nature of religion are theological. What face men may rightfully give to the supernatural is a theological question. What place they give to the pursuit of it and how and why they engage it are sociological questions. If there be any who do not concern themselves with the supernatural explicitly yet devote their lives to values, it comes to the same thing so far as "wholeing" is concerned. For values are ends men seek for their own sake, and anything set above the mundane in that way envelops it in a unitary meaning. Dogma or no, there is a beginning of religion in values. Conversely, the worship of holiness is not strictly distinguishable from the passion for wholeness in value commitment.[34]

The connections existing between values and religion still need a thorough dissection. But we will need to adopt some point of view on the question for the purposes of this book. Parsons is one who has seen values to be important both to the ordering of culture and to the constitution of religion, but he is somewhat vague about their inter-relationships.[35] He does not, at any rate, equate values with all of culture, but sees them to make the highest level of generality in culture. This conveys the idea of an organizing operation, which seems entirely necessary.

For my part, I would suggest that the connection between religion and values be viewed in the following way. First of all, they do have a certain independence of one another. A religion has a specific set of beliefs about man's total situation which can be valid only for a particular time span. When wider experience and new knowledge cause these beliefs to crumble people may either hold to values purely and simply or, lacking a vindication for them, may let go of them. A religion is thus a kind of elaborated underpinning devised to vindicate a commitment to values. It can be thought of as the source of man's morale in persevering in his commitment to ends which may themselves outlive any one particular system of vindication that can be given to them. Depending on the point of view adopted, either element can seem the more fundamental. There is no authority for pursuing values unless man's situation is such a one as religion describes. On the other hand, religion can give only a relatively adequate account of man's situation and is therefore time-bound, whereas values are more perennial. We may readily illustrate the distinction. To aim to realize social unity by expressing love in relationships is to be committed to love as a value. To believe that God is love is to find a religious vindication in the nature of reality for perseverance in this course.

While values are any ends men make self-sufficient, it is spiritual values which may assume a special importance for religion. In a much earlier paper I set out to show what we mean by spiritual values.[36] Briefly, I defined them as that class of *satisfactions* in which the person experiences something like exhilaration, release, euphoria or ecstasy, where he "loses himself," by shedding self-consciousness and self-concern through engrossment in a system of meaning. The system could be personal relationships in a fellowship of trust or a cultural symbolic system; most commonly, it is both of these together. It is a meaningful order because its parts, including the person, are reconciled in a unity—even, possibly, things that seem to be contradictory until you look more deeply. The idea of a relieving, supporting and controlling self-inclusion, as opposed to an anxious, isolating, resisting self-assertion, was central to it. There is a going out of oneself by involvement, absorption, commitment, immersion, surrender. Yet there is, of course, a vast reward for the self. By being a part, a member of the whole, the person internalizes that whole for his new self. If you want examples of this kind of experience that stop short of the religious experience of identification with the divinity, you can find them in patriotic loyalties and loyalty to family, kin and friends, in sociability and in games.

Now the pursuit of such values is quite pervasive in everyday life and much of it never invokes the name of religion. I was suggesting, in a way like Luckmann, that man's whole life is spiritual simply because his situation is social and cultural. I do not consider that religion is exhausted by this everyday manufacture of miscellaneous meaningful worlds, but I think it is important to give recognition to it. Later, in *The Sociological Task,* I suggested that delight in art is also a cognate experience, in that the person finds release in another world by surrender to shared conventions of fiction and form.

People can find "delight" in art and "fun" in games because they are the sort of creatures that can find "service" in institutions and "blessing" in religion. These are not the same things, by any means, but they are the same kinds of things. Their achievement rests on the same kinds of conditions. It is a precarious prize always, but it is a prize that

*is taken when a set of persons surrender to rules that im-
merse them in a system where they "lose themselves."*[37]

Finally, may I briefly remind you that Simmel is enlisted in
the contingent of those who have found religion, so to speak,
everywhere. The concern to find unity in one's social experience
is, for Simmel, the religious impulse in itself, and he considers
it to be universal. He takes this to be the constant substratum
of different religious systems, the thing that remains with men
when specific religious beliefs lose their hold over them. He
does not imply that this natural capacity for religion will serve
in place of religious belief systems. The implication is that we
might expect religious systems to be perennially renewed since
this capacity is constant. But there *is* an implication that there
is more religion in life than necessarily goes by the name, that
it is a diffuse, ubiquitous thing. Just as there can be economic
and power dimensions to every transaction between men, so
there can be a religious one. Our most intimate and most dis-
tant relationships can all have it.

> *To comprehend the origin and the continuance of religion
> it will be advantageous to unravel from the multiplicity of
> relations and interests which exist beyond or rather on this
> side of religion certain religious motives, those rudiments
> of that which achieved independence and self-reliance as
> "religion." I do not think religious emotions and impulses
> are expressed only in religion; they are experienced in mani-
> fold combinations upon many occasions, but religion exists
> as the acme and isolation of the religious element as an
> independent condition of life.*[38]

Insofar as a person is guided by his intuition of unity with that
with which he has to do, he is giving expression to this impulse.
Simmel calls it "piety." He does not, of course, mean the kind
of self-conscious religiosity for which we commonly use the
term. What he means is closer to what we mean when we say
that a person is "sympathetic" or, better still, "sincere"—or
even "nice." He means a spontaneous surrender to a non-utilitarian, non-self-seeking social constraint.

Religious Surrogate or Religion without the Capital?

With these evidences now before us, we can turn to the question
of how we are to classify a phenomenon that is not full-blooded
religion in the conventional sense. One thing we have to settle
quite early is whether it is a religious surrogate or true even
though uncapitalized religion. And we may take warning of how

much caution we have to exercise if we choose to call anything at all a religious surrogate. There are two problems here. The first is that we have to assume not one but several large questions already settled. We assume we know what religion is and we assume the thing we are talking about is not religion but that it functions in the same way. But this ushers in the second problem, for we have to be able to specify in what way or ways its function is the same. Rarely does a substitute function in every respect like the thing it replaces. And if it copies only one or several out of a large number of functions, it can be quite misleading to call it a surrogate for the original thing, since the term can suggest a general equivalence.

I am reminded of William James' eulogy of the religious truth in alcohol in which he presents it as a religious surrogate.[39] He states:

> The sway of alcohol over mankind is unquestionably due to its power to stimulate the mystical faculties of human nature, usually crushed to earth by the cold facts and dry criticisms of the sober hour. Sobriety diminishes, discriminates and says no; drunkenness expands, unites, and says yes. It is in fact the greater exciter of the Yes function in man. It brings its votary from the chill periphery of things to the radiant core. It makes him for the moment one with truth. Not through mere perversity do men run after it. To the poor and the unlettered it stands in the place of symphony concerts and of literature; and it is part of the deeper mystery and tragedy of life that whiffs and gleams of something that we immediately recognize as excellent should be vouchsafed to so many of us only in the fleeting earlier phases of what in its totality is so degrading a poisoning.[40]

Alcohol is seen as inducing the exhilarating, liberating aspect of religious consciousness I have referred to, and to that extent one would willingly call this use of it a religious surrogate. Yet there are many functions served by religion that alcohol leaves completely unsupplied, such as a comprehensive world view, petitionary prayer, guidance, the baptism of infants and the burial of the dead—to name a very random few. Clearly, if we speak of surrogates at all we must specify the function in which there is equivalence.

On the other hand, should we want to classify anything as not a religious surrogate but true though uncapitalized religion, we will need to have a definition of religion sharp enough to discriminate it yet broad enough not to exclude it. In either case, to dispel the disorder and confusion that threaten to engulf this entire field of study we need a definition of considerable sophistication and subtlety. Taking my lead from Durkheim I will now attempt to produce this. That done, we will see how the various phenomena we have been considering are to be arranged relative to one another. But what definition can sociology supply?

Defining Religion Sociology:
In the Wake of Durkheim and Swanson

It seems to me that Durkheim isolated the differentiating thing about religion in a very satisfactory way.[41] For his position allows us to hold a great diversity of phenomena together, without diminishing the fact that there is something that marks religion off from all other human activities, making it *sui generis*. He says we might be unnecessarily restrictive if we required a belief in personal gods or spirits in order to say we had religion, but that religion exists where men make a categorical distinction between two discontinuous, incompatible realms of experience, the sacred and the profane. He points out that men may formulate this distinction in terms of a distinction between a transcendent and material realm, or in some different way. But, in any case, I do not think we misrepresent Durkheim if we take him to mean that it is *always* a distinction between the natural and supernatural as this is most meaningfully made by ourselves. I am set on maintaining this even though Durkheim rejects that way of formulating it. It is only because he construes "the supernatural" as meaning the bizarre and miraculous that it seems to him an inappropriate formulation. But that is not the sense in which I think we use the word most meaningfully. We use it rather for a realm of influences or forces that is qualitatively different from what we experience as "nature"—which is exactly what Durkheim means by the sacred. When he discusses the transcendence of the totemic principle and, indeed, that of every religious force, he stresses that people do not find the sacred character of objects in their intrinsic properties but in something added: "The world of religious things is not one particular aspect of empirical nature; *it is superimposed upon it.*"[42]

It is this, then, that I would accept from Durkheim as distinguishing religion—the freedom of being able to go into a second and qualitatively different world from that which is given naturally in ordinary experience. This sacred world, this circle furnished maybe with sacred beings and objects, will vary in diameter according to the religion. Durkheim states:

> *That is how Buddhism is a religion: in default of gods, it admits the existence of sacred things, namely, the four noble truths and the practices derived from them.*[43]

It does not seem to me to be stretching things to say that these immutable truths and rules supply a Buddhist supernatural, even though no personal divinity is envisaged.

Anyone who has equated the idea of a supernatural with that of personal divinity may think it disingenuous to take commitment to life-guiding truths for a case of supernatural faith. But this does not seem unjustified to me. I think we must consider *super*natural any influence for which empirical proof is not given in nature but by which men nevertheless acknowledge themselves constrained. Truths of life, like the four noble truths of Buddhism, are clearly *super*natural in this sense. Their validity and authority cannot be proven and one can only commit oneself to them in faith. At the same time, to the believer in them they are acknowledged imperatives. If one should fail to be conformed to this *way* one would fail to find fulfilment. They also provide the added depth of freedom I referred to. For the four noble truths are believed to be true eternally and are thus beyond contingency.

It is, of course, interesting to ask why men ever come to conceive of such things as truths of life to which they long to be conformed. But that they do this very commonly we may acknowledge right away. Every time we observe that men choose to pursue values we acknowledge that they are doing the same kind of thing as the Buddhist who follows the four truths. They are ascribing unconditional worth to something, and without being able to adduce proof that this is warranted. Now I cannot see how belief in a supernatural ever entails anything more than this, so far as adding a sacred dimension to life goes, even if one ascribes personality to the principle of worth. Indeed, what makes it possible for anyone to find a realm of experience that is incommensurable with the realm of ordinary experience is the simple fact that we distinguish ends from means. Anything made an end in itself has a status categorically different from that of the instrumental things pressed into its service: it is sacred, they profane.

Durkheim considers that the source of our experience of the sacred is society. He was the originator of this idea and, as is often the case, the new idea begged for an explication and qualification that could not be given to it all at once. Some lasting ambiguity in Durkheim's thinking about it makes it necessary for me to say in what respect I can entertain the notion. When that is done I want also to show that what is viable in Durkheim's view is also enshrined in Swanson's view of religion.[44]

On the face of it, it seems that Durkheim is wanting to say that the sacred and the social are identical, that divinity is society. There have been followers and critics alike who have been willing to take that bald statement for Durkheim's message: "God is society worshipping itself."[45] Yet this would *not* be consistent with the way Durkheim characterizes the sacred, if we understand by "society" in that statement *nothing but* the empirically knowable "society" of everyday. The society given directly in ordinary experience cannot be sacred to us. It is not only because it is riddled with imperfections either—but also because it is directly knowable. Durkheim explicitly considers the particular objection that an imperfect, actual society could not inspire religious veneration, and that it is perhaps the ideal society that he is thinking does this. It is extremely important to notice in what way he answers. He says that to make a distinction between the real and the ideal in this matter is to make a false dichotomy. For the ideal which a society forms of itself is part of its own reality and, in any case, this ideal is cradled by its imperfect actualities. The very persons who perpetrate society's imperfections are the ones who conceive an alternative ideal for their action at the same time. Calling this ideal world a new world, he says: "For society has constructed this new world in constructing itself, since it is society which this expresses."[46]

Note well, then, that Durkheim is not found to deny that an ideal of society is necessary for the generation of religion. He accepts this, but insists that even ideals of society have a social reality of their own. Yet once he makes this the issue Durkheim really diverges from the question posed. Can I emphasize this? Because he diverges he leaves us without an answer. The question he had begun to take up was not whether social ideals have a social reality, but whether or not it is these *exclusively* that generate the religious sentiment. What he does at least make clear, though, is that this idealization *added,* the emergence of this "new world," is absolutely essential to religion.

> *Therefore it is necessary to avoid seeing in this theory of religion a simple restatement of historical materialism: that would be misunderstanding our thought to an extreme degree. In showing that religion is something essentially social, we do not mean to say that it confines itself to translating into another language the material forms of society and its immediate vital necessities. It is true that we take it as evident that social life depends upon its material foundation and bears its mark, just as the mental life of an individual depends upon his nervous system and in fact his whole organism. But collective consciousness is something more than a mere epiphenomenon of its morphological basis, just as individual consciousness is something more than a simple efflorescence of the nervous system. In order that the former may appear, a synthesis sui generis of particular consciousnesses is required. Now this synthesis has the effect of disengaging a whole world of sentiments, ideas and images which, once born, obey laws all their own. They attract each other, repel each other, unite, divide themselves, and multiply, though these combinations are not commanded and necessitated by the condition of the underlying reality. The life thus brought into being even enjoys so great an independence*

that it sometimes indulges in manifestations with no purpose
or utility of any sort, for the mere pleasure of affirming
itself. We have shown that this is often precisely the case
with ritual activity and mythological thought.[47]

Is God society worshipping itself? Clearly, whether this is
Durkheim's view depends on what we mean by "society" when
we make the assertion. It is *not* his view if we mean by "society"
nothing but the palpable activity and interaction that unfolds
before our gaze.

While Durkheim allows the worshipping church to call its
god god, he does not think the observing sociologist should do so.
The student of society should be hard-headed enough to see it is
only society that is constraining men. He says that in trying to
account for the source of moral constraint some theorists have
postulated it came from god. But he says that *we* can see it comes
from society—and so, he says, between god and society it is
necessary to choose. Here the issue is starkly enough put! Pre-
senting us with the challenge of this choice certainly seems to be
giving complete equivalence to divinity and society. But a second
later, with characteristic ambiguity, Durkheim goes on to say:
"I can only add that I myself am quite indifferent to this choice,
since I see in the Divinity only society transfigured and symbolically expressed".[48] If they *are* equivalent, he now says, choice
between them is not possible. The choice is not between two
things but between the two names for the one, apparently. And
yet, not really that either. They are not exactly equivalent.
Divinity is not society simply, but society "transfigured and
symbolically expressed." What aspect of society is that? Since it
is not "society" altogether unqualified that men worship, one is
tempted to follow convention and name this reality "God" to
give it a distinguishing name. Since Durkheim does not take us
as far as we need to go we must go forward on our own. I want
to suggest a way through these ambiguities, a way that leads via
Swanson.[49]

Like Durkheim, Swanson maintains that the supernatural to
which men turn is a reality and that it is constituted by society
in some sense. His special contribution in *The Birth of the Gods*
is in specifying the sense. Let us see on what he narrows down.
He is convinced that "social relationships inherently possess the
characteristics we identify as supernatural."[50] But he is just as
emphatic that we have to be more discriminating than to say
simply that. He adds: "Nevertheless a critic would be right in
saying that . . . groups, as such, are not worshipped or venerated
as supernatural. What features are associated with them that
provoke the notion of supernature?"[51]

Swanson knows that social relationships and groups are never
solely made up of what meets the eye, of those activities of
which we may experience the passing flow, whether as partici-

pants or observers. What is enacted between people is the result of shared expectations between them concerning the interaction that will be rewarding. Sociologists commonly accept the shared expectation as a feature of social interaction, of course; but it has not been common to locate the experience of the supernatural in it, which is what Swanson does.

Insofar as shared ideals of action crystallize; insofar, that is, that there is some purposive resultant of the diverse interests involved, Swanson says we may witness the emergence of individualized divinities. These divinities are accepted as the guardians and directors of right action: men acknowledge their constraining powers. Insofar as the expectations are diffuse and fluid they are simply felt as impersonal power, a sort of *mana*. Both expressions of the supernatural are commonly found. Swanson refers to the former as the "constitution" of the group, a term very happily chosen. It is not a formally written constitution, like that of the U.S.A., and where a constitution like that does exist, the constitution Swanson has in mind will be something more inclusive in any case. Like every divinity men have worshipped, it is much vaguer, probably always to some extent hidden in shadow. But for any group of a kind Swanson calls "sovereign," a more or less defined profile of divinity can emerge. By sovereign groups he means those having some independent jurisdiction in their members' lives. In most societies the family, for instance, is a sovereign group in this sense, and, in the U.S.A., the national state and the separate states of the union. In other societies, clans, chiefdoms and extended families supply examples. The second, less individualized expression of the supernatural Swanson calls the "primordial conditions" of interaction.

The supernatural that men experience, then, is their experience of the constitutions of their sovereign groups and the primordial conditions of their collective life in general. Swanson considers that religion springs from the former and magic from the latter. I would not endorse a separation along this line, for I think that the unindividualized power is recognized in religion too. I would differentiate between religion and magic by the attitude taken to the power. Insofar as men submit to it they approach it religiously, and insofar as they try to manipulate it they use it magically. But apart from this, I would accept Swanson's position in its main outline.

Ancestral spirits supply an example of Swanson's individualized divinities. They personify the constitution of the kinship organization, where that makes a sovereign group of the society. High gods like Yahweh of the Israelites, Earthmaker of the Winnebago, and the supreme beings of the Nuer and Azande, supply other examples. Swanson sees hierarchical order appearing among gods when it appears among groups. There is a high god when there are at least three different *types* of sovereign group (kingdom, village and nuclear family for instance), one of which is supreme in that it undertakes to resolve the diversity among the others and weld them into a unity. The high god personifies the constitution of the sovereign group exercising supremacy.

We see how Swanson adds a precision that Durkheim failed to afford us. Yet even here I want to make qualifications. The supernatural could be the objectively existing constitutions and the objectively existing primordial conditions—or it could be what men suppose them to be. There is a distinction between the objective reality and men's knowledge of it. If the supernatural is simply men's knowledge of these things, men do indeed make their own gods. But if the supernatural is some ideal imperative in the constitution of social relationships which men grope after and endeavour to interpret in their shared expectations, they may be said to make, not their gods, but an image or picture or doctrine of their gods. This will be a more or less faithful representation of the reality; yet even though it distorts the reality, that will still have its own independent character. Now it is only in this understanding of what Swanson's position *could* be taken to imply that I would care to accept it. Ultimately, I would want to say, the supernatural is constituted by the necessity men are under to come together in cooperation if their needs are to be supplied; by the fact that they are made social in the profoundest meaning of that word.

Can I emphasize this? I do not take the shared expectation to be the divinity that constrains: I take the shared expectation to be the doctrine of it. Distinguishing thus between the reality and belief about it preserves a great potentiality—a sort of open-endedness—for the supernatural powers, quite beyond that which men may actually ascribe to them. Yet, even so, this *is* a characteristic commonly allowed to the supernatural by religious men themselves. It is common to give up when in pursuit of the supernatural's character. God cannot be pinned down by their own knowledge of him, religious men will say. He is lost in ineffable light, moves in a mysterious way, is past finding out. He must be left to himself. As the powers constraining men make themselves specifically felt, divinity may indeed be revealed to them, but with a margin of darkness. Even a religion like Christianity, which makes much of the fact that God has not left men in darkness but has made himself known, insists that at best he is seen "through a glass darkly." Taking this view allows that there will be an objective reality behind religion, but that a particular system of belief does not necessarily interpret it accurately or completely.

When I go on now to speak of the *ideal* personal relationship or the *ideal* society, it is to the power of this objective constraint I will be referring. Lest the spectre I have exorcised rise at once to haunt us, may I make the same kind of distinction again? Very commonly, when we talk of "ideals" we mean the inventions of the mind. "Ideal" personal relationships and "ideal" societies of that kind do also exist, but they are the shared expectations. For some purposes they can be bracketed with the objective ideal which they seek to represent, and the two treated as one. But we have to remember their separate existence. It is the objective ideal society—and it alone—that I take to be the supernatural constraint to which men respond. This would be my answer to the question Durkheim answered so incompletely. This ideal is a reality, a most exacting reality, and not a dreamed-up fiction. It goes *before* the activity that unfolds in social life and has a shaping influence on it.

And here, not without a certain excitement, I want to diverge for a moment to draw attention to a parallel. It is extremely interesting to me that this idea of the supernatural, which is reached along a sociological path, accords so well with the idea of it that William James reached along a psychological path.[52] James concluded that the supernatural to which the religious man responds is a kind of continuum with a near and further side, the near side of it being his own subconscious self. But of the further side James said this:

> *The further limits of our being plunge, it seems to me, into an altogether other dimension of existence from the sensible and merely 'understandable' world. Name it the mystical region, or the supernatural region, whichever you choose. So far as our ideal impulses originate in this region (and most of them do originate in it, for we find them possessing us in a way for which we cannot articulately account), we belong to it in a more intimate sense than that in which we belong to the visible world, for we belong in the most intimate sense wherever our ideals belong. Yet the unseen in question is not merely ideal, for it produces effects in this world. When we commune with it, work is actually done upon our finite personality, for we are turned into new men, and consequences in the way of conduct follow in the natural world upon our regenerative change. But that which produces effects within another reality must be termed a reality itself, so I feel as if we had no philosophic excuse for calling the unseen or mystical world unreal.*
>
> *God is the natural appellation, for us Christians at least, for the supreme reality, so I will call this higher part of the universe by the name of God. We and God have business with each other; and in opening ourselves to his influence our deepest destiny is fulfilled. The universe, at those parts of it which our personal being constitutes, takes a turn genuinely for the worse or for the better in proportion as each one of us fulfills or evades God's demands. As far as this goes, I probably have you with me, for I only translate into schematic language what I may call the instinctive belief of mankind: God is real since he produces real effects.*[53]

It is because of the real constraint of the ideal that religion is a supernatural or transcendent thing. Even a religion of materialism or purely natural good would be a supernatural religion in this sense of the word. It is made that because it has a transcendental reference to an ideal state of affairs. Ahead of that which is, is placed that which should be and could be, and it is the discontinuity between these that introduces the profound sense of displacement and disquiet that distinguishes the religiously awakened. There is no difference between an ethereal heaven and a material utopia—so far as their being constitutive of religion is concerned. Both of them are out of this world. There is no difference between an ideal conformity to the law written into nature or history and an ideal conformity to the will of God—so far as their being constitutive of religion is concerned. Both of them surpass the fulfilment we see actualized.

But it is not enough to stress transcendence. I must make explicit two other features that the position being taken implies for the definition of religion. The second feature is comprehensiveness—a cosmic purview. For the whole of life calls for an ideal programming. Each particular relationship or sphere of action could have its divinity or they could all come under the one, but in either case they will all need attention. However, when I say this is implied, I do not mean that any concrete society will have an actual religion exhibiting this in perfection. I merely mean it will exhibit this interest in comprehensiveness in principle, and that it will be relevant to ask how far and what ways it has actually been worked out.

It seems to be the challenge religion faces to countenance *everything* that constrains and to view these constraints in relation to one another. It can, therefore, be particularly conscious of three things: (1) of life's multiplicity or many-sidedness; (2) of the felt contradictions, discrepancies and antinomies of life; and (3) of life's extremities—the individual's beginning and end and those of the universe. It may seek, though not necessarily successfully, to find a reconciliation for the incompatibles. The community of religious souls may be considered to have engaged in an operation analogous to that of the physicist who seeks to find the resultant of multiple and diversely directed forces. A variety of achievements have been the result of this unifying effort: a monotheistic belief system, for example; mystical union with the divinity; values, which are very general principles of wide application; a comprehensive life-ethic; ritual for the full life cycle.

The third feature that has to be made explicit I will call "closure." Religious truth is not decided by discussion and the babble of irreverent, egoistic private opinions is silenced by the authority of revelation. All teachings are to be tested for orthodoxy. This is the aspect of religion that most alienates the scientific temper, yet it seems to be indispensable to religion and there is no reason to think it will disappear. Religious beliefs cannot be entertained tentatively as hypotheses for testing: they have to be assumed dogmatically as the grounds for action. I would presume that this is precisely because they issue from that objective constraining ideal that men sense to be the best real possibility for their life. The initiative is out there and what is known in religion is received. If men held their religious beliefs purely as hypotheses for testing they would be paralyzed in a world that requires good morale for action, and they could languish and die as their needs went unsupplied. In sum, then, the three distinguishing criteria I propose to use are these: transcendence, comprehensiveness and dogmatic closure. But one last thing remains to be done before we apply these criteria to the material we have reviewed. This is to distinguish cultism from true religion.

It is a fact that any religion is disposed to charge any other with idolatry, thereby imputing a cultic character to it. But this does not plunge us into bottomless relativism. It does not mean that sociology cannot have its own criterion of false religion, and it is extremely important that it should have, since this is a constantly occurring thing and the war between it and true religion a constant war. Perhaps the simplest approach is to recall how in everyday life a person can be accused of making a cult out of something or making a religion of it. Usually, he is not being advised to give it up altogether but to cease giving it an exaggerated importance. This ascription of undue importance, the worship of something not worthy of it, is the essence of what I mean by cultism.

When we look at the practice of art as a social institution we find that not only is provision made for the production of works of art, provision is also made for their evaluation. The same occurs in science. It is recognized that not everything that purports to be art or science will in fact be so and the unwary have to be warned. Well, the same is also true in religion, of course, and a large part of religious life consists of distinguishing the true from the false in its own domain. Religious people can be highly practised in making these discriminations. They are found saying that Satan is very deceptive and that they have been seduced into worshipping things close to the divinity rather than the divinity. They may confess, for example, that they have gone astray because they have worshipped the church, or the Bible, or even their experience of God or knowledge of God, instead of worshipping God. This not only highlights the importance of a line between the sacred and the profane, it highlights the importance of knowing and remembering *exactly* where it lies. On the far side, in the sacred, lies the ideal only. Nothing actualized has that same character or is entitled to that same veneration.

Cultism, then, is ascribing sacred status to anything in the profane, actualized world. *Within the culture, everybody knows* that same worshipped thing in a different character since it is part of the furniture of their mundane world. The great prevalence of this setting up of systems of false worship shows a great deal about man's religious need, of course. It is as though he has to organize his disorderly experience somehow by hanging it all on a peg outside of itself. If necessary to get the job done, he will make something from the inside act as if it were outside. He will make it transcendent, all-embracing, authoritative. He will force a sense of significance into life by worshipping, it may be, a lover, a career, a sport, a talent, a drug-state, health of body or mind, science, civilization, empire.

Classification of the Material Reviewed

What now are we to make of the material we reviewed in the first part of the chapter? It seems fairly obvious that the totalitarian ideologies exhibit all three criteria. They qualify on all counts to be religions in the same way as Christianity and Judaism are. It might be better to treat them directly as that and not make them out to be surrogates of religion. Nazism and communism are religions. But although I would be willing to say this, I would not agree with people who speak of them as "political religions" and invoke them as proof that you can have politics for your religion, or that political and religious considerations are really the same, or at least equivalents or alternatives. I am wanting to call them religions because they exceed political concerns and glow with a supernatural light. Of course, like Arendt, I am thinking of them as very pervasive movements in thought and society and not simply as the forms of government or political strategies these produced.

As for the other "isms" one is never sure how inclusively such terms are applied, but it seems possible for "humanism," "nationalism," and comparable terms, to be used with the same content of sacredness that we found in nazism and communism —in which case they designate religions. In contrast to this, however, there does not seem to be anything genuinely religious about psychoanalysis as a therapy. It is properly a technical, instrumental matter like plumbing and surgery. On the other hand, if the sufficiency of mental health it seeks is made sacred, it can provide the occasion for cultism. Yet if it is made to serve as a totalitarian ideology it makes a religion.

Regarding the psychedelic experience, we saw that this could present itself in four different aspects: as an experience that is non-religious, as a religious experience, as a non-religious experience given cultic significance, and as an ingredient of a totalitarian counter-culture. This last we can now, of course, accept as religion. Concerning the religious experience purely and simply, some comment is needed. First we recall that two kinds of experience were possible: first and second blessing we might call them. We also recall that it was common for the latter to come to people with a long preparation having nothing to do with drugs. But the important consideration is this one: How much religion is there in a religious experience? Although that may sound a silly question it is not.

If religion be defined in the way I have chosen to define it, it involves much more than one or two experiences, even if these are repeated. It is an involvement with the collectivity and its cosmos and entails moral discipline and intellectual belief, both of them many-sided. There is a sense in which no experience is entitled to be called religious except insofar as it occurs in that context. But, leaving that objection aside, if we do accept the experiences in question as religious we can only accept them as *elements* of religion. What the psychedelic record points to is that some of the elements of which religion is made can crop up at random in our experience. And this same observation has relevance for interpreting the more diffuse, everyday religiosity of which our other authors speak. That there can be a random and even unsolicited occurrence of religious elements is illustrated in Eliade's everyday enactment of religious forms; Berger's signals of transcendence; Goffman's interaction ritual; Luckmann's culture and socialization; my own meaning-making through institutionalization and sacralization, and meaning-finding through spiritual values; Simmel's piety. Perhaps if we are prepared to talk of religious elements we can avoid talk of religious surrogates altogether, with its attendant snags.

All of that, I take it, is religion without the capital. Giving recognition to it does not seem to me to be suggesting that religion can do as well or better without its capital. But it provides a sociological vision of man's religious capacity that shows it to be more diffuse and more perennial than any one religious system with its capital R. To build such systems is, of course, essential for man's religious need. No one imagines that our capacity for music will serve in place of symphonies or our capacity for language in place of plays and poetry. It would be just as absurd to expect our capacity for religion to serve in place of a religion. Yet in contrast to the religious capacity, a religion with the capital is a dated phenomenon, only compelling until widening experience makes it obsolete. Should he be present at its passing, the sociologist at any rate need not be so naive as to suppose that man's religiosity has passed with it or that new capitalized religion will never come again.

When Luckmann says there will be no more official religion I do not take him to mean that henceforth there will only be religion without the capital. It is under culture and socialization that uncapitalized religion receives attention from Luckmann. When he analyzes the contemporary scene he moves to another topic, and his observation is that capitalized religion now wears an unfamiliar form. Whether the form of religion most recently made obsolete has been superseded by the ultra-Protestant kind of invisible religion of Luckmann's account I scarcely know. It would hardly be surprising to find that it has, since cultural offspring, like their human counterparts, have a habit of scandalizing their parents by wholeheartedly applying what they were taught. Protestantism *has* taught that the individual alone will know what is true for him to believe and right for him to do. On general grounds, besides, one would expect an increasing individualism to be the direction of development.

Yet greater individualism is the fruit of greater social responsibility accepted, and one would expect to see it accompanied by public affirmations of that ever more demanding common duty. You would hardly expect to see religion generated in the everyman-for-himself atmosphere where each one clamoured for self-realization. You would get it, though, where men took the constraining ideal of love to mean that each must work as much for his brother's individually tailored self-realization as for his own. But a religion acknowledging the authority of that ideal could not be private or invisible, it seems to me—except, perhaps, in a twilight hour of unheralded birth. In its fullness, it would have to have its own publicly shared worship, doctrine and ethic.

Notes, Chapter 1

1. Roland Robertson, *The Sociological Interpretation of Religion*, Oxford: Basil Blackwell, 1970.
2. Glenn M. Vernon, *Sociology of Religion*, New York: McGraw-Hill, 1962, p. 57.
3. *Christian Century*, Vol. 69, Oct. 22, 1952, p. 1215.
4. Nicolas Berdyaev, *The Origin of Russian Communism*, London: Geoffrey Bles, The Century Press, 1937.
5. Hannah Arendt, *The Origins of Totalitarianism*, London: George Allen & Unwin Ltd., 1967.
6. Sigmund Freud, *New Introductory Lectures on Psychoanalysis*, New York: W. W. Norton & Co. Inc., 1933; *An Outline of Psychoanalysis*, New York: W. W. Norton & Co. Inc., 1949.
7. Erich Fromm, *The Sane Society*, New York: Holt Rinehart and Winston, 1955.
8. Edwin A. Burtt, *Man Seeks the Divine, A Study in the History and Comparison of Religions*, New York: Harper & Row, 1964.
9. *Ibid.*, pp. 6-86.
10. Cited in Willis W. Harman, "The Issue of the Consciousness-Expanding Drugs," *Main Currents in Modern Thought*, Vol. 20, No. 1, Sept.-Oct. 1963, p. 6.
11. Aldous Huxley, *The Doors of Perception and Heaven and Hell*, Harmondsworth: Penguin Books in association with Chatto & Windus,

1959; Timothy Leary, *High Priest*, New York: World, 1968; *The Politics of Ecstasy*, New York: Putnam, 1968.

12. Aldous Huxley, *op. cit.*, pp. 51-61.
13. Aldous Huxley, *op. cit.*, p. 60.
14. Aldous Huxley, *op. cit.*, p. 60.
15. R.E.L. Masters and Jean Houston, *The Varieties of Psychedelic Experience*, London: Anthony Blond Ltd., 1967.
16. *Ibid.*, p. 5.
17. *Ibid.*, p. 257.
18. Walter Terence Stace, *Mysticism and Philosophy*, Philadelphia: Lippincott, 1960.
19. R.C. Zaehner, *Mysticism, Sacred and Profane, An Inquiry into some Varieties of Praeternatural Experience*, Oxford: The Clarendon Press, 1957.
20. R.E.L. Masters and Jean Houston, *op. cit.*, p. 259.
21. Theodore Roszak, *The Making of a Counter Culture, Reflections on the Technocratic Society and Its Youthful Opposition*, Anchor Books edition, New York: Doubleday & Co. Inc., 1969.
22. See, for example, Allen Ginsberg, *Howl and Other Poems*, San Francisco: City Lights Books, 1956; *Empty Mirror*, a Totem/Corinth Book, 1961; *Kaddish and Other Poems*, 1958-1960, San Francisco: City Lights Books, 1961; *Planet News 1961-1967*, San Francisco: City Lights Books, 1968; Jack Kerouac, *Satori in Paris*, New York: Grove Press, 1966; Alan Watts, *The Way of Zen*, New York: Pantheon, 1957; *Psychotherapy East and West*, New York: Pantheon, 1961; *This Is It*, New York: Collier Books, 1967.
23. Timothy Leary, *op. cit.*
24. Theodore Roszak, *op. cit.*, *p.* 167.
25. Mircea Eliade, *The Sacred and the Profane, The Nature of Religion*, translated from the French by Willard R. Trask, New York: Harcourt, Brace and World, 1959; Peter L. Berger, *A Rumor of Angels, Modern Society and the Rediscovery of the Supernatural*, Garden City, New York: Doubleday & Co., 1969; Erving Goffman, "On Face-Work: An Analysis of Ritual Elements in Social Interaction," pp. 3-36 in *Where the Action Is, Three Essays*, London: Allen Lane, The Penguin Press, 1969; Thomas Luckmann, *The Invisible Religion, The Problem of Religion in Modern Society*, New York: Macmillan, 1967.
26. Harold Fallding, "Secularization and the Sacred and Profane," *Sociological Quarterly*, Summer, 1967, pp. 349-364; *The Sociological Task*, Englewood Cliffs, New Jersey: Prentice-Hall Inc., 1968; Georg Simmel, *Sociology of Religion*, translated from the German by Curt Rosenthal, New York: Philosophical Library, 1959.
27. Mircea Eliade, *op. cit.*, pp. 201-13.
28. Enid Welsford, *The Fool*, Garden City, N.Y., Doubleday, Anchor Books, 1961, p. 326.
29. Thomas Luckmann, *op. cit.*, p. 48.
30. *Ibid.*, p. 104.
31. Harold Fallding, "Secularization and the Sacred and Profane."
32. *Ibid.*, p. 351.
33. *Ibid.*, p. 350.
34. Harold Fallding, *The Sociological Task*, pp. 96-97.
35. Talcott Parsons, *The Social System*, London: Tavistock Publications, 1952, pp. 326-83; Talcott Parsons and Edward A. Shils, editors, *Toward a General Theory of Action*, Cambridge, Massachusetts: Harvard University Press, 1962, pp. 159-89.
36. Harold Fallding, "Towards a Definition of the Term 'Spiritual,'" *Journal of Christian Education*, Vol. 1, No. 1, June, 1958, pp. 29-44.
37. Harold Fallding, *The Sociological Task*, p. 122.
38. Georg Simmel, *op. cit.*, p. 74.

39. William James, *The Varieties of Religious Experience, A Study in Human Nature*, with a new introduction by Reinhold Niebuhr, New York: Collier Books, 1961.
40. *Ibid.*, pp. 304-5.
41. Emile Durkheim, *The Elementary Forms of the Religious Life*, translated from the French by Joseph Ward Swain, London: George Allen & Unwin Ltd., 1968. (First published 1915.)
42. *Ibid.*, p. 229.
43. *Ibid.*, p. 37.
44. Guy E. Swanson, *The Birth of the Gods, The Origin of Primitive Beliefs*, Ann Arbor: University of Michigan Press, 1964.
45. See, for example, Edward A. Tiryakian, *Sociologism and Existentialism: Two Perspectives on the Individual and Society*, Englewood Cliffs, N.J.: Prentice-Hall, 1962, p. 35.
46. Emile Durkheim, *The Elementary Forms of the Religious Life*, p. 423.
47. *Ibid.*, pp. 423-4.
48. Emile Durkheim, *Sociology and Philosophy*, translated by D. F. Pocock with introduction by J.G. Peristiany, London: Cohen & West, 1953, p. 52.
49. Guy E. Swanson, *op. cit.*
50. *Ibid.*, p. 22.
51. *Ibid.*, p. 21.
52. William James, *The Varieties of Religious Experience*.
53. *Ibid.*, pp. 399-400.

Chapter 2

Illusion or Reality?

While it is Durkheim and Swanson who delineate the super-natural most clearly, a whole group of modern writers have a convergent approach. They share the belief that men are orienting themselves to a reality in religion, and the profiles they draw of that reality overlap. In this chapter I shall try to bring into focus a common core in the thinking of Eliade, Otto, van der Leeuw, Burridge, Tillich, Weber and Parsons.[1] But first it will be well to give heed to dissenting voices. For the opposite point of view, that religion is an illusion, has also had its modern protagonists. Feuerbach, Marx and Freud have taken this line.[2] Their thought has a quite tantalizing fascination. One does not wish to consider it *simply* to dismiss it, for there is much in these writers also that converges on the point of view I adopt. Some things these men have said would only need to be placed in a different context or given a different emphasis, for them to fall in line with the other thinking. Rather than representing them as opponents, one is tempted to draft them as unwitting supporters.

Feuerbach, Marx and Freud as Unwitting Supporters of Religion's Reality

Feuerbach: Man's Ideal and Collective Being

It is appropriate to begin with Feuerbach for, of the three, he is the one most with us in spirit. Only in stated intention is his position atheistic. He does not doubt the reality of real religion. It is because he wants to uncover the real basis of religion that he makes an attack on conventional religion. Moreover, we find Feuerbach groping after the religious constraint just where Durkheim locates the sacred—in the collectivity and, in addition, in the ideals of thought and life. He recognizes that experiences both of the collective and of the ideal underlie the religious sentiment, although he does not bring them together by naming the ideal of the collectivity the vital element. A particular statement will illustrate the Feuerbachian ambivalence over religion. In his *Principles of the Philosophy of the Future* we find him saying:

> *The old philosophy possesses a double truth—the truth for itself, which was not concerned with man, that is, philosophy, and the truth for man, that is, religion. The new philosophy, on the other hand, as the philosophy of man is also essentially the philosophy for man; it possesses an essentially practical—and indeed in the highest sense practical—tendency without damaging the dignity and independence of theory, indeed in closest harmony with it. It takes the place of religion and has the essence of religion within itself. In truth, it is itself religion.*[3]

Here, then, is the philosopher attacking philosophy—in the name of an improved religion.

Feuerbach's main thesis is that man does himself violence by making himself subservient to God, for his God is merely an aspect of himself. For this reason, he says, theology must give way to anthropology, as men come to see that the constraining power in their experience is a human thing. (This use of "anthropology" is perhaps unfortunate, since Feuerbach scarcely means the loose collection of sciences currently grouped under that name.) Because of this expected transfer of worship to the divinity in man, Feuerbach thinks the really modern thing is to emphasize the incarnation. You might say that he goes beyond Christianity by affirming the incarnation, as opposed to the unitarian way of rejecting it. Luther strikes a sympathetic response in Feuerbach for this reason, for he finds Luther giving prominence to the human Christ as the means by which men may fathom God. But the point where Feuerbach's position is most clouded is in identifying what it is about man that deserves worship. When he says that "God in man is nothing other than the essence of man,"[4] what is meant by "the essence of man?"

As I intimated, Feuerbach *appears* to find this essence in two places. Expressed more precisely now they are: (1) man's sense of the possibility of a more ideal being for himself, and (2) the fact that his real being as well as any awareness of ideal possibilities in it, are products of the human collectivity and not of the separate individual. It is true, as Marx complained, that Feuerbach does not use sophisticated sociological concepts to express the idea of collective man when he wants to draw attention to its importance.[5] He sometimes speaks of the "race" or "species," rather than "the ensemble of the social relations" —which is how Marx would have said it.[6] But the social and cultural bond is implied and sometimes actually explicit, and we may be sure that if he had had sociological vocabulary Feuerbach would have used it. Three selected statements will serve to epitomize Feuerbach's thought. They illustrate the volatile and tortuous qualities generated in it by the necessity of distinguishing God from man when these have no existence apart from one another.

> *Our positive, essential qualities, our realities, are therefore the realities of God, but in us they exist with, in God without, limits.*[7]
>
> *Idealism is, therefore, in the right when it looks for the origin of the ideas in man; but it is in the wrong when it wants to derive them from the isolated man determined as soul and as a being existing for itself, in short, when it wants to derive them from the "I" without a given sensuous "thou". Only through communication and conversation between man and man do the ideas arise. Not alone, but only with others, does one reach notions and reason in general. Two human beings are needed for the generation of man—of the spiritual as well as of the physical man; the community of man with man is the first principle and criterion of truth and generality.*[8]
>
> *Solitude is finiteness and limitation; community is freedom and infinity. Man for himself is man (in the ordinary sense); man with man—the unity of I and Thou—is God.*[9]

Here, then, is the atheist delineating—God. It is really against an abstract, over-intellectualized theology that Feuerbach takes his stand. But he insists that there *is* a divine something in man's experience and, though human in a profound way, it is *not the concrete, fallible, individual human being.* This venerated "man" is an "essential humanity" that stands over against the concrete individual as something more and other than himself, even though he has a root in it. Feuerbach is driven to use terms like "divinity" and "God" to distinguish it from "man (in the ordinary sense)."

Marx: Ideology from Unfulfilment

Although he was his critic, Marx followed Feuerbach in viewing religion as a fictional perfection that compensates for society's imperfection. This idea, in fact, becomes altogether incandescent in Marx: men locate in heaven the fulfilment denied them on earth. And it is inevitable that they do this, he believes.

> *If in all ideology men and their circumstances appear upside down, as in a camera obscura, this phenomenon arises just as much from their historical life process as the inversion of objects on the retina does from their physical life process.*[10]

For Marx, men make and need religion only because they are unfulfilled, alienated. This condition occurs because they are victims of exploitation in the production process. They will cling to the illusion of religion for compensation for as long as that condition lasts. It is therefore pointless to try to demolish the religious illusion by argument. What is necessary is to change the social conditions that give rise to it by accomplishing the socialist revolution. That done, religion will wither away.

> Religious *distress is at the same time the* expression *of real distress and the* protest *against real distress. Religion is the sigh of the oppressed creature, the heart of a heartless world, just as it is the spirit of an unspiritual situation. It is the* opium *of the people.*
>
> *The abolition of religion as the* illusory *happiness of the people is required for their* real *happiness. The demand to give up the illusions about its condition is the* demand to give up a condition which needs illusions. *The criticism of religion is therefore* in embryo the criticism of the vale of woe, *the* halo *of which is religion.*[11]

Whereas Feuerbach gives back what he takes away and acknowledges reality in the kind of religion he approves, Marx never weakens. His insistence that religion is an illusion keeps him categorically apart—at least as a theorist of religion. Yet it is an astonishing paradox that, as a practitioner, Marx generated more religion than most men in generating the communist ideology.

But, for all his divergence from it, Marx is with the tradition I am defending in perceiving religion to be generated by social experience. What is more, he is even in tune with the sharpened definition of the sacred I have proposed, as being the expression of the ideal possibility in society. Is it not men's propensity to idealization in the face of their unfulfilment that holds his attention? Astounding as it may seem to some readers, then—and it would certainly have astounded Marx—I want to propose that Marx is in step with my argument in the main. Were his emphasis but slightly different, he would seem in accord with the defenders of religion, even some of the most orthodox. It is commonly acknowledged by religious people that religion is a resource only for the vale of woe. Were we ever to come to utopia, paradise, heaven, it would indeed be expendable.

One feels entitled to remonstrate with Marx for so peremptorily writing off idealization as phantasy and illusion. It is precisely here that I take issue with him. Whereas I claim that the objective, ideal society is a most exacting reality, Marx calls it illusion. Yet, were it illusion, his own ideology would come under the same condemnation as the religion he attacks. Without idealization how would men ever conceive of a utopia for which to strive and for the advantages of which they will tear down the present good? What reality and authority could there be in such an ideal goal? What kind of truth and appropriateness could the vision have? If the heaven of the religious person is phantasy so is the Marxist utopia. Yet I would prefer to affirm their common reality and say they are the same kind of thing.

Marx was angry because allegiance to the religious ideal seemed to weaken the will to change the world, but he believed allegiance to the utopian ideal would strengthen it. This point deserves consideration. But we now know enough not to be able to admit that religious commitment *necessarily* induces indifference to the state of the world. Much world-changing motivation has sprung from it, while the *variety* of possible attitudes in this regard is one of the salient facts of religious history. It appears that a religion that views its god as active in the world may inspire its followers to work with him to redeem it. This is conspicuously so in certain expressions of the Judaeo-Christian tradition, and the utopian ideology of Marx looks like a variety of the same thing with the god taken out and a substitute inserted. Marx and the prophets of Israel are not all that far apart. At least in their messianic outlook they are the same.

Yet, as they have actualized in life, the militant stance in Judaeo-Christianity has differed from that of the Marxist ideologist in a number of ways. Since the religious person hoped in God and not only in God's improved future, he has enjoyed perfection even now to some degree, by union with God. Secondly, his reforming zeal has lacked the ruthless terrorism of the totalitarian ideologist, because it was not in a purely natural, Darwinian struggle that he saw himself engaged. Since it was God in the world and not nature in man that was making the advance, the way of overcoming has been the way of the sacrificial lamb. (I refer, of course, to the uncontaminated concern that has issued in the form of martyrdom, service, social reform, industrial enterprise and civilizing influence. It has to be allowed that religious action has been easily drawn into unholy alliance with the totalitarian outlook, when things like religious wars and the Inquisition resulted.) And, finally, the religious activist was proofed against impatience and disillusionment, since he had no exaggerated expectation about the short-run improvement to be gained through change. A mile nearer the infinite distance was still infinitely far.

Freud: Help in Frustration

Freud's book on religion, *The Future of an Illusion,* conveys by its title his attitude. The complaint it makes is that religion is a prop that men invent when the frustrations of nature and society make them feel weak and helpless. Not until they give up this illusory consolation and comfort will they learn maturity by coping realistically. It is like the Marxian view in that it sees religion as a compensating reaction, but different in that the reaction is to frustration rather than alienation. As Freud depicts the human situation, the frustrations men must expect from both nature and society are by no means negligible. So the challenge of growing to maturity without divine assistance is really of heroic proportions. Freud does not himself have much specific guidance to give on the way to do it, except to encourage us in the habit of facing reality. It is by way of this stoic discipline rather than by a Marxian class revolution that emancipation from the religious illusion will come to pass. But, as in Marx, the end of religion *does* wait upon the arrival of utopia. Men will only dispense with religion entirely when their perfect maturity has transformed them into a perfect humanity. The earlier, less perfect generations can give the later generations an advantage in this upward climb by perfecting the method of child-rearing.

What is of greatest interest to us is the form Freud sees the religious illusion take. Essentially, it is an infantile, regressive reaction. In the general helplessness generated by our situation we resort to a stance we have learnt in childhood: we appeal to the protective father. In childhood we have learnt a two-sided attitude to the father. We fear him because of his power to frustrate us but we also appreciate the protection he affords us. When, subsequently, we are frustrated by nature and society we are disposed to think this external frustrating power must be two-sided in the same way. It must be protective as well as frustrating. So, although we see no father there, we put one there and address our supplications to him. Thus, as father figures, are the gods born. (One is compelled to comment that if this is what happens it is being more infantile than children ever are, since it is in a real father that children trust.)

Freud's explanations of the way men came to have their mixture of feelings for divinity are so speculative and involuted that one cannot present them seriously. For instance, in *Totem and Taboo*, he proposes that in mankind's early history the sons of the tribe performed one of their first acts of cooperation by joining forces to slay and eat the father of the tribe. This was an act of vengeance because he had monopolised all the women. The totem feast observed till modern times by the Australian aborigines commemorates this highly important criminal act. It is memorable because social organization, moral restrictions and religion all had their beginning in it. Yet that was only because remorse set in, and to make up for their crime men disallowed any killing of the father substitute, that is, of the totem, and renounced the women they had liberated, thereby creating exogamy. From this same ancient source, the sense of guilt and wish to make amends in relations with father figures lingers on and, apparently, can crop out anywhere. For instance, it explains why in Christianity reconciliation with the father is sought through the son's sacrifice and why communion amongst the brothers is celebrated now by eating the flesh and blood of the son instead.

I will not waste words by attempting to answer such proposals in evaluating the Freudian contribution. What is significant in his view is the idea that divinities are fictions made in the image of the father, with his dual power of control and support, and the idea that these fictions are generated by the painful discrepancy between ideal aspirations and frustrating actualities. It is only necessary to look at these propositions in a somewhat different light for them to weigh in favour of the idea that religion is oriented to a reality. It is possible to consider the father not as the primary figure that the divinity copies but as the secondary figure that copies the divinity. The father is a mediator to the child of the reality that constrains them both. Why do fathers behave towards their children as they do anyway? Why do they assume this dual role of thwarting and supporting? Is it not because the constraint of the ideal society deals that way with them, and their duty to their children is to show them the reality of the situation they are in? Furthermore, I take issue with Freud when he imputes illusion to representations of the ideal, just as I do with Marx. It need not be wishful thinking to picture heaven in the midst of earth's woeful realities but a timely reminder that the ideal has its own reality too.

Convergent Views on Religion's Reality

I have paid attention to the objectors and, at the same time, have salvaged some further support for my thesis from an unexpected quarter. I will now try to demonstrate the convergence with the Durkheimian approach that I claim to see in the other authors. Most of them use different terms from those that Durkheim and Swanson employ. But Eliade speaks of the sacred and Otto of the holy. So it will perhaps be appropriate to preserve continuity by considering these formulations first. Van der Leeuw and Burridge employ the same kind of formulation as one another, so they may be grouped and considered next. In yet a different way, Tillich, Weber and Parsons use an approach similar to one another's, so these may be treated as a third group.

The Holiness of the Religious Object: Eliade and Otto

We have already had occasion to refer to an aspect of Eliade's work, but here we will be considering his view of religion in general. He is in step with Durkheim in accepting that men may have religion without invoking deities and in defining it by their orientation to the sacred. As a student in the comparison and history of religions, Eliade is confident that religious man can be seen assuming a mode of existence that is always recognizably the same.

Whatever the historical context in which he is placed,
homo religiosus *always believes that there is an absolute*

> *reality,* the sacred, *which transcends this world but manifests itself in this world, thereby sanctifying it and making it real.*[12]

Eliade lays considerable stress on the *reality* and *absoluteness* that men impute to that which they consider sacred. If this is qualitatively different from the profane world of ordinary experience, it is in the direction of being *more real.* Moreover, Eliade also gives considerable attention to the interpenetration of these worlds. The distinction between the sacred and profane is indeed a categorical one, but it does not necessarily mean that the sum of things divides into two, with profane things excluded or outcast. The sacred, in a certain way, may overwhelm the profane and give it a derived reality—hence the notion of sanctification. Religious man sees life originating in the sacred, and sees human existence realizing its potentiality insofar as it participates in it. The gods create man and the world, and the culture heroes continue the work. The account of all this sanctifying work is preserved in the myths. By imitating in various ways the divine behaviour there recorded man keeps himself close to the gods, and thereby makes his own life real. In *The Sacred and the Profane* Eliade shows how relative things— space, time, nature and human existence—have all been sanctified in various systems of belief by inserting them in the sacred envelope of the absolute.

Otto speaks of the sacred reality to which religious man turns as "the holy." A feature of it to which he gives special attention is the paradox of its being simultaneously transcendent and a present possession. Religion is a real knowledge of something above knowledge. Since it is categorically different from the person because it is free from limitations, he experiences it with awe as "otherness"—and would for that reason draw away. In this aspect it is the *mysterium tremendum.* But he experiences it also as available strength—and would for this reason draw near. In this aspect it is the *mysterium fascinans.* To be *touched* by the holy in this approach can be a ravishing, transporting, intoxicating experience. In the attitude of worship the drawing away and drawing near are welded together. One enters into worship to be touched by the beyond. Otto writes as a theologian centrally concerned with the holy as an object of direct experience. He does, of course, accept the reality of it. It is also very important that he treats it as a highly generalized object, available for approach through diverse systems of belief. He does not suggest any social source for this reality in the way I have done. Yet it would seem to me entirely in keeping for the sacred as I have presented it to have the characteristics that Otto ascribes to the holy. Because of its ideal character it is wholly other. Because of its being a real constraint and a real possibility for one's life it can be intimately felt.

The Perfect Power of the Religious Object:
Van der Leeuw and Burridge

Insofar as the student of society pays attention to the ideal character of the religious object he will stress its sacredness, but insofar as he pays attention to its constraining power, he may stress power. That can be an alternative way of naming the same thing and some students of religion prefer to name it that way. Religion is the response to power. Yet, because the capacity to make an impact, to be a force, is something the sacred shares with profane things, it has to be related to profane forces and differentiated from them. How does the divine power stand out from the power of the wind in the storm, the power of fertility in nature, the personal power of the huntsman and warrior and father and king?

It seems that the short answer is that *any* power, *any* efficacy or ability, can be viewed one way or the other, and it will be sacred or profane accordingly. It is not what anything is in itself but the quality of what can be added that makes sacredness a consideration in any instance. This was Durkheim's point, and the force of it comes home to us again and again in a variety of contexts. The idea of *mana,* as efficacious power, is quite widespread, and men can see it residing in things as diverse as physical force and natural human ability, like prowess in war. All such natural powers are profane in themselves. But if any such demonstration of natural power is *impressive* it is likely to be attributed to *mana.* That puts it in a different category. But what would make it impressive? It is by its being particularly effective or successful, which means that it reaches towards the ideal expectation for things of its kind. Van der Leeuw refers to Codrington's saying this makes it "in a way supernatural."[13] And, while that statement might seem to some too categorical to make the point properly, van der Leeuw thinks it "appears to have expressed the accurate implication."[14]

Thus we see it is not natural power that is made sacred but the supernatural power demonstrated through it on extraordinary occasions. Anywhere that men believe they see the power of the ideal break forth they may make obeisance. This may be in physical nature as much as in man. But what has the vision of an ideal in nature to do with the ideal in social relationships and society? We must wait till Chapter 7 for the extended answer to this question. But since it has become relevant here we must anticipate briefly. I believe it is rightly understood as making part of and being incorporated in the ideal of society, since nature supplies the properties for the drama enacted there. When religion takes an interest in nature it is for that reason.

Van der Leeuw is one of those who represent the reality behind religion as power. He has bequeathed us an encyclopaedic interpretation of religious data in these terms in the study *Re-*

ligion in Essence and Manifestation. He shows man's religious consciousness being forged by his response to extraordinary demonstrations of power which, because of their extraordinariness, betoken a second power added to the natural. Manifestations of this transcendent power are identifiable at distinct levels of experience. They can be seen to break forth in the most elemental way in nature: in trees and plants and animals, earth and rock, wind and running water. But their most significant occurrence at this level is in the principle of fertility in nature, in the power of *life*. New life, in reproduction and the renewal of spring, has a special importance. Manifestations are seen again in the power of exceptionally gifted and influential people: the king, the medicine man, the speaker and preacher, the consecrated, the saint. They are seen yet again in the power the person feels within himself, in his possessing a "soul," and in his ability on occasion to be more than himself through ecstasy. Van de Leeuw finds the three major expressions of institutionalized religion in ritual, mysticism and ethics. He shows them to be nothing more nor less than ways of formalizing and routinizing the recognition and response given to power on these various occasions.

Burridge is another who chooses to view religion as a response to power. His special interest lies with millenarian activities, and these are movements in which concern with the ideal society is transparently in evidence, of course. But they are also movements in which religious aspirations are often mixed pell-mell with political aspirations. So they raise in an acute form the question of the relation between the supernatural power and the earthly, political power. Along with the question of the relation of the supernatural power to natural forces, this is a very important one. As with that other question, the reader must wait till Chapter 7 for the extended answer to this one. But I would make the observation right away that it is possible to borrow directly from Marx here and present the religious power as an illusion that men entertain only for as long as direct political action is denied them. Politics and religion are then represented as the real and fanciful alternatives for pursuing the same end. Some writers do this, whether or not they explicitly acknowledge Marx for their teacher. It will be clear, however, that anyone who considers religion a reality would not endorse this approach. Burridge's approach illustrates the non-Marxist answer.

Burridge thinks it is important to recognize something *sui generis* in religious ideology which political action and ideology cannot supply. He says that the religious ideology is generated to perpetuate the tremendously motivating vision of *man transfigured*. Political aspirations will seek to bring about a change in actual power relations between different social groups. So they will be directed to such ends as liberated man, enfranchised man, equalized man, justly rewarded man. But religion is concerned with man *redeemed*. Burridge uses this term deliberately for he finds no other that is equal to his thought. By redemption he means freedom from the conditions that block man's perfect fulfilment. This ideal state will be differently pictured in different societies: man may loom up as "a free-mover in heaven, enjoying nirvana, or joined with the ancestors."[15] In any case, the religious element in millenarian movements will picture man in this more than life-size image, even though the political element pictures an improvement in actual life at the same time. The millennium is not the new political regime but the great day of redemption when the supernatural power will be untramelled and man and his world transfigured by it.

The Meaning-giving Totality of the Religious Object: Tillich, Weber and Parsons

The final group of three—Tillich, Weber, Parsons—have an approach to religion that is formulated in another way again, yet it is complementary to those we have considered. This formulation is not made in terms of the sacred or of power, but in terms of "meaning." Religion is that which gives meaning to life. In all of this discussion I think we see it implied that anything takes on meaning insofar as it is placed in a context. A particular action or problem is made meaningful by being included in any larger sphere; it is made still more meaningful by being included in a sphere that is larger again; it is given ultimate meaning by being included in the all-inclusive sphere, in the totality. In addition, of course, it is implied that these context-supplying spheres are themselves internally organized and unified, and that the ultimate sphere makes an all-inclusive unity. Order is a paramount consideration: for *anything at all* to be meaningful, *everything* has to be in order. Thus viewed, religion is essentially an operation of drawing attention away from the disorderly foreground of life to the orderly background.

Tillich approaches this question as a philosopher of religion rather than as a social scientist, yet that scarcely makes it a different question. Of course, as a philosopher, he has many qualifications to make that could be used to differentiate his position from that of Weber and Parsons. But a broad affinity can nevertheless be claimed. For Tillich, the concept of religion is derived from a concept of unconditional being as the *ground* of all separate beings. It is this being that constitutes the religious object. Individual beings have their being in it, so they are not to be thought of as additional entities apart from it. They exist, so to speak, with this outrigger. It is the meaning-giving context, envelope, anchorage, underwriting or insurance of their own being. This is how the notion of religion as the source of meaning becomes essential in Tillich's thinking. Also, it is because the religious object has the character of *unconditional* being that an idea of *ultimate* meaning becomes involved. By locating any being in the unconditional being, the ultimate meaning of it is disclosed. This, in Tillich's view, is the great and unique thing that religion does for man: it reveals the ultimate meaning of his life. By the same token, it is the alleviator of the anxiety attaching to his "ultimate concern."

Tillich makes full use of this notion of ultimate concern: it affords him a way of defining religion which is fairly independent of the content. For he can simply say that a man's religion is that which concerns him ultimately. In this way he achieves the same freedom from particulars that Durkheim achieves when he defines religion in terms of the sacred. And, indeed, it becomes much the same thing—they are virtually alternative expressions. Is not the thing that concerns us ultimately the thing we make sacred? Furthermore, Tillich's definition achieves the same functional objectivity and universal applicability as Durkheim's. In both views, religion is that which functions as such, regardless of whether the person in question names it for religion. What a person makes "ultimate," "sacred," is categorically beyond the mundane realm, and is *thereby* a "god." It functions thus no matter what character it has: whether it be material or immaterial, personal or impersonal, singular or plural, or worthy or unworthy in other men's eyes. So defined, any man and society will have something that functions as religion. (We should note, of course, that we would still have to inquire in addition whether this might possibly be false, cultic religion, which would be the case if ultimate concern were attached to something not considered ultimate in the culture in question. But Tillich's definition is intended to be a broad one which will allow us to recognize the religious quality of true and false religion alike.)

Adopting an evolutionary stance on the development of religious consciousness, Tillich says that the divine and demonic principles are not at first differentiated. But this does in time occur, so that, "in the consciousness that has become split God the bearer of meaning struggles against God the bearer of hostility to meaning."[16] Apparently, this differentiation is one in which orderliness is discovered to characterize the meaning-giving being and disorder to characterize all that can be experienced in isolation from it. The secular, natural world explored by reason exhibits the same orderliness as the divine, so it is allied with it.

> *The Holy in the sense of the divine and the secular are therefore simultaneously subsumed under the category of the pure. Divine and secular alike stand over against the demonic. In common they affirm form, in contrast to the demonic which shatters it.*[17]

The ultimate and all-inclusive boundary of life as the thing that supplies the source of its meaning, is also central to the understanding of religion developed by Max Weber. He saw men being driven beyond the empirical world of common sense by the fact that it contained profoundly disturbing discrepancies that could not be resolved within itself. That which meets the eye had to be subsumed under a more inclusive order before one could be reconciled to it. Parsons represents Weber's view in the following way.

> ... the search for grounds of meaning which can resolve the discrepancies must lead to continually more "ultimate" reference points which are progressively further removed from the levels of common sense experience on which the discrepancies originally arise. The "explanations", i.e., solutions to the problems of meaning, must be grounded in increasingly generalized and "fundamental" philosophical conceptions.[18]

Such a philosophy of moral meaning Weber calls a "theodicy." "Meaning," in this connection, does not refer to naturalistic explanations of phenomena but to the teleological and personal question of "why." Why is any particular person's experience of the world exactly what it is? And how can the pursuit of values be vindicated in such a world, since short-run perspectives can give cause to doubt them? Things like suffering and evil, and everything that mars, have to be reconciled with everything sublime. Apparently it was simply an observation Weber made, that men resorted to religious thinking when in this kind of sensed contradiction. That is to say, they then took account of non-empirical realities in a systematic way.

In the history of religion, Weber suggested, only two (and those divergent) major paths have been followed in the quest for an enlarged context to ensure meaning in life. The one is that exemplified in the Hindu and Buddhist doctrines of karma and transmigration. As Parsons' introduction to Weber's studies puts it, this is a path which "seeks to ground meaning in progressively greater extension of the time span to which it applies, and in increasingly higher 'levels' of participation in the sources of ultimate 'satisfaction.' "[19] This means that, in the case of Hinduism and Buddhism, if present experience is defective with respect to meaning, one has to learn not to expect it there, knowing that time will be given, in however many lives, to learn this lesson fully. Eventually, then, by the extinction of misdirected desire one will come to true satisfaction. (This, we may note, is a negative or agnostic way. The meaningful totality is not given any concrete character. The only thing concretely conceived is the meaningless fragment given in present experience. One does not actively attach oneself to meaning but actively detaches oneself from meaninglessness.) The other path is that exemplified in the Jewish and Christian faiths. Here the world which exhibits discrepancy is itself believed to be in process of transformation, transfiguration, redemption, by the continuing action of its Creator. With the consummation of this work, the discrepancy will have been done away with. While these are the two available patterns for the resolution of discrepancy, there can be a variety of actual expressions for each principle.

Weber's views on the dynamics of religion are of special interest. When the state of culture is such that a new all-inclusive order has to be forged, the charismatic prophet may appear. Charisma is essentially the introduction onto the scene of the new vision of larger order. It is because of its occurrence that Weber considers religion capable of taking the lead in social progress—and in this he places himself in direct opposition to the Marxian view. Furthermore, although religion and reason are often thought to be in tension, Weber sees rationality to be basic in generating religion's unifying systems of belief and ethics. The prophet's mission is simply a phase in the effort to introduce greater rational consistency and system into the cultural order. Protestantism was of singular interest to Weber because it exhibited this rationality in a very advanced degree, and he believed that the discipline of life that resulted from it was responsible for the Western capitalist economy. His studies of the religions of India and China showed them to lack any comparable development of rationality, and he attributed to that the absence there of the European-type economy.

It is appropriate for us to consider Talcott Parsons' view of religion immediately following the consideration of Weber's. Parsons' study *The Structure of Social Action* includes a critical review of the thought of Durkheim and Weber, and it would seem that Weber's view of religion earns Parsons' general acceptance, whereas he can accept Durkheim's only in a highly qualified way. Interestingly, it is the same ambiguity in Durkheim's thinking I have mentioned, that makes Parsons demur. But he does not, as I do, give Durkheim the benefit of the doubt. I judge that Durkheim is inclining to stress the ideal society insofar as he equates the sacred and the social. Parsons judges that he stresses the empirically real society, whereas he should have meant the ideal. Parsons therefore takes Durkheim to be saying that religion is an illusion, in spite of Durkheim's own avowal to the contrary. Yet that is what Parsons understands to be Durkheim's clear implication.

> *Religious ideas must, then, be distorted representations of an empirical reality which is capable of correct analysis by an empirical science, this time sociology.*[20]

But Parsons is convinced there is a non-empirical side to life which has its own reality and which becomes religion's concern. Hence we find him siding against Durkheim in order to champion religion's reality—which seems an odd posture.

Even in the form he understands it to take, Parsons is willing to concede an "immensely important scientific truth in Durkheim's view."[21] He is alluding to Durkheim's notion that it is religious ideas that give intellectual formulation to the ultimate value-attitudes the members of a society hold in common. As Parsons pursues this he inevitably comes to view Durkheim's thought more after my manner of viewing it—and apparently for the reason that values are ideal ends. So we find Parsons conceding:

> . . . it is clear that the fundamental significance of Durkheim's "equation" . . . is not in the relating of religious ideas to a known "material" entity but rather the reverse—it is his proof of the great extent to which the empirical, observable entity "society" is understandable only in terms of men's ideas of and active attitudes toward the nonempirical. If the "equation" is to be accepted at all the significant way of putting it is not "religion is a social phenomenon" so much as "society is a religious phenomenon". This is naturally the more strikingly true when one realizes that Durkheim's reasoning is applicable not to the concrete phenomenon society so much as to the abstract social factor. This, defined as a system of common ultimate-value attitudes, is indeed inseparable from religious ideas. Thus the charge of "materialism" is not justified. Durkheim arrives at the equation of religion and society by emphasizing not the material aspect of religion, but rather the ideal aspect of society.[22]

What Parsons finds altogether compelling in Weber's approach is the idea that through religious systems men grapple with the problems of meaning. Parsons notes that Weber recognizes some subjective factor at work in this, some sort of "will to believe," as if the discovery of meaning by this means was partly a function of the need to find it.[23] But, as Parsons also notes, Weber does not elaborate on this. However, in *The Structure of Social Action*, we find Parsons willing to fall in with Weber's whole line of thinking so far as it goes. In a paper delivered in 1942 and published subsequently in *Essays in Sociological Theory*, Parsons represents this Weberian view as the end of a progressive rounding out which begins in Pareto's thought and passes through Malinowski's and Durkheim's.[24] However differently they expressed it, he sees them all insisting that there are features of the human situation that prevent men from stopping short at the empirical world that science explores. For Pareto it is the fact that knowledge alone cannot vindicate sentiment. For Malinowski it is the anxiety created by the uncertainty in all our important undertakings. For Durkheim it is the respect generated by moral authority. Because they experience these constraints, as well as the constraining imperative to find life meaningful, men orient themselves not to one world but two. The two worlds are incommensurate and men do not expect to apply the same criteria to them.

It is clear from Parsons' other work that the Weberian legacy becomes his own possession. In *The Social System* we find him continuing to assert that religion has to do with non-empirical realities and that it is by making reference to them that men seek to resolve their problems of meaning. In *Theories of Society* he sees taxonomic usefulness in recognizing a subsystem within culture which is "rooted in the most generalized orientations of meaning," and which finds its expression in religion.[25] But it seems fair to say that, like Weber but unlike Durkheim, Parsons has no way to account for this turning to non-empirical realities. He has no way of giving them a character, either, or of showing how they relate to or arise from the experience of empirical things. That is not a line of inquiry that Parsons displays any need to pursue. What he, as a scientist, is mainly in need of is some way of classifying this department of human experience that will enable him to represent its uniqueness. That he has equipped himself to do so, is apparent whenever he writes on religion.

For instance, in an early paper on "Religious Perspectives" he argues that religion is generated in response to the strain in man's worldly situation, and that it consequently gives him an unworldly elevation where he can build a platform for great creative innovations in culture.[26] In perceiving this capacity for religion to spearhead cultural change Parsons shows a direct indebtedness to Weber. In a more recent paper on "Christianity and Modern Industrial Society" we find him still elaborating the same kind of theme.[27] There he suggests that the modern, secular world is not as hostile to religion as some seem to expect, simply because Christianity has worked like a transforming leaven to christianize it from within. He seems to imply that the secular world is itself the product of the religious endeavour to transfuse the actual world with the ideal order.

Finally, in any comment on Parsons' views, reference should be made to his notion that all groups include "integration" and "pattern-maintenance" amongst their functional imperatives. While Parsons certainly does not lead us to believe that either of these is equivalent to religion, he gives them the character of very pervasive constraints that call forth a variety of actions. It would seem that religion has a good deal to do with both of them, and with "integration" especially. We might even consider actions taken to further integration to be "religious," whether they are done in the name of religion or not. Thus it could make the same kind of substratum to particular religions as Simmel's piety. In addition, we could think of the integration imperative as being very close to the sacred constraint issuing from the ideal society and to Swanson's constitution of the sovereign group.

It may not be directly obvious that finding meaning for life, in the face of its apparent meaninglessness, is related to the real constraint of the ideal society. I would not imply that Tillich, Weber or Parsons took them to be related. Yet I would claim that they are related, and I think we can trace the connection between them. We may recall that meaning is only found by *exceeding* what is given in actual experience, yet it is to something in actual experience that meaning is given. This suggests that the context considered relevant for understanding an actual situation is the potential, real possibility inherent in it. But the potential in any single situation is partly a function of the potential in all the constraints on it, so we are led to the potential in the totality. That would be how the ideal society comes to be drawn in, how it is implicated in the interpretation of the actual. For the totality finds its boundaries in the ideal society—nature, for instance, being included within society as I have already briefly indicated. Also, just because it is the ideal totality it is beyond the realm of instrumental means and contingency. It has the character of an end in itself, and this would account for the place these writers give to ultimacy in the religious quest for meaning. Finally, it is only because the ideal society affords a vision of more perfect order that charisma and rationality force themselves on the attention of denizens of the imperfect world and introduce a dynamic for transforming it.

It must be clear, from the literature reviewed in these first two chapters, that the reality prompting man to the religious response has been a burning question for a number of modern minds. I hope it has also become clear that there is a considerable agreement in the conclusions they eventually reached about it —and more than may at first appear. There is an abundance of support for the idea that the constraining divinity in men's experience is the real constraint of the ideal social relationship or society. I therefore propose to use this notion throughout the remainder of the book, and I believe it will make facts intelligible that would only seem puzzling and disjointed otherwise. Religion has a number of sides to it, it is made up of distinct components, and in the next two chapters we shall see how they all hang together because they have this constraining ideal for their common focus. Doctrine, fellowship, ritual, ethic and experience are all needed to make a religion. They are very different things in themselves, yet men employ each of them to affirm in a different way the reality of the ideal.

Notes, Chapter 2

1. Mircea Eliade, *The Sacred and the Profane, The Nature of Religion*, translated from the French by Willard R. Trask, New York: Harcourt, Brace & World, 1959, and *Rites and Symbols of Initiation, The Mysteries of Birth and Rebirth*, translated from the French by Willard R. Trask,

New York: Harper & Row (Harper Torchbooks), 1958; Rudolf Otto, *The Idea of the Holy, An Inquiry into the Non-rational Factor in the Idea of the Divine and Its Relation to the Rational*, translated by John W. Harvey, London: Humphrey Milford and the Oxford University Press, 1926; G. van der Leeuw, *Religion in Essence and Manifestation*, translated by J.E. Turner, New York: Harper & Row, 1963; Kenelm Burridge, *New Heaven, New Earth; A Study of Millenarian Activities*, Toronto: Copp Clark, 1969; Paul Tillich, *What is Religion?* New York: Harper & Row, 1969; Max Weber, *The Sociology of Religion*, translated by Ephraim Fischoff with an introduction by Talcott Parsons, Boston: Beacon Press, 1964; *The Protestant Ethic and the Spirit of Capitalism*, translated by Talcott Parsons, London: George Allen & Unwin, 1930; *The Religion of China, Confucianism and Taoism*, translated and edited by Hans H. Gerth with an introduction by C.K. Yang, New York: The Free Press, 1951; *Ancient Judaism*, translated and edited by Hans H. Gerth and Don Martindale, New York: The Free Press, 1952; *The Religion of India, The Sociology of Hinduism and Buddhism*, translated and edited by Hans H. Gerth and Don Martindale, New York: The Free Press, 1958; Talcott Parsons, *The Structure of Social Action, A Study in Social Theory with Special Reference to a Group of Recent European Writers*, New York: The Free Press, 1949; *The Social System;* "The Theoretical Development of the Sociology of Religion," in *Essays in Sociological Theory, Pure and Applied*, New York: The Free Press, 1949, pp. 52-66; *Religious Perspectives of College Teaching in Sociology and Social Psychology*, New Haven: Edward W. Hazen Foundation, 1951; "Christianity and Modern Industrial Society," in Edward A. Tiryakian, editor, *Sociological Theory, Values and Sociocultural Change. Essays in Honor of Pitirim A. Sorokin*, London: Collier-Macmillan, 1963, pp. 33-70; Talcott Parsons, Edward Shils, Kaspar D. Naegele and Jesse R. Pitts, editors, *Theories of Society, Foundations of Modern Sociological Theory*, New York: The Free Press, 1961.

2. Ludwig Feuerbach, *The Essence of Christianity*, translated from the German by George Eliot, New York: Harper & Row, 1957; *The Essence of Faith According to Luther*, translated by Melvin Cherno, New York: Harper & Row, 1967; *Lectures on the Essence of Religion*, translated by Ralph Manheim, New York: Harper & Row, 1967; *Principles of the Philosophy of the Future*, translated with an introduction by Manfred H. Vogel, Indianapolis: Bobbs-Merrill Co., 1966; Karl Marx and Friedrich Engels, *Basic Writings on Politics and Philosophy; Karl Marx and Friedrich Engels*, edited by Lewis S. Feuer, Anchor Books, Garden City, New York: Doubleday & Co., 1959; Loyd D. Easton and Kurt H. Guddat, *Writings of the Young Marx on Philosophy and Society*, Garden City, New York: Doubleday & Co., 1967; Sigmund Freud, *Totem and Taboo, Some Points of Agreement Between the Mental Lives of Savages and Neurotics*. Authorized translation by James Strachey. London: Routledge and Kegan Paul, 1950; *The Future of an Illusion*, translated by W. D. Robson-Scott, revised and newly edited by James Strachey, London: The Hogarth Press and the Institute of Psycho-Analysis, 1962.

3. Ludwig Feuerbach, *Principles of the Philosophy of the Future*, pp. 72-3.

4. *Ibid.*, p. 58.

5. Karl Marx and Friedrich Engels, *Basic Writings on Politics and Philosophy*, pp. 243-5.

6. *Ibid.*, p. 244.

7. Ludwig Feuerbach, *The Essence of Christianity*, p. 38.

8. Ludwig Feuerbach, *Principles of the Philosophy of the Future*, pp. 58-59.

9. *Ibid.*, p. 71.

10. Karl Marx and Friedrich Engels, *op. cit.*, p. 247.
11. *Ibid.*, p. 263.
12. Mircea Eliade, *The Sacred and the Profane*, p. 202.
13. Van der Leeuw, *op cit.*, pp. 24-25.
14. *Ibid.*, p. 25.
15. Kenelm Burridge, *New Heaven, New Earth; a Study of Millenarian Activities*, p. 6.
16. Paul Tillich, *What is Religion?*, p. 87.
17. *Ibid.*, pp. 87-88.
18. Max Weber, *The Sociology of Religion*, pp. xlvii-xlviii.
19. *Ibid.*, p. xlviii.
20. Talcott Parsons, *The Structure of Social Action*, p. 420.
21. *Ibid.*, p. 426.
22. *Ibid.*, p. 427.
23. *Ibid.*, pp. 658-672.
24. Talcott Parsons, "The Theoretical Development of the Sociology of Religion."
25. Talcott Parsons, *et al.*, *Theories of Society*, p. 983.
26. Talcott Parsons, *Religious Perspectives of College Teaching in Sociology and Social Psychology*.
27. Talcott Parsons, "Christianity and Modern Industrial Society."

Chapter 3

Affirming the Reality of the Ideal in Myth, Dogma and United Hearts

---

Doctrine, fellowship, ritual, ethic and experience: it is a fact of great interest in itself that religion makes this five-pointed star. Why it should be so, how each point relates to the others, and what is the nature of each, are questions we shall explore in this chapter and the one to follow.

Religious Knowing is *Sui Generis*

Religious doctrine has seemed a particularly provoking thing ever since the dawn of the scientific era. For it claims with great confidence to be knowledge, but it does not observe the scientific method. Scientifically minded people were therefore often impatient with it and some rejected it altogether. It appeared to them a primitive way of trying to do what science now did properly. Yet the idea that religious knowing is *sui generis* has persisted, and we have recently witnessed a florescence of thought about the question. It focuses on the nature of myth and, while not all myth is religious, it is a fact that religious doctrine has come to us largely in the mythical form. Of course, if we are to benefit from an excursion into this discussion, we must appreciate that "myth" is used just in that sense—as a legitimate *form* of statement. In this context, we have to dispel that other understanding of the term wherein "myth" implies an erroneous fiction. In the present understanding, on the contrary, myth is seen to be employed in a serious attempt to grapple with truth of a certain kind. If it can be presumed that there *is* truth of another kind from that which science explores, myth—and religious doctrine generally—may claim an esteemed place still. This would not be bad or primitive science but knowledge about things that science does not touch because they are non-empirical. I shall use "religious doctrine" as the inclusive term for knowledge of this kind, and we shall see that as well as being expressed in mythical narrative it can be expressed directly as dogma in general statements.

Precisely because it is transcendent things that are figured, mythical form might be expected to have features that startle common sense. Precisely because it purports to be knowledge about that which, empirically speaking, is unknowable, what it intends to convey could scarcely be given in a literal or face meaning. I would want to claim that what religious doctrine is striving in its own way to do—though with varying success in the particular instance—is depict the nature of man's total situation in order to vindicate his pursuit of values. It is not a detached but a deeply involved account. It does not ask man to reflect and consider but hands him his situation as an incentive for action. Focally, in representing his situation to him, it will speak for the real constraint of the ideal—it will be, in the parlance of our own tradition, "the word of the Lord" to him. But let us see how far the recent appraisal of myth accords with this.

The Quest for an Understanding of Myth

One has to admit that the explanation of myth-making has been a challenge. We have, by now, a vast assortment of collected myths, and it may be part of the problem that we are embarrassed by riches. Yet the difficulty of explanation really arises from the characteristics of myth as a form of expression. For one thing it is fictional. Yet the fact that men give it serious and repeated attention indicates that it has something to do with a knowledge of truth. But what sort of truth does it enshrine and how can it be extracted? Clearly, myths are not exactly fables, parables or allegories—forms of expression in which moral and spiritual truths are conveyed by direct analogies. Nor are they representative stories in which, as in the modern novel and drama, truth about life is communicated by inventing a narrative that has verisimilitude. For, quite contrary to this, it is typical of many myths that the action is capricious and fantastically improbable. Not only can the laws of nature be infringed but the laws of character and morality also, and gods and heroes can commit atrocities that their devotees would never dream of. Nor are myths indistinguishable from legends. While these two terms may indeed be used as rough equivalents, and often are, it is useful to distinguish separate things by them. There is something appropriately called legend which is an embroidery of fact but which people like to consider true, perhaps because it adds prestige to their past. The legend may simply attribute unsubstantiated feats to an historic character, as when miracles are attributed to a monarch, or it may fabricate a new character or set of characters who are believed to be historic, as in the Arthurian cycle. The importance of this distinction is that it separates a class of narrative which is not supposed to be taken as factual in time and space from another class which is.

Müller: The Puzzle of the Gods' Caprice

In the second half of the nineteenth century an ambitious attempt to account for myths was undertaken by Max Müller.[1] Andrew Lang demolished his theory, and it does seem a strange one now.[2] But it did take cognizance of the bizarre and crude conduct that can be encountered amongst the gods. It was not, Müller suggested, that anyone had ever been so perverse as deliberately to represent divinities in that light. In the Veda, the early Aryans had originally given a noble character to the divinities. But in the subsequent migrations both the language and the myths underwent change. Dorson, in his review of Müller's work, summarizes the rest of the argument as follows.[3]

> A time came when the original meanings of the names of the Vedic gods were forgotten, and survived only in mythical phrases and proverbs of uncertain sense. Stories then developed to explain these phrases. From this "disease of language" myths were born.[4]

Thus the myths of the Greeks were not invented to explain the supernatural but to explain bits and pieces of surviving language from the Vedic tradition. What originally inspired religious awe in the Aryans, Müller had deduced, were natural phenomena like the dawn and sun and light and darkness. Their divinities represented their experience of these things and, for this reason, this mythology, as depicted by Müller, has been called "solar mythology."

It is unfortunate that this early engagement with myths had the appearance of disingenuousness. It has made the field of study suspect to the outsider and may even have licensed adventurers within. For there can still be a tendency to exploit this field for demonstrations of mystifying cleverness. Although, of course, any field with puzzling data and little order is probably exposed to that. In regard to the particular puzzle of the "unseemly" conduct of some divinities, let me make this comment. Our surprise over this is occasioned by our own cultural perspective, since in our tradition we have learned to expect the divinity to model conduct for us. But it is not impossible that extraordinary powers could have seemed more important marks of divinity in earlier times to other people. It is not uncommon amongst ourselves for the working of miracles to be accepted as evidence of supernatural power. To be above or outside the order of nature in that way is to be of the transcendent order from which nature has issued. The same sentiment could easily have been extended to the moral order. For the divinities to be above or outside the constraints of conventional morality and *able* to achieve their ends by whatever means they chose, could have seemed part of their legitimation. It was not that they would be seen to be setting men an example of licence but to be demonstrating their freedom in their capacity, as it were, of prime movers. In a way, this is also an aspect of the grotesque, which Bolle takes to be one of the distinguishing traits of mythical form.[5] As a matter of fact, Bolle makes an analysis of the features of myth which is basic because, being made in terms of form, it can be applied to myths of any kind. Since it is basic, it will pay us to take note of it before going on. It should help us to read the very language of myth, as it were, and develop a feeling of familiarity with features that might otherwise disconcert us.

Bolle: The Characteristics of Mythical Form

Bolle entitles his study *The Freedom of Man in Myth* and his leading idea is there expressed. It is that the very form of myth is designed to give us freedom from the determinism of the natural world by intimating that we belong to a world that is larger than that. It does this negatively, really. It shows up the limits of the natural world, exposing its attempt to appear complete in itself by revealing that it has gaping holes. What is ultimate is not contained within it. Strictly, what myth does is laugh at the natural world for making it appear that our ultimate concerns are circumscribed by it. Myth is thus marked by humour preeminently, and Bolle sees Jean Paul's four elements or constituents of humour exemplified in it, namely, the dimming of the opposites, the inverse effect, subjective reservedness, and the grotesque.[6]

The first means a dimming or obliteration in the myth of lines of basic distinction observed in everyday life, such as those between what is truly great and what is very small, between what is high and what is low. This confers a freedom which is not chaotic but cosmic, for it intimates that there is a larger perspective where these distinctions fade. The inverse effect is where what is expected to have a bad outcome has, surprisingly, a good one. This indicates that to rely on limited, natural understanding is to lay oneself open to being misled. Subjective reservedness is where the listener to the myth is made aware of the fact that there is a teller of the tale with his own estimate of it. This relativizes the myth and implies an outside point of vantage, a larger, liberating world. The grotesque, finally, indicates the existence of a realm qualitatively different from that of the ordinary and everyday. To speak of grotesque things and affirm them is to defy nature's claim to ultimacy. I think if one is prepared to accept that myth is like this and that it reminds man of his supernatural freedom by its very form, then any myth will have a general message which may even be its main message. It might not always be of overriding importance to find significance in the particular story. Viewed in this way, myths are variations on one exhilarating theme.

Burke: Narrative and Dogma as Alternative Ways of Saying the Same Thing

Further help in understanding what I have called the language of myth comes to us from Kenneth Burke in his book *The Rhetoric of Religion, Studies in Logology.*[7] Burke points out that there are two ways of expressing a set of life-truths or principles: "tautological" and "rectilinear." The former means that if we want to expound any large idea—such as the idea of "order" for instance—we will show that this one term logically implies a number of others. We expound it by advancing a set of propositions that logically imply one another. It is a matter of indifference where we start, Burke says, since any one implies the remaining ones, which is his reason for calling it a tautological cycle. (We must realize that he does not use "tautological" here in any way disparagingly. It is accepted as a property of terms which unify or summarize an entire sphere of implied understandings.) He shows that a whole chartful of terms are intrinsic in the idea of "order"—understanding that term in the social sense of control by authority. Disorder, covenant, fall, righteousness, law, sin, will, reward, punishment, grace, sacrifice and redemption: all these and more are implied from the start.

But narrative affords a second way of expressing the same set of principles, and this is what Burke calls the "rectilinear" method. Here, logical implication is replaced by active causation. Instead of saying that b follows from a by logical deduction, it is said that an action a of some person causes b to happen. Personality assumes importance and plausibility in this translation, Burke seems to think, because it is persons who use symbols, the means by which terms are always designated and their implications drawn out. Thus the separate traits that would characterize the essence of something are replaced by a sequence of phases in time. It also seems that pristine beginnings and final eventualities in time—first and last things—are the phases that have a particular aptness for this way of rendering truths. (Although Burke remarks that this is the case, he does not say why. Possibly it is because we accept the end of anything as the real test—the "judgment"—of its nature, and its beginning as the action that bestows its nature on it. At both moments its nature is exceptionally transparent.) It is this rectilinear, more pictorial, action way of expressing the truth of principles that is characteristic of much religious expression. Burke demonstrates how the first three chapters of Genesis set forth in narrative style a set of things that are implied in the idea of order. Thus, for example, instead of saying the contents of the world fall into six major classifications, Genesis says that six different classes of things were created, separately and in sequence. Instead of saying "that completes the first broad division, or classification, of our subject matter," it is said that "the evening and the morning were the first day."

But it is mainly towards the inevitability of atoning sacrifice, as the condition of redemption, that Burke sees the opening chapters of Genesis to be leading. If we follow his exposition of this right through it will give us a concrete understanding of what he means by the equivalence of the two ways of stating truth.

> *Whereas, the terms of Order, considered tautologically, go round and round like the wheel seen by Ezekiel, endlessly implicating one another, when their functions are embodied in narrative style the cycle can be translated into terms of an irreversible linear progression. But with the principle of authority personalized as God, the principle of disobedience as Adam (the "old Adam in all of us"), the principle of temptation as an Aesopian serpent, Eve as mediator in the bad sense of the word, and the idea of temptation reduced imagistically to terms of eating (the perfect image of a "first" appetite, or essential temptation, beginning as it does with the infantile, yet surviving in the adult), such reduction of the tautological cycle to a narrative linear progression makes possible the notion of an* outcome.
>
> *Thus when we read of one broken covenant after another, and see the sacrificial principle forever reaffirmed anew, narratively this succession may be interpreted as movement towards a fulfilment, though from the standpoint of the tautological cycle they "go on endlessly" implicating one another.*[8]

One outcome of God's authority is man's obedience. Obedience requires mortification, since no one can obey authority without "putting to death" some natural impulses. Mortification is thus a voluntary self-control exercised for the sake of giving obedience to the sovereign ruler. In its fullness mortification can constitute an atoning sacrifice for the disobedience of others.

> *The companion principle to such an idea of graceful, voluntary subjection being, of course, sovereignty, the other side of the sovereign-subject relation is presented in terms of the ultimate rewards in store for those of good will who subject themselves to the principle of governance. That is, as with the two advents of Christ, the logical contrast between sovereignty and subjection is resolved by translation into terms of narrative sequence whereby the principle of subjection, of mortification first prevails, but is finally followed by the sovereign principle of boundless rejoicing.*[9]

The rejoicing celebrates the redemption.

> *Then comes the Grand Rounding Out, where the principle of reward as payment (from the Order side) merges with the principle of punishment as payment (from the Disorder side), to promise redemption by vicarious atonement. Sover-*

> *eignty and subjection (the two poles of governance) are
> brought together in the same figure (Christ as King and
> Christ as Servant respectively)—and the contradiction be-
> tween these principles is logically resolved by a narrative de-
> vice, the notion of two advents whereby Christ could appear
> once as servant and the second time as king.*[10]

Burke is saying that there is something inherent in the logic
of the situation that enables the obedience of one man to have
far-reaching effects that cancel the (also far-reaching) effects
of the disobedience of another. Apparently it works somehow
like this: if one person voluntarily undertakes obedience in a
situation already made disorderly by another's disobedience he
assumes a second load of mortification. But he thereby deprives
the first man of even the punishment due to him and simultaneously changes it for something else: it is exchanged for a
share in the enlarged reward the enlarged obedience earns. The
compounded mortification is proportionately rewarded. The suffering servant becomes the sovereign lord, his mortification having successfully re-established order. In some such way as this
we could express the principles of redemption abstractly as a
set of propositions that logically imply one another. If we speak
of two advents of the Christ we express the same truths nar-
ratively.

As one reads Burke, many large questions on which he is
silent arise in the mind. It would be interesting to know, for
instance, why these two alternative modes of expressing principles are available and why one is sometimes preferred over the
other. One thing he does make clear, at least in one context, is
his belief that both modes have to be acknowledged as valid and
even perhaps, that both are necessary for a complete statement
of truth. Thus he supports Pascal's defence of the orthodox interpretation of the mass against Luther's interpretation, for the
reason that he thinks Pascal is acknowledging both a tautological and rectilinear aspect to it while Luther makes the mistake of rejecting one in order to affirm the other.

> *In terms of essence, the Mass re-enacts Christ's sacrifice,
> and Christ is present. It is the Crucifixion, which in this
> sense is not a temporal event at all, but simply an unchanging
> moment in the logic of the Christian nomenclature. (In this
> sense, it would be no more "temporal" than the relations
> among the parts of a syllogism. It "goes on constantly.")*
> *However there is also the interpretation of the Crucifixion
> as an event that took place in one particular time in history.
> Viewed in this sense, the sacrament of the Mass, when cele-
> brated now, could be taken as the commemoration of one mo-
> mentous single past event.*
> *Luther's "heresy," Pascal says (in* Pensée *788, on the
> Church) derives from using one of these interpretations to
> the exclusion of the other.*[11]

(Parenthetically, if I may comment on this, it seems that Burke is in any case misapplying his own concept here. Crucifixion purely as a principle and not a temporal event at all, can no more be a present thing than a past thing. So it would seem that the tautological aspect of the crucifixion has no bearing at all on the question of whether the celebration of the mass constitutes a crucifixion of Christ in the present moment. It simply indicates that crucifixion is a timeless principle of life. Burke's new tool does not really give us any new leverage on this ancient controversy.)

What Burke brings to the understanding of the language of myth, of the mythic idiom, is the very suggestive notion that logical connections can be represented in myth by narrative sequence. If one is willing to accept that narrative structure is found in myths because of some convention like that, it makes the handling of them much more deft. One is further proofed against the natural tendency to understand the story factually or literally, for one thing. For another, it helps one to relinquish the naive expectations that the sequence should have verisimilitude with real life sequences and that it will be a significant myth in proportion as it makes a convincing tale.

Bultmann: Stripping the Myth Away

One thinker who has contributed decisively to our contemporary myth-consciousness is the Christian theologian Rudolph Bultman.[12] Unfortunately, he does not leave an entirely clear impression about the evaluation he places on the use of myth. But if we follow his thought we learn a great deal about myth, since he shows how it operates as a component of one of the most elaborate systems of religious doctrine we know. At the risk of some oversimplification, I shall try to give an interpretation of what appears to be his main concern. First of all, we find that Bultmann is very conscious of the fact that myth does not deal with the things that can be known empirically: it is used to figure the transcendent. In his definitional statement in the renowned paper "New Testament and Mythology" there are things completely in tune with the position I have been developing. Religious man responds to the constraining reality of the ultimate power: it wields authority over him and gives him freedom.

> *The real purpose of myth is not to present an objective picture of the world as it is, but to express man's understanding of himself in the world in which he lives. Myth should be interpreted not cosmologically, but anthropologically, or better still, existentially. Myth speaks of the power or the powers which man supposes he experiences as the ground and limit of his world and of his own activity and suffering. He describes these powers in terms derived from the visible world, with its tangible objects and forces, and*

*from human life, with its feelings, motives, and potentialities.
He may, for instance, explain the origin of the world by
speaking of a world egg or a world tree. Similarly he may
account for the present state and order of the world by
speaking of a primeval war between the gods. He speaks of
another world in terms of this world, and of the gods in
terms derived from human life.*

    *Myth is an expression of man's conviction that the origin
and purpose of the world in which he lives are to be sought
not within it but beyond it—that is, beyond the realm of
known and tangible reality—and that this realm is perpetu-
ally dominated and menaced by those mysterious powers
which are its source and limit. Myth is also an expression
of man's awareness that he is not lord of his own being. It
expresses his sense of dependence not only within the visible
world, but more especially on those forces which hold sway
beyond the confines of the known. Finally, myth expresses
man's belief that in this state of dependence he can be delivered from the forces within the visible world.*[13]

In *Primitive Christianity in Its Contemporary Setting* Bultmann shows how the writers of the New Testament used the
myths available to them in order to express the full significance
of the life and death of Jesus. They employed principally the
messianic expectation of Judaism and the redemption myth of
Gnosticism. Certainly the *meaning* of Jesus could not be conveyed
by a purely factual account of the career of Jesus for all that
met the eye was an exceptional and controversial teacher who
came eventually to an ignominious end. Bultmann believes that
it is an important part of the Christian faith to affirm the resurrection of Jesus, but this is itself part of the hidden meaning that
only myth can express. For the resurrected Christ was a succession of appearances made to believers only—he did not resume
a career under the ordinary material conditions of life. His resurrection was *not* a part of his historicity, and Bultmann considers it a disservice to Christianity to claim that it was.

Christians have always made much of the fact that theirs is an
historic faith, and it is doubtless of great importance that the
person to whom they attribute so much actually lived. Yet it
is definitely not the case that the significance they attribute to
him was lived. Bultmann's signal contribution is to make us
aware that the most important part of what Christians believe
was not and could not be empirically proved in the historical
Jesus. Christ is nothing if he did not also live before and after
that incarnation. The Jesus of history is significant in Christian
faith only because his character made it appropriate to lay him
into the *entirely mythical* cosmic figure who is the Alpha and
Omega of all existence.

On the one hand, Bultmann writes as though he considers
myth to be indispensable for the expression of truths that cannot be expressed without it. But, on the other hand, he thinks

we must strip it away and bare the abstract truth beneath. Otherwise, apparently, we may fall into one or both of two kinds of error. We may interpret its assertions literally or historically, whereas if it refers to temporal things it is only as metaphor for non-material reality. Secondly, we may fail to see that any particular myth is arbitrarily related to the truth it expresses and that other myths might do just as well. (This is similar, presumably, to the arbitrary relation between thought and language. Just as it can be a matter of indifference, for many thoughts, whether they are expressed in English, German or Greek, so it can be a matter of indifference whether Jesus' role in the new humanity is expressed in terms of the Jewish Messiah or the Gnostic Lord endowed with a cosmic body.) In "New Testament and Mythology" Bultmann argues that a true understanding of New Testament theology requires a de-mythologizing of New Testament thought forms. His own *Theology of the New Testament* brings the whole of New Testament teaching under that kind of scrutiny.

Yet it seems that Bultmann is in a dilemma. If mythology is indispensable for the expression of certain kinds of truth, how can one express that truth without some myth or other? Bultmann's motive is to free modern, scientific man from any obligation to subscribe to archaic thought forms, lest that obligation be an obstacle to faith. Yet he proceeds as if this meant freeing him from all necessity for mythical thinking—and there Bultmann appears to forget his own wisdom. For he knows very well that the *scientific* beliefs of modern man refer exclusively to the realm of tangible reality. It is because religion claims there is more than this of which to take account that it adds mythological expression to factual expression. If modern man feels awkward with ancient myths will he not need modern myths to replace them? This would mean that some sort of re-mythologizing is needed, rather than a mere de-mythologizing.

It is instructive to see what the message of the New Testament boils down to in Bultmann's view, once the mythology is stripped away. It comes to a challenge to make an individual, existential decision to turn from sin to God. Sin is the expectation that material, temporal reality can give security and satisfaction. The New Testament is asking us to cast ourselves on God's act of mercy in giving Jesus to be crucified to take the guilt of that false expectation away. If we do this we are identified with Jesus in that we die to sin and this present world with him, and we enter a new life which is identical with his resurrection life. This new life is simply a kind of inversion of former values. By rejecting any false promise of fulfilment in the things that pass away, including the body that dies, we have victory already over the world and death. It is to God's grace alone, and to whatever future it may bring us, that our hope of fulfilment now attaches. As a consequence of adopting this attitude we do not expect any consummation in or for the material, temporal world, but live in it as persons already translated beyond it. This non-attachment in present-day living is the de-mythologized equivalent of the messianic hope of the coming of the Son of Man on the clouds of glory: it is living eschatologically, for it is putting an end to time momentarily.

But one has to protest that there is still mythology in this abstract of New Testament doctrine. The messianic and redemption content has been reduced but not removed. The references to God as an actor, to an atoning death and to resurrection, still reach beyond temporal realities for a larger context to give them meaning. It is true that there is virtue in juxtaposing the statement in narrative with the statement in terms of principle, just as with Burke, for that does elucidate the meaning we can give to both. Indeed, Bultmann's "de-mythologizing" seems to be nothing else than translating doctrine from one to the other of the two forms of expression that Burke recognizes. It might also be that Bultmann, if pressed further, could give us a statement more purely in terms of abstract principles. But, even were Bultmann to do his de-mythologizing perfectly, it seems that in giving an ultimate meaning to personal experience, the modern Christian would still ask for myth. He would still need a way of representing the cosmic end in which he partakes. If the Son of Man coming on the clouds of glory will not serve, what new image is there to express the corporate triumph? How will the modern Christian express the eventual triumph over sin and death not of himself only but of the new humanity that will reflect in unison the ideal reflected by Jesus? However, let us be fair. The very fact that we have these questions to ask results from what Bultmann has taught us. No one has done more than he to make us see why it is necessary to add mythical expression to the factual, and how it can express truth without being true literally.

Frye: Myth-making Still Goes On

The student of literature, Northrop Frye, has some observations on myth which depict it as ever present.[14] Were we inclined to think myth-making was left behind with the primitives, we have Frye to remind us that we do it ourselves all the time. For man to act in the world at all it is inevitable that his belief shall exceed what is empirically known. Modern, scientific man is not exempt from this pressure. In *The Modern Century* Frye states:

> *In every age there is a structure of ideas, images, beliefs, assumptions, anxieties, and hopes which express the view of man's situation and destiny generally held at that time. I call this structure a mythology, and its units myths. A myth, in this sense, is an expression of man's concern about himself,*

about his place in the scheme of things, about his relation to society and God, about the ultimate origin and ultimate fate, either of himself or of the human species generally. A mythology is thus a product of human concern, of our involvement with ourselves, and it always looks at the world from a man-centred point of view. The early and primitive myths were stories, mainly stories about gods, and their units were physical images. In more highly structured societies they develop in two different but related directions. In the first place, they develop into literature as we know it, first into folktales and legends of heroes, thence into the conventional plots of fiction and metaphors of poetry. In the second place, they become conceptualized, and become the informing principles of historical and philosophical thought, as the myth of fall becomes the informing idea of Gibbon's history of Rome, or the myth of the sleeping beauty Rousseau's buried society of nature and reason.[15]

Frye thinks that in the history of Western culture there have been only two primary mythological constructions. One was the vast synthesis that the Christian Church made from its Biblical and Aristotelian sources. At its peak in the Middle Ages, this persisted into the eighteenth cenury. The other is the "modern" mythology that was born with the modern world. Frye sees the definitely modern world to be about a century old (1867-1967), although it was incubating for a century before. Two features distinguish the modern mythology from the preceding one. There is a stress on man as maker, even the maker of his own institutions, rather than on God as Creator. Secondly, there is a Darwinian idea of man being immersed in a nature which is blindly growing rather than teleologically directed. The consciousness expressed in this mythology is pessimistic: it is an agonized awareness of the alienation of progress. The tide that is moving modern man forward is bearing him away from values and meaning. Frye names two plays that epitomize the doleful theme: Beckett's *Waiting for Godot* and Albee's *Who's Afraid of Virginia Woolf?*

The modern mythology filters to us at two levels, corresponding with the common sense of elementary education and the "confused" sense of the advanced education dispensed, for example, in liberal arts courses. The elementary mythology, which Frye rather unhelpfully calls "social mythology," is a kind of survival.

Social mythology in our day is a faint parody of the Christian mythology which preceded it. 'Things were simpler in the old days; the world has unaccountably lost its innocence since we were children. I just live to get out of this rat race for a bit and go somewhere where I can get away from it all. Yet there is a bracing atmosphere in competition and we may hope to see consumer goods enjoyed by all members of our

society after we abolish poverty. The world is threatened with
grave dangers from foreigners, perhaps with total destruc-
tion; yet if we dedicate ourselves anew to the tasks which
lie before us we may preserve our way of life for generations
yet unborn.' One recognizes the familiar outlines of paradise
myths, fall myths, exodus-from-Egypt myths, pastoral myths,
apocalypse myths.[16]

The more complicated mythology is a conglomerate of the
thought of influentials like Rousseau, Marx, Freud and the
existentialists. It comes to flower in art and scholarship as well,
and in a wide variety of books expounding seminal ideas.

> *On the bookshelves of my study in front of me as I write*
> *I see works of history: Spengler's Decline of the West, Toyn-*
> *bee's A Study of History, Hannah Arendt's Origins of Totali-*
> *tarianism. Works of philosophy: Whitehead's Science and the*
> *Modern World, Sartre's Being and Nothing. Works of science:*
> *Eddington's Nature of the Physical World, Sherrington's Man*
> *on his Nature. Works of criticism: McLuhan's Understanding*
> *Media, Fiedler's An End to Innocence, Harold Rosenberg's*
> *The Tradition of the New, Irving Howe's Steady Work. Works*
> *of psychology: Norman Brown's Life Against Death, Mar-*
> *cuse's Eros and Civilization. Works of religion: Buber's I and*
> *Thou, Tillich's The Courage to Be, Cox's The Secular City.*
> *This is a purely random list, but it should give an idea of the*
> *kind of book that helps to shape our contemporary mythology,*
> *and to give coherence and co-ordination to our views of the*
> *human situation. All these books deal with ideas, but occa-*
> *sional words in the titles, 'Decline,' 'City,' 'Eros,' 'Innocence,'*
> *indicate their origin in myth. In a sense they are all philo-*
> *sophical, even though most of them are clearly something*
> *other than actual philosophy. What I am here calling myth-*
> *ology has in fact often been regarded as the rightful function*
> *of philosophy, and we note that philosophers, especially of*
> *the existentialist school, have been particularly fertile in*
> *naming our central myths, such as the alienation, absurdity,*
> *anxiety, and nausea dealt with in my first lecture.*[17]

Throughout these Whidden Lectures, Frye is saying that in
order to depict the human situation in terms of our hopes and
fears, in order to have an orientation and motivation for action,
we must always exceed proven knowledge by beliefs assumed
true. This "filling in" is what he understands mythology to be.
It is interesting that he sees it differentiating into two expressions in advanced societies—although they are not strictly
the narrative and logical forms that Burke recognizes as alternatives and on which Bultmann also plays the changes. Frye, I
think, is really suggesting that modern myth-making neglects
the archaic mythical narrative form to concentrate on the form
of general principles. Modern myth-making's own use of narrative, in the novel and drama, is not really a continuation of the

narrative of archaic myth. It is rather a method of illustrating dogmatic principles by a story that has verisimilitude.

Frye's depiction of myth shows clearly that there is a distinct difference in the way belief is entertained in myth from the way in which it is entertained in hypothesis, even though it may be the same thing believed. The hypothetical belief is the idea provisionally held and the action that proceeds from it is simply experimental, designed to arrive at reliable knowledge by testing. But the mythological belief is the idea dogmatically held in order that action proceeding from it can be action with commitment. Thus it is entirely possible for the theories of science to be adopted by mythology, yet when that occurs they are given new status. Hence Freudian notions are made to justify a belief that unconscious motivation must override reason, or Darwinian notions a belief that human life must be a struggle of man against man. Perhaps people in general are not as conscious as they should be of this. We can move from science to mythology simply by the way we use a belief, without change in the content of belief.

Some scientists have been willing to oblige as myth-makers too and present the same belief in two ways. But no doubt there have been times when scientists were astonished and embarrassed by this transmutation. What they propose to the scientific community as provisional knowledge for testing and refining *as knowledge,* is seized by the lay public unquestioningly *as grounds for action.* Yet there is no evading this. It simply illustrates that closure of belief is a condition of action. Frye accepts this. But he does not think it necessarily means blinding ourselves to new truth. He thinks we may have reached the stage where an open mythology is possible; where our dogmas, though still dogmas, will be continuously subject to revision on the basis of scientific advance.

I have wanted us to be entirely aware that myth-making is something that still goes on, before we gave fuller consideration to myth in the cultures of antiquity and the primitives. For that material is viewed quite differently according to whether we see it as an early expression of something that is constant and universal, or the expression of something that is simply early and later outgrown. It matters a great deal whether we think we are getting an understanding of primitivism or of mankind in general when we look at some aspect of less advanced societies. I would suggest that we may learn more if we view their mythologies as the early phases of a constant. There is, indeed, one way in which primitive expressions can even make a special contribution to our understanding of constants. Societies which are simpler may reveal the nature of certain human pursuits more clearly. Before leaving this question, there is also another point to make. Often when people come eventually to accept that moderns are continuing some practice observed amongst primitives, they do so only disparagingly, their implication being that "we are still as primitive as they were." They speak as if although we still do it we shouldn't, and wouldn't if we were properly grown up. But that has emphatically not been my implication in demonstrating that myth-making still goes on. I have wanted to suggest that it can be as respectable and mature as it is inevitable and lasting.

Dumézil: Gods and Men in Mirrored Hierarchy

Comparative study of the mythologies found with the languages in the Indo-European group has been revived by Georges Dumézil along a more plausible line than Müller's.[18] Dumézil's hypothesis is a fairly simple diffusionist one. He tries to show that the peoples in question share what he calls a common ideology which issues in a common form of social stratification and a stratification of the pantheon that corresponds with it. This is essentially his argument in *L'idéologie tripartite des Indo-Européens.* What he calls ideology is a very fundamental habit of thought—in this case a tendency to divide experience into three divisions, a tripartition. Classical India exemplifies the social-stratification facet of this tripartition in its priestly, warrior and cultivator castes. The hierarchy among its gods exemplifies the corresponding stratification of the pantheon. Mitra and Varuna, for instance, are located at the highest level, Mitra presiding over the legal aspects of sovereignty and Varuna over the magico-religious aspects. Divinities in this class further the same function as the priests. At the second level appears the warrior god Indra and the other divinities who, along with him, further the function of the warriors. At the third level are the Asvins and the gods who, because of their interest in fertility and growth, further the cultivator function.

While the individual features differ, of course, this same pattern is found, Dumézil claims, throughout the Indo-European language area—in Iran, for example, and even as far afield from India as Italy and Scandinavia. It does not occur outside this area: the ancient Near East, Nile Valley and China, for instance, know nothing of it. That there is this wide diffusion of the same pattern is one interesting consideraton. But another consideration is the support that Dumézil's observations might possibly lend to some of the Durkheim-Swanson notions. There are suggestions here of a sacred realm that is the expression of the ideal society and of the constitutions of sovereign groups.

Lévy-Bruhl: Men Achieving Synthesis by the Collapsing of Classes

To know the nature of the primitive mind, as this can be inferred from the primitives' mythical thought, is the way in which some scholars have formulated their problem in this area. Lucien Lévy-Bruhl and Claude Lévi-Strauss are two of these.[19] They seem to have more in common than Lévi-Strauss —the one to write later—is willing to allow, although they do of course have quite different approaches. It would also be my judgment that what they show about the structure of thought, although learned from the primitives, applies to mankind in general, and that this is mainly why it is important. The point made above about learning lessons *from* primitives which apply *to* other men besides, is particularly relevant to this work.

In spite of Lévi-Strauss's impatience with him it seems to me that Lévy-Bruhl has a contribution to make. In *Primitive Mentality* Lévi-Bruhl imputes what he calls a mystical and pre-logical character to primitive mentality. Perhaps the terms are misleading, but I think he is simply saying that in the less advanced cultures men are less fastidious in sustaining their discriminating judgments. It is not that they do not make differentiations in their world, but they simply let them dissolve when they want to affirm their awareness that separate things are joined by causal connections—lacking, as they do, any better way to indicate cause. Consequently they see things and forces participating in one another and have a sense of the identity of things which, under the aspect of common sense, they also know to be separate. Thus in New Guinea crocodiles may participate in the nature of witches and so become equally possessed of lethal power. But it is also true that they may be regarded as quite separate from one another.

Lévi-Strauss: Men Achieving Synthesis by Dwelling on Resemblances

Now this scarcely seems to be incompatible with Lévi-Strauss's own depiction of the primitive mind. For in his analysis of it, as it is expressed in primitive myths, he sees it to be a mind bent on resolving the contradictions of experience. This points to the presence in the primitive mind of some kind of impulse to have life all of a piece—yet to have it all. Moreover, Lévi-Strauss does not see the primitive achieving this resolution by logic, even though he calls it *a* logic to suggest the use of a method. Precisely how he sees it to be done is one of the obscure things in Lévi-Strauss, but it is not by logic. It is rather by some intuition that *participating* in each of the contraries there is a third thing, the same in each of them, which eventually allows you to let the difference between them dissolve; that is to say, to drop out of attention. This third thing is the mediating principle between the two things that are felt to be contrary. It may intervene explicitly as a third term between the two opposites. Or it may be implicit, in that the distance between two opposites can be progressively closed by substituting another pair of terms for them, each of these being more like one another than the terms of the preceding pair. In this latter case it must be the increasing likeness that would embody the now implicit mediating principle.

Mary Douglas draws attention to an instance of the implicit mediating principal in Lévi-Strauss's treatment of the *Story of Asdiwal*.[20] "Above" and "below" are the two terms which are at first opposed; this is replaced by an opposition of "water" and "earth," and this again by an opposition of "maritime-hunting" and "mountain-hunting." She concludes:

> *In the sea hunt the gap is almost closed between sea- and mountain-hunting, since Asdiwal succeeds where his brothers-in-law fail because he clambers onto a rock.*[21]

Lévi-Strauss presents an instance of the explicit mediating principle in the carrion-eating creature—coyote, raven—of American mythology.[22] It is brought in, he claims, to mediate between agricultural and prey animals. This it can do since it has a certain resemblance to each of them. The carrion-eating animal is like prey animals in that it eats animal food. But it is also like the producers of food-plants in that it does not kill what it eats. In his *Mythologiques* Lévi-Strauss analyzes a large number of myths, from South America and elsewhere, to demonstrate the recurrence in them of this dialectical form of thought.

This form of the thought is what Lévi-Strauss calls its "structure" and at once a warning has to be given to the student of sociology. For this structuring of thought is not the same thing as the structuring of social action that has traditionally been called "social structure." (Yet it is interesting, of course, from the point of view of the unity of science, that this same property of structure can be treated in such different phenomena.) In addition, the reader must be told that what we have considered is but the most rudimentary element of Lévi-Strauss's structure. There can be different levels in a myth on which mediations are effected and the configuration of them all may then comprise its structure. A myth in any case is not one single statement but the sum of the variants. The structure, moreover, is a superindividual thing. It will not, most likely, be consciously put there by anyone inventing a myth, but will come there because culture habituates him to resolve contraries in this way and even because the human mind as such inclines to that.

I must confess that I do not find Lévi-Strauss convincing in the details of this dialectic. When he applies them to particular cases, the oppositions and resolutions he discovers are arbitrary, tenuous and forced. The formula is too standardized to seem credible anyway. The net impression, to me, is one of disingenuousness. But his *general* thesis, of an endeavour in myths to face and resolve contraries, is persuasive and attractive. It is in step with much I have already said. Lévi-Strauss, along with Lévy-Bruhl, must be added to that group of observers who have taken note of a powerful propensity in man to unify his experience of what life contains. The method for doing it observed by Lévy-Bruhl is a simple collapsing of classes that brings separated things together again. The method observed by Lévi-Strauss is a synthesizing of diverse things by dwelling on resemblances amongst them of any kind. Lévy-Bruhl stresses that the primitive's world is closed. Lévi-Strauss does the same, in effect, when he says the primitive always makes a great effort at synthesis. He considers that the imperative to synthesize again what it has analyzed, is the distinguishing trait of the savage mind.

> *The exceptional features of this mind which we call savage and which Comte described as spontaneous, relate principally to the extensive nature of the ends it assigns itself. It claims at once to analyse and to synthesize, to go to its furthest limits in both directions, while at the same time remaining capable of mediating between the two poles.*[23]

I would want to add—so does the modern mind. I would want to propose, also, that analysis makes the scientific phase of the cycle and synthesis the religious phase.

Kirk: The Need to Discriminate between Different Types of Myth

An evaluation of the work of Lévi-Strauss, along with that of other writers on myth, is included by Kirk in a wide-ranging review of the literature, *Myth: Its Meaning and Functions in Ancient and Other Cultures.*[24] Reminding us that not all myth is concerned with religion, Kirk points out that his subject is myth as such. His main plea is that most students of myths make statements about them in general which are only likely to be true if applied to a particular type. He therefore develops a typology which should make future discussion of the subject less doctrinaire. Illustrative of the doctrinaire approach was one dear to classicists like Cornford and anthropologists like Malinowski and Kluckhohn.[25] This was an idea that all myths are associated with rituals and, according to one variant, necessarily secondary to them, in that the myths' *raison d'être* is to give an explanation or validation for the rituals. It is surprising how this idea has persisted in some quarters and not as a hypothesis for testing but as dogma. Yet there is ample evidence that in many instances myth and ritual do not occur in association with one another. Often, when there is association, there is no trace of a suggestion that the myth is explaining the ritual.

Kirk divides myths according to whether their primary purpose is (1) narrative and entertainment, (2) operative, iterative and validatory, (3) speculative and explanatory, or (4)—a supplementary class—descriptive of the after-life. The second class includes the myths that are repeated on ritual or ceremonial occasions, and it is here those myths that do have a close complementarity with rituals belong, such as the myths of origin and increase, for instance. Myths which provide a model or charter for social institutions make an important subdivision of this class. It is in the third class that myths reflecting life's problems and contradictions fall.

What Kirk has to say about the way these problems are handled in myths is illuminating. He does not suggest that the myths necessarily resolve the problem, in the sense of giving an intellectually satisfying answer. Rather, what they do is ease the burden of the problem. They make the person better reconciled to the situation in some way or other. Simply to reflect the problem may serve to do this. Or the myth may state in affective terms that the problem is inevitable and inescapable, part of the divinely ordained order. The Mesopotamian epic of Gilgamesh is a myth of that kind. Gilgamesh is eventually reconciled to his mortality only by being told on higher and higher authority that it is impossible for mortals to evade death. Even a king with divine ancestry is not exempt, it is part of the human condition. When a myth does actually dispose of a problem, there are several methods by which it may do so, the Lévi-Strauss method of mediation between opposites being only one. One alternative method is to make the problem seem irrelevant or non-existent; another is to domesticate threatening aspects of nature by reducing impersonal forces to personal, more familiar forms; another is to use some other kind of allegory so that the fresh set of terms suggests associations that make the problem less severe.

We may note, finally, Kirk's awareness of the distinctively mythic language or idiom. In his view myths are distinguished above all by the fact that they make use of a special kind of imagination—he calls it "fantasy" for want of a better distinguishing term. It tends to express itself "in a strange dislocation of familiar and naturalistic connections and associations." Infringements of order, proportion and logic are all licensed, reminiscent of the way they are in dreams. It is true that folk tales, of which fairy tales and animal fables are varieties, may exhibit this feature too. But narrative interest is their first appeal; supernatural elements are subsidiary. It is only in myths that serious subjects are treated and deep problems and preoccupations reflected. Myths, then, can be given an altogether distinguishing definition, Kirk believes. They are traditional stories, usually envisaged as taking place in a timeless era, and dealing with serious subjects, such as establishing and confirming rights and institutions or exploring and reflecting problems or preoccupations, with their main characters supernormal—if not actually supernatural gods they are at least semi-divine or more-than-life-sized heroes. Their conduct and their world have their own freedom.

The accounts of myth we have reviewed show a remarkable compatibility with one another, yet there is some residual discrepancy that must be ironed out if we are to weld them into a single view. Frye gives a more comprehensive meaning to the term "myth" than the other authors. He equates it with doctrine in general. He includes under it both the narrative form and the dogmatic statement made in terms of abstract principles, and he understands the modern expression of myth in the vehicles of literature and philosophy. Burke and Bultmann give a place to the dogmatic statement made in terms of principles, but they reserve the term "myth" for the narrative form. What are we to do about this? The narrower use, which restricts the term "myth" to narratives, is the one most obviously in line with usage. Yet it seems there is also a certain virtue in employing the term in the wider sense, particularly when we have to convey the idea that moderns employ this more differentiated complex to achieve what primitives achieve by narrative almost entirely. It seems we may not be greatly handicapped if we try to have the best of both worlds and use the word in both ways, provided each context makes clear the sense intended.

There is also another discrepancy. I said earlier that myths are not representative stories like novels and dramas, yet I am now wanting to accept Frye's notion that the conventional plots of fiction are part of the modern's mythology. Yet this discrepancy is tied to the one already noticed of two meanings for "myth" having crept into our discussion. The plot of a modern novel is included under "myth" in the more comprehensive sense of doctrine in general, but it can still be distinguished from the narrative "myth" of primitive and classical cultures. It is important, though, to appreciate in what way the modern novel makes a doctrinal statement—and poetry, drama and our our other literary forms do it in the same way. We have only to recall the literary critic's insistence that literature is not a photograph of life but an interpretation of life. It gives us more than the raw experience of life can give. That raw actuality is exceeded by a context of assumptions about our nature and situation, and on the basis of this it is interpreted. It is from the author's dogmas that these assumptions are derived. So we must remember that modern literature uses quite different conventions of expression from those we have identified above as the mythic idiom.

What Is Meant When It Is Said Myths Depict Man's Total Situation

The appraisal of myth and dogma that we have reviewed accords well with the view I advanced early in the chapter, and I hope this will now be plain. I said that religion uses doctrinal statement to depict the nature of man's total situation in order to vindicate his pursuit of values. One can still maintain this while accepting Kirk's breakdown of myths into different types. What I asserted would be claimed only of his last three classes of myth, in that these could have to do with religion, and it would also be claimed of dogma expressed in general principles. It seems it is probably the case that, with the course of evolution, the mythical narrative form is supplemented increasingly by the dogmatic form in which religious truths are expressed as general principles. Whether the latter can or will eventually displace the former remains very doubtful. Yet it is certainly true that myths from other cultures, presented without a simultaneous translation into dogma, look very strange to modern man. But I think Frye is entirely right in showing modern man to be just as much an exponent of doctrinal thought as any primitive. He simply leans more to the dogmatic mode.

The writings we have reviewed should have helped to clarify what I mean when I say that myths depict man's total situation. I do not mean that we will always find them drawing vast panoramas. I do not mean either that they will always show life's antinomies to be smoothly ironed out and life a polished apple. The main point is that they will be found insisting on transcendence, and they will find a variety of ways for doing it, many of them oblique and veiled. They will do this in order to show that man's total situation is only to be apprehended from a larger perspective than the one natural perception can command. If there is a discrepancy or contradiction in experience or knowledge they will not need to suppress it at the level at which it occurs. They will simply have to indicate that its resolution requires removal to another level. We have to examine actual myths to appreciate what a loose fitting a particular myth may have for the total situation to which it is a pointer. Let us consider two in illustration.

Can we take first the Sumerian myth of *Enki and Ninhursag,* which dates from the third millennium B.C. I shall reproduce Kirk's summary of this myth and then make a comment on it.[26]

> *Ninhursag appears once more, this time in her usual role as earth-goddess, in the most fascinating of all surviving Sumerian myths, 'Enki and Ninhursag'. The action takes place, before the creation of man, in the paradise-land of Dilmun, imagined as lying to the south of Sumer, either at*

the mouth of the great rivers or in the Persian Gulf. Dilmun is 'clean' and 'bright', and that is somehow associated with Enki's lying with his wife Ninsikilla, 'pure lady'—an epithet, probably of Ninhursag, that may explain the emphasis on Dilmun's purity. In spite of this purity and the absence of old age and death, Dilmun is still short of water. Ninsikilla asks Enki, the god of sweet water, to supply it, and he does so by calling on the sun- and moon-gods for help, as well as by making it come up from the earth. Then (or perhaps as part of this same water-supplying sequence) Enki impregnates Nintu, 'the mother of the land', who is definitely Ninhursag; she bears a daughter after nine days. Enki has forbidden anyone to walk in the marshes, but this young daughter, Ninmu, does so; Enki catches sight of her, crosses the river in his boat, and impregnates her. She too bears a daughter, Ninkurra, who also lurks around in the marshland with the inevitable consequences; her daughter is called Uttu. But now Nintu-Ninhursag decides to intervene; she tells Uttu to require that Enki bring her, out of the desert, cucumbers, grapes, and some other fruit. Enki irrigates the uncultivated places to the delight of an unnamed gardener, who gives him the fruit. Uttu receives it and now at last allows Enki to impregnate her. But along comes Ninhursag and removes Enki's seed from within Uttu—or so it seems from a fragmentary text; next we are told that eight different plants are growing, and it is probable that Ninhursag has placed Enki's seed within herself—in the earth—to make them grow. Enki catches sight of them and eats each in turn, apparently so that he may know their name and nature and decree their fate. Ninhursag is infuriated; she curses Enki and withdraws from him 'the eye of life', so that he sickens. She disappears, and because of this and the water-god's illness there is a drought. The great gods are in despair (a common motif), but the fox says that he can bring Ninhursag back (another common motif, of folktale type) and does so. Ninhursag now seats the dying Enki in her vagina; Kramer misleadingly translates 'in' as 'near', although he identifies the literal sense in a footnote. Enki is diseased in eight different parts, presumably corresponding to the eight different plants he has so destructively eaten; and Ninhursag causes to be born eight deities, one to heal each part. The deities are a miscellaneous lot, chosen solely because their names happen to resemble, superficially, those of the different diseased parts of the body. And so, with Ninhursag's assignment of functions to these deities, the myth ends.[27]

This myth confronts us with a realization that sexual fertility and nature's fertility are linked together, and also that they can become problematic in the same kind of way. For there is a proper norm to be found for regulating each of them. This norm is like a transcendent law worked out through the interaction of the gods, and it is one and the same for both of them, in fact, since it is a mean which avoids excess. To promote nature's fertility successfully through irrigation the water god must not squander water either by overfilling the irrigation system or by extending cultivation to the desert. To secure a proper use of the sexual function the earth goddess has to intervene and stop the galloping irregularity. What was very valuable to the Sumerians was both their own sexual fertility and the fertility of the fields. They are vindicated in their pursuit of these by the knowledge that, in the total result, the gods have their procurement regulated.

For our second example let us consider some mythical narratives from Shintoism, as they have been summarized by Woodward.[28] These myths are recorded in chronicles compiled as late as the eighth century, but derive from the ancient tradition.

> The creation myth starts with a pre-existing universe likened to an ocean of mud veiled in darkness. Three gods appeared from this—how, we are not told—Amé-no-minaka-nushi-no-kami (Divine Ruler of the August Centre of Heaven) and two other creation deities whose long names may be rendered High August Producing God and Divine Producing Goddess. These proceeded with the task of creation until heaven and earth were distinguished, but earth was still fluid like oil or foam on water. At this point the three deities retire and are never heard of again. A number of gods and goddesses appear and disappear without trace until we come to the divine couple, Izanagi and Izanami, the first god and goddess of any real significance in the Japanese Pantheon.
>
> Izanagi, 'The Male who Invites', and Izanami, 'The Female who Invites', were ordered by the gods of heaven to descend to earth and create the land. They stood therefore on the Floating Bridge of Heaven, pushed down a jewelled spear and stirred up the brine until it curdled, whereupon they drew up the spear, and the drops which fell from it formed an island, stated to be the island of Awaji in the Inland Sea. They descended to this island and started their courtship there. They walked round the island in opposite directions until they met, whereupon Izanami exclaimed, 'O beautiful and attractive youth!' and Izanagi replied, 'O beautiful and attractive maiden!' Marriage was immediate and without ceremony, and from their union began to be born islands, plains, and the elements and forces of nature. But the first two to appear were failures. They realized that Izanami had made a mistake in speaking first. The courtship was repeated and on their meeting this time Izanagi exclaimed, 'O what a lovely and beautiful maiden!' and Izanami responded. After this all went well, and from their union the Islands of Japan and many nature deities were born—gods of rocks, of winds, of seasons, of seas, of trees, of mountains, and of food and fire.
>
> When the fire-god was born, he scorched his mother and she died and went to the nether world of the dead. Izanagi killed the fire-god, and followed her to the underworld to try to bring her back, but found her in a state of filth and putrefaction, with eight thunder-gods born inside her. She tried to seize him and confine him to the nether world also, but

he narrowly escaped after a fierce pursuit by furies. From the filth which he washed from himself were born numerous other deities, the most notable being Amaterasu-ōmikami, the Sun-goddess, who was born from the washing of his right eye. She is for all practical purposes the most important deity of the Shinto Pantheon, being the divine ancestress of the Japanese Imperial Line. From the left eye of Izanagi was born the Moon-god, Tsuki-yomi, and from his nostrils, Susa-no-o, the Rainstorm-god.

The story is then taken up with the adventures of Amaterasu and Susa-no-o. Izanagi having retired, the rule of the universe was divided between sister and brother. She ruled benevolently and instituted religious rites. He, however, being a storm-god, was arrogant and disobedient. He behaved so outrageously to his sister that she took offence and shut herself in the Rock-Cave-of-Heaven, whereupon the whole universe was thrown into darkness. There follows a story which is at the very centre of Shinto mythology, and one which reflects and has helped to preserve the ritual of the time at which it was recorded.

In consternation at the darkness, the gods held a conference in the dry bed of the River of Heaven to discuss how she should be induced to come out and give light to the world again. In the end a plan was agreed upon. A mirror was made, jewels hung on the branch of a sakaki tree, a platform erected before the cave, and a goddess performed a lewd dance which so amused the assembled gods that they burst into loud and prolonged laughter. Amaterasu was overcome by curiosity and opened the door of her cave a little. She saw the reflection of her own brilliance in the mirror, and emerged a little further to examine it. Upon this, the god Strong-hand, who had been hidden in readiness, seized hold of her and pulled her out. Susa-no-o was barbarously punished and banished from heaven. In the course of his adventures on earth, however, Susa-no-o rescued a maiden from an eight-headed serpent and found a divine sword in the dead serpent's tail. The mirror, the jewels, and the sword became the three Imperial Treasures of Japan, and it is claimed that they survive to this day.

The next story of significance concerns Ō-kuni-nushi, Great Lord of the Land, one of the numerous sons of Susa-no-o. He ruled the province of Izumo on the Sea of Japan, facing the Asiatic continent, an ancient haunt of the gods. He is worshipped at the Great Shrine of Izumo (Izumo Taisha). Unlike his boisterous father, he ruled the land gently and beneficently and had many useful children such as the Harvest-god and the Food-goddess. But Amaterasu had decided that the rule over the land of Japan was to be given to her grandson, Ninigi-no-mikoto, and his descendants for ever in unbroken line. Ō-kuni-nushi humbly gave way to the wishes of Amaterasu and has been worshipped as the model of loyal and obedient self-sacrifice ever since.

When Amaterasu committed the government of the land to

Ninigi-no-mikoto she is reported to have said: 'The Luxuri-
ant Reed-plain Land of Fresh Rice-ears (Japan) is the land
over which my descendants shall reign. Do thou, Imperial
Grandson, go and rule over it, and the prosperity of the Im-
perial Succession of Heaven shall be as everlasting as Heaven
and Earth.' This very important decision of Amaterasu is
known among Shintoists as the 'Divine Edict' and is claimed
as the divine sanction for the Imperial System of Japan.[29]

In these narratives I think we are carried through to the transcendent from springboards placed at three distinct levels. We
might designate them the levels of creation, life's complementar-
ities and social institutions. The main message regarding creation is that what now comprises the closed system of the universe
issued from beyond it. This added dimension makes it meaningful and acceptable. The same dimension added to life's comple-
mentarities is precisely what makes them that. Things that would
otherwise be opposed are shown to be in meaningful association
because the supernatural acts through them. The following pairs
are all harmonized in this way: male and female, life and death,
sunshine and storm, light and darkness, the kingdom of earthly
rule and the rule of Heaven. There are human institutions that
are likewise made meaningful—because they are copying an
archetype laid down in the other world. Parenthood, male initiative in love, female curiosity and vanity, masculine valour, the
practice of loyalty and obedience, and the imperial throne: all
these are hallowed. Taken together, the narratives outline the
nature of man's situation. Because of its being thus he may
confidently pursue his cherished ends: human fertility; nature's
fertility with its result in harvest and food; conquest; prosperous
rule.

While individual myths and dogmas may depict only isolated
aspects of the human situation, they aim to convey something of
its total depth. Its total breadth is something they convey in
combination. In order that this comprehensiveness will not remain completely implicit, it is common for some of the later
writing in a religious tradition to embark on a systematization
of the dogmatic teaching contained in the earlier writings. In
this way religious dogmas can become codified. If a very suc-
cinct summary is made, this becomes a creed or doctrinal statement. Giving assent to such a statement can be a basis of membership in the body of believers, the church. Repeating that
statement in unison can become a part of the church's ritual.

Union of Hearts through Shared Belief

So we have been led now to take note of the fellowship of kindred
minds, the union of hearts, that religion establishes. It is a fact

of supreme importance that religious doctrine provides a *shared* definition of their situation for a set of people, thereby making them a community. A system of religious belief is not the creation of an isolated individual, nor is it created for the isolated individual. It is part of the symbolic system that governs a group's life. When people agree on any particular thing a bond of sympathy is created between them, but when they agree on the definition of their total situation the sense of unity can be overwhelming. What is shared between them is what is deepest for each of them, and they are in fellowship with one another because each is in fellowship with the divine. The divine communion and human community coincide and resonate. They *can* resonate because they *are* alike, the divine being the ideal community. The exhilaration in this unity gives men morale to face life, for they believe it is the same challenge they face and that they face it with both divine and human aid. The exhilaration has sometimes caused believers to call their joy in fellowship "a sweet foretaste of heaven." In saying this they make a double reference to the ideal. They have figured the ideal society in dogma as heaven: it is part of the meaning-giving background for their imperfect earthly experience. In their present unison they feel their actual association drawn palpably nearer that ideal.

This communal aspect of religion is one that Durkheim emphasized.[30] The beliefs and practices related to the sacred "unite into one single moral community called a Church, all those who adhere to them,"[31] he said. The word "church" is meant to be taken representatively not literally. The fact that the characteristics of the modern church, from which the word is taken, may not be reproduced in other religious communities, is unimportant. What *is* important is that men will attribute their communal tie to their religious affinity because religion defines their situation in the profoundest way. They may even transfer the terms of kinship to this relationship, saying that their true "brothers" and true "kindred" are those with whom they are united not by blood but by faith; although, of course, it is possible for the fellowship of faith to coincide with blood relationship. The actual constituency of a group comprising a religious community—a "church" in this Durkheimian sense—can be quite variable, and we shall try to account for that in the second part of the book. The basic differentiation that occurs is one between naturally occurring groups, like families, cities and nations, which add a religious function to their other functions, and groups that are expressly created for a religious purpose. In either case, however, the sharing in myths and dogmas that depict their ideal union generates solidarity between the persons concerned.

This sharing aspect of religious belief can help us to appreciate why orthodoxy can be taken for one of the criteria of truth in religion. That is something the scientific mind usually finds surprising and even repugnant. For the scientist is trained to find truth by thinking critically and independently. But if religious doctrine voices the constraint of the ideal union, its viability will partly be a function of the extent to which men are able to agree on it. The same kind of grounding of belief in a practical constraint helps us to understand why totalitarian governments exercise strict thought control. It also helps us to understand, incidentally, why political parties, even in democracies, feel entitled to compromise the independence of their members to some extent, by dictating policy to them. Political constraint and religious constraint are not the same thing, the former being the constraint of actual powers and the latter that of the ideal, but they share the element of constraint.

The Inherent Limitation in Religion's Instruments

Each of the five sides of religion has its severe limitation, as we shall see. It is as though the instruments men can devise for navigating on their most important journey have to be the most faulty: their ingenuity is unequal to its rigours. The limitation may be reached very abruptly, before the person knows he is there. Or he may know it, yet not know what to do about it. The limitation in doctrine (and the fellowship in it) is obvious and often lamented: the closed mind it can produce as a result of its inevitable closure. I mentioned Frye's hope that it might now be possible to have an open mythology, to have dogma which is open to continuous revision. This has been the perennial hope, and it is the only hope of deliverance from the trap that turns religious conviction into prejudice and in-group fellowship into out-group hostilities. Yet how would anyone be disposed to that openness? Only by distinguishing very definitely between the divinity and the doctrine of it. By this means dogma is balanced with agnosticism, since it insists that the constraint we are under is from the divinity and not from the doctrine that struggles clumsily to define it. When believers have done their utmost to express the unspeakable glory of the ideal, they have to give it all back and cancel their distorting work, saying: "Who hath known the mind of the Lord? . . . For of him, and through him, and to him, are all things: to whom be glory for ever."[32]

There are yet other mysteries on which light dawns once we appreciate the pervasive place in our experience of the real, constraining ideal. For instance, truth, beauty and goodness are often separately enjoined as authentic values—but we rarely have any insight into why they make a trinity. Of what round orb are they the separate faces? Is it not of this very thing—the real, constraining ideal? And is this not why we regard them with awe, as though they were the divinity's impersonal names? Its reality is our truth, its constraint our goodness, its ideality our beauty. Our more secularized consciousness differentiates these but in religion we approach them in their unity. Yet even in that approach there can be a differentiation in that each aspect elicits a distinct response. Experience and doctrine register its truth, fellowship and ethic its goodness, ritual its beauty. I would suggest that this is why religion has its five distinct aspects. Our cognitive, conative and affective faculties have each to make their distinct appraisal of the ideal.

Notes, Chapter 3

1. Max Müller, *Chips from a German Workshop*, Vol. II, London: (printed in Oxford), 1867; *Contributions to the Science of Mythology*, London: Longmans & Co., 1897.
2. Andrew Lang, *Myth, Ritual and Religion*, London: Longmans & Co., 1887; *Modern Mythology*, London: Longmans & Co., 1897.
3. Richard M. Dorson, "The Eclipse of Solar Mythology," in Thomas A. Sebeok, editor, *Myth, A Symposium*, Bloomington: Indiana University Press, 1958, pp. 15-38. Bibliography and Special Series of the American Folklore Society, Volume 5, 1955.
4. *Ibid.*, pp. 19-20.
5. Kees W. Bolle, *The Freedom of Man in Myth*, Nashville, Tennessee: Vanderbilt University Press, 1968.
6. His reference is to Jean Paul, Vorschuleder Ästhetic, in *Werke*, (ed. Norbert Miller), Vol. V., München, Carl Hanser Verlag, 1963.
7. Kenneth Burke, *The Rhetoric of Religion, Studies in Logology*, Berkeley and Los Angeles: University of California Press, 1970.
8. *Ibid.*, p. 217.
9. *Ibid.*, pp. 200-201.
10. *Ibid.*, p. 191.
11. *Ibid.*, p. 251.
12. Rudolf Bultmann, "New Testament and Mythology," in Hans Werner Bartsch, editor, *Kerygma and Myth, A Theological Debate*, translated by Reginald H. Fuller, London: S.P.C.K., 1953, pp. 1-16; *Primitive Christianity in Its Contemporary Setting*, (Fontana Library), translated by R.H. Fuller, London: Collins, 1960; *Theology of the New Testament*, London: S.C.M. Press, 1952.
13. Rudolf Bultmann, "New Testament and Mythology," pp. 10-11.
14. Northrop Frye, *The Modern Century, The Whidden Lectures 1967*, Toronto: Oxford University Press, 1967.
15. *Ibid.*, pp. 105-6.
16. *Ibid.*, p. 111.
17. *Ibid.*, pp. 112-13.
18. Georges Dumézil, *L'idéologie tripartite des Indo-Européens*. Collection Latomus, Vol. 31, Brussels, 1958. See also C. Scott Littleton, *The New Comparative Mythology, An Anthropological Assessment of the Theories of Georges Dumézil*, Berkeley and Los Angeles: University of California Press, 1966.
19. Lucien Lévy-Bruhl, *Primitive Mentality*, authorized translation by Lilian A. Clare, London: George Allen & Unwin, 1923; Claude Lévi-Strauss, "The Structural Study of Myth," in Thomas A. Sebeok, editor, *Myth, A Symposium*, Bloomington: Indiana University Press, 1958, pp. 50-66;

Structural Anthropology, translated from the French by Claire Jacobson and Brooke Grundfest Schoepf, London: Allen Lane The Penguin Press, 1968; *Mythologiques, Le Cru et le Cuit*, Paris: Plon, 1964; *The Savage Mind (La Pensée Sauvage)*, London: Weidenfeld & Nicolson, 1966.

20. Mary Douglas, "The Meaning of Myth, with Special Reference to 'La Geste d'Asdiwal,' " in Edmund Leach, editor, *Myth and Totemism*, London: Tavistock, 1967, pp. 49-69.

21. *Ibid.*, p. 56.

22. Claude Lévi-Strauss, "The Structural Study of Myth."

23. Claude Lévi-Strauss, *The Savage Mind*, p. 219.

24. G.S. Kirk, *Myth, Its Meaning and Functions in Ancient and Other Cultures*, Cambridge: Cambridge University Press, and Berkeley and Los Angeles: University of California Press, 1970.

25. *Ibid.*, pp. 8-31.

26. *Ibid.*

27. *Ibid.*, pp. 91-93.

28. S.C. Woodward, "Shinto," in J.N.D. Anderson, editor, *The World's Religions*, London: Inter-Varsity Fellowship, 1950, pp. 136-60.

29. *Ibid.*, pp. 140-42.

30. Emile Durkheim, *The Elementary Forms of the Religious Life*, pp. 42-47.

31. *Ibid.*, p. 47.

32. *The Holy Bible*, Authorized Version, Rom. 11: 34,36.

Chapter 4

Affirming the Reality of the Ideal in Ritual, Ethic and Hearts Alight

That the ideal is our nourishment for life in the real world, and that we must partake of it repeatedly and regularly, is the message of religious ritual. A general message can be discerned in ritual just as in myth: particular messages for particular types of occasion and concern are additional. The fact that a ritual is a repetition helps us to see what the general message is. It is a reminder, lest we forget, that our life in time is passed under the shadow of the eternal. Again and again and again it has to be said. Our practical, mundane life is lived in the precinct of the mystery: very near is the very far away. We cannot live a utilitarian life.

Religious Ritual as the Purely Expressive Response to the Ideal

In its very form religious ritual affirms the non-utilitarian. For this is how we distinguish it from other kinds of action: it is non-utilitarian, it is not designed to be the real cause of practical effects. Even though practical benefits might be included in the results expected from performing it, such as rain or an ample food supply, it is not itself the practical cause. The performers do not think their ritual action makes the rain or food in the way that other actions would make, say, a tool or a meal. This action is directed to and expressive of the *other* reality, through whose overflow of power rain and food may well in turn come.

Because religious ritual is oriented to nothing in the mundane world, the observance of it is cardinal evidence of men's distinguishing between the sacred and profane. Worship is ascribing worth to the sacred, and the form it takes is dictated by that. The actions, gestures, vestments, utensils, music, speech and song of ritual are all designed for that. In their modest way they mirror the ideal order by creating the little order of ceremony. That order has the same kind of disinterestedness as appears in the order of a game or a work of art. Order for order's sake, we could call it, pure formality, provided we are not misunderstood.

It is the little order for the sake of the great order, not for the sake of itself. Ritual is pure affirmation of the ideal. It celebrates it in the aspect of its ideality specifically, in its character as the fountainhead of beauty or—to say it in the religious way —as glory.

Man is full of apprehension when on the threshold of the sacred for a mixture of reasons. As Otto says, he wants both to draw near and draw away. He draws near so that the power of life may come to him from beyond but draws away because, being qualitatively different from his creatureliness, the power beyond could destroy him. Each of these imperatives separately is cause for apprehension, since he may fail to achieve the correct stance for it. He is therefore man on the alert, and van der Leeuw reminds us that the very word *religio* indicates this alertness.[1] But since the two causes for apprehension are presented together, and since they pull in contrary directions, his apprehension is doubly compounded. How do you stand at the doorway that you must not cross but must open so that the power of the divine may cross to you? It is clearly a matter of right balance, of exquisite poise. How, in other words, do you draw the line between the sacred and profane in exactly the right place? Religious ritual is a way of marking the place. It positions the barrier which is impermeable from one side but permeable from the other. If there were nothing he could do to achieve this balance and poise, man would presumably be more apprehensive still and be in torment. But the exact balance is to be found, and when it is achieved the release and exhilaration are immense. This explains why worship is such a peak of intensity of emotion: first the apprehension, with one's very being at stake, then the relief when life is assured. To do nothing practical is part of what has to be done to achieve the exact balance, since it is not a practical end. Simply to be expressive is what is needed and, thanks be, this is possible. So man mirrors the glory in the little order of ceremony and shows that no more glory than that could ever be borne by him, while in ascribing glory to the ideal only he opens the door to its inflow of life.

Magical ritual differs profoundly from religious ritual. Whereas religious ritual shows man victorious, magical ritual shows him defeated. For in both he is simply being expressive, and while this supplies all that is needed to accomplish the religious end successfully, it is not enough to secure practical ends. Yet it is to secure practical ends that magic is invoked. Magic is brought into play when men lack the practical means to procure some practical end. They may want food, health, fair weather, a good harvest or good fortune, for instance, and lack the practical means for securing it with certainty. So they perform magic. Different from what they suppose of the ritual of religion, they suppose it to be the real cause of the effect desired. It relieves their anxiety to perform it: better to do something than nothing.

It relieves their anxiety to believe the ritual act will be a practically effective act when they know of no other that will, as Malinowski says.[2] It relieves their anxiety to know the society has supplied a standard ritual for standard uncertainties, according to Radcliffe-Brown.[3] For these reasons confidence can be heightened through practising magic. Yet I say we see men defeated because magic, as we all know, is not the efficient, instrumental means to practical ends. If men have more knowledge or more control over their circumstances they use them and abandon the use of magic.

Even more defeated is the man who is mastered by the compulsive ritual of an obsessive neurosis. In this mental abnormality the person cannot help repeating some act which is out of step with the rational ordering of his life, such as washing his hands or tidying his room. Because it is repetitious it can be called a ritual, but insofar as it is compulsive it differs from the voluntary and scheduled repetition of religious ceremonies.[4] In life, magical ritual and even obsessive compulsions may become associated with the practice of religion and even so confused with it as to be advertised as part of it. But we need to be able to recognize them from one another: they are procedures for handling entirely different anxieties. The student of religion does not have to accept as religion everything advertised as such.

Every Society Has Its Ritual

A random list of ritual practices shows by what miscellaneous acts and objects it is possible for men to acknowledge the sacred. While the frequency and meaning given to any one has varied, all of the following have been employed: a natural object such as a tree, stream or rock; the orientation and architecture of the place of assembly; the act of assembling; pilgrimage, shrine, image, ikon, procession, liturgy; the order of service; the recitation of myth, creed and scripture; preaching, prayer, glossolalia, silence, hymn, chant, song, instrumental music, drama, fasting, feasting, festival, intoxication, trance, sexual act, posture, dance, divination, sacrifice, consecration, blessing, cleansing, totem, fetish, taboo, initiation. Such a list helps us to see how independent ritual is of the mundane meanings of things, how much its own meaning is a function of the conventional significance ascribed to a form. No society will have everything in this list, yet it will have some ritual-set of its own that will be just as miscellaneous.

The ritual-set observed by primitive peoples has differed from that of more advanced societies. For one thing, amongst primitives the intermixture of magical rituals is much greater; so much greater, in fact, that some students refuse the attempt to distinguish religion from magic in it. Besides this, the viability of the primitive community is more directly tied to health, skills, and the bountifulness of the immediate environment, and its ideal of life is more circumscribed by those concerns. Its religion consequently focuses on the solidarity needed to secure things near at hand and largely nature-made. Since its purposes are thus diffuse, short-term and less differentiated, Swanson's "primordial conditions" can play a larger part in the composition of its supernatural. It is characterized by notions like *mana*, taboo and totem for that reason. *Mana* is the power for which man draws near to the sacred, and is ritually secured by contact. Taboo is his drawing away from its dangerous voltage, by ritual avoidance. Totem, while meaning different things to different people in addition, is at least a way of identifying the critical groups whose ideal operation funnels the people's requisites to them.

To the South Sea Islanders *mana* was equally expressed in skilful diving, potency, victory in war, the authority of the chief and the happiness of the people.[5] We have an illustration of the taboo in the Andamanese expectant parents described by Radcliffe-Brown.[6] The child is named while still in the womb, and from then till some weeks after the birth nobody may use the personal name of either parent nor may the parents eat certain of their normal foods. It appears that this is because the importance of the occasion gives the parents an abnormal ritual status. At such a time they are especially vulnerable to being hurt by the sacred power, unless they observe taboos to fend it off. The moiety totemism found amongst aboriginal Australians will serve to illustrate totemism.[7] A group of people who make a moiety by being matrilineally related, will adopt for a moiety totem some natural species like eagle hawk, crow, black cockatoo or white cockatoo. This represents their group identity. They may call themselves one flesh with the totem species and avoid eating it unless driven to do so by hunger. The same individuals may also be joined with different sets of people to make yet other groups—for example, clan, section or cult society—each of which will have its own totem.

The Sacred Calendar and Sacred Career Express Religion's Comprehensiveness

Both in primitive and advanced societies two different ritual cycles are commonly found. One imposes a sacred calendar on the natural year so that a succession of celebrations unfolds as the year passes and is then repeated annually.[8] The other imposes a sacred career on the human life cycle, so that a succession of rites of passage unfolds as the individual passes from birth to death through one phase of life to the next. Each institution illustrates both the comprehensiveness of religion and the repetitiveness of ritual. While the same rite of passage is not repeated for the same individual it is nevertheless repetitive for the society. Since different cohorts of the membership reach the same phase of life at different times, the rites have to be repeated for each cohort. The comprehensiveness of religion is illustrated in rites of passage in that, as a set, they make provision for all life's major turning points. The calendar of celebrations illustrates this comprehensiveness in that, over a year, it reminds the community of the full scope of the creed. Thus the lifetime and the year-life each takes on a ceremonial pattern that is complete in itself.

1. The Sacred Calendar

The Gregorian Calendar of Western civilization is really a memorial to the sacred year. It still celebrates classical and Teutonic divinities in some of its month and day names, yet it is punctuated by Jewish sabbaths to make weeks, except that these have been transformed into Sundays to commemorate the day of resurrection of the Christian Lord. Many of the holidays observed in Christendom originated as the holy days of the church year. Commonly, the yearly cycle of celebrations divides into festivals and fasts which are respectively times of rejoicing and sorrowing. Commonly, they commemorate past events of special religious significance. Sometimes, too, they seek to phase the religious mood with the seasonal mood of nature. The Christian year commemorates mainly events in the career of Christ. Forty days of fasting are observed during Lent, a period that commemorates the time leading up to the crucifixion of Christ, and this is followed in the spring by the feast of Easter which commemorates his resurrection. Holy Week is the last week of Lent and commences with Palm Sunday, which commemorates his triumphal entry into Jerusalem. Advent is a four-week preparation for Christmas, the celebration of Christ's birth which is observed close to the winter solstice. Epiphany commemorates the baptism of Christ as marking the coming of light to the Gentiles. Circumcision and Transfiguration commemorate those events in his life. Whitsunday or Pentecost, seven Sundays after Easter, commemorates the descent of the Holy Ghost. With the historical development of Christianity so many other feasts were added that eventually congregations could only select from the repertoire. Feasts like Trinity Sunday and Corpus Christi were instituted to impress people with the importance of theological points. A host of saints days were instituted to commemorate the exemplary lives of the saints.

The religious year of the Hebrews celebrates events and occasions from their history. Mazzoth, the Feast of Weeks and the Feast of the Ingathering were pre-exilic institutions. Mazzoth is the feast which includes Passover. In it the first lambs of the season are offered to Jahweh and there is a wave offering of the first sheaf of barley. Passover commemorates the exodus from

Egypt, when unleavened bread is eaten. The Feast of Weeks is the feast of the wheat harvest, when the first fruits are offered to Jahweh. The Feast of the Ingathering or of Tabernacles (also known as Sukkoth) takes place at the end of the year and, at Jerusalem, assumes the character of a New Year festival. It is an autumn festival of thanksgiving for the produce of the threshing floor and winepress. After the exile this was connected with the Feast of Trumpets, which announces the New Year with resounding music. The Feast of the Dedication (Hanukkah or Feast of Lights) commemorates the purification of the Temple after Judas Maccabaeus defeated the Syrian Greeks, whose Antiochus Epiphanes had introduced idolatrous worship. (It is thought that its date might have suggested a date for the Christian Christmas.) The Feast of the Wood Offering recalls the offerings of wood made for the Temple. The Feast of Purim celebrates a notable deliverance during the Persian exile. The Feast of Nicanor celebrates the victory of Judas Maccabaeus over Nicanor. The periodical fasts are the Day of Atonement (Yom Kippur) and the fasts of the fourth, fifth, seventh and tenth months. The Day of Atonement probably perpetuates the idea in the early practice of an annual purification of the holy places. The fasts of the months commemorate events connected with the siege and capture of Jerusalem.

Traditional Chinese religion has a cycle of six great festivals that unfold in the course of the agricultural or moon year. Three are festivals of the living, three of the dead. There are many festivals that are local only in their observance. Each temple, for instance, has a principal deity and there will be an annual festival in honour of that deity that may involve a fair and theatrical performances. But the six great festivals are observed throughout all China. Of the festivals of the living, the Dragon-boat Festival of the fifth moon and the Autumn or Harvest Festival of the eighth moon are of dwindling importance. But the one that is of increasing importance is the Festival of the New Year. It continues for fifteen days and much effort goes into preparing for it. It is a time of general festivity and elation. Ancestors and household gods are honoured and worshipped. There are gatherings of kinsfolk and friends; good-will is expressed on all sides; debts are cleared; houses are freshened up for another year. At Ch'ing Ming, one of the festivals of the dead, celebrants visit graves, set them in order and offer sacrifices to the dead. At the Festival of Hungry Ghosts or All Souls' Day masses are said for the souls of the dead. At the Festival of the First Day of the Tenth Moon clothing to equip the spirits is burned at the graves.

2. The Sacred Career

Van Gennep it was who made us very conscious of rites of passage.[9] He saw them as having been instituted to facilitate the whole set of changes that occur when a maturing individual's status changes radically. The major occasions are pregnancy and childbirth, birth and childhood, entry into adulthood, betrothal, marriage and death. Characteristically, the ritual marking such crises exhibits three phases: separation, transition and incorporation or reintegration. The individual is plucked out of his former situation and returned to the bosom of society in a new character. But the change in status is made only after a phase of suspension between the two, and this extraordinary condition is sacred. The pattern is illustrated most typically in the way adolescents are often admitted to adulthood. There can be a ritual death. Then comes a period of seclusion in which the novitiate learns the tribal law and mythology and other things necessary for adulthood. After this again comes a ritual rebirth. Van Gennep's analysis dwells more on the socially integrating function of such rites than on their supernatural character, and Eliade has tried to bring our attention back to the latter.[10] Whether or not the actors formulate this supernatural element in an explicit way, the rite of passage does imply that at this point the person is more transparently open to the sacred, not simply that he becomes more psychologically and socially mature. Through these occasions the individual and society are refreshed by closer contact with the sacred power. And is not this connected with the fact that the sacred is the ideal society? In admitting a person to a new status the society has to expose him to the best that can be conceived for itself, both for his sake and its own. In any case, according to the Goffman account noted in Chapter 1,[11] to receive a new social self would be to be made sacred over again.

The Toda women of India may be used to illustrate pregnancy rites.[12] At or about the fifth month the woman leaves the village to live in a special hut and is ritually separated from the dairy. Then when she leaves this hut she drinks sacred milk ceremonially. In a subsequent ritual a social father is established for the child. After the birth the woman, accompanied by the child, goes to live apart again, and they eventually return to ordinary life by drinking sacred milk again. In some societies, particularly those where a belief in reincarnation exists, birth itself can be considered a transition period for the infant. Amongst the Ainu of Japan the father, mother and child are all in a transitional state after the birth, being segregated from ordinary contacts. This is because the father is believed to give the child his soul during the twelve days following birth.

For an instance of entry into adulthood—sometimes called initiation or puberty rites—we may take the practice of the Yuin and Murring tribes of Australia.[13] The boys are first separated from their mothers and given instructors who teach them the myths. These instructors bring them to a specially cleared ground in the forest and there they are shown a drawing of the divinity Daramulun on a tree. After the chief medicine man has knocked out an incisor of each youth with a chisel and small hammer, the youth is told the secrets regarding Daramulun. Dances and pantomimes follow where each performer represents some ancestral individual from the Dream-time. When the entire group are ready to return to camp, first they bathe in a stream to wash away everything connected with their life in seclusion, so that the women will know nothing about it. As they re-enter, the initiates come decorated with red ochre, to resemble other men. Their mothers have a band of white clay across the face, as a sign of mourning. After this, the initiates return to the bush where they live, observing dietary prohibitions, for six or seven months.

In the betrothal and marriage practised by the Chaga of Tanganyika there are two ritual cycles to be distinguished, the termination of the first being the beginning of a second.[14] The separation phase of the first cycle is when the young man obtains consent to marry from the girl, and his father obtains consent from the girl's father. This is followed by the transition phase of betrothal, which lasts several years. In that time the young man pays off the bride price in instalments and the girl makes visits to the house of the young man's mother, living there continuously for the last two months. The wedding, which is attended by all the relatives of the betrothed pair, is the incorporation phase of this cycle; yet it becomes a rite of separation in that the relatives of the girl lament their loss. It is then followed by another transition phase, in that for three months the girl is not supposed to do anything. All the work is done by her mother and mother-in-law who are teaching her to keep house. The young man is under instruction from his father and father-in-law at the same time. This period of apprenticeship terminates in the celebration of the *wali,* with much dancing, singing and feasting. It is attended by all relatives, and neighbours and friends. Only with this second incorporation is the marriage really validated, for by it the union is given public recognition.

If it seems surprising that death should give occasion for rites of passage having this same three-phase character, it is to mourning that we must pay special attention. For this is essentially a transition—at least for the survivors, but sometimes also for the departed. The survivors enter it through rites of separation and, at the end, are reintegrated into society through rites of the lifting of mourning. The departed may enter it with death and may leave it after an interval with entrance to the final abode. When a person dies among the Ostyak of Salekhard he is put in a dugout canoe.[15] In this he is placed on the frozen ground of the clan's burial place, feet to the north, surrounded by the things he will need in the next world. The mourners eat a meal there, of which the deceased partakes. His female relatives make a doll in his image and this is dressed, washed and

fed every day. The practice continues for two and a half years if
the dead person was a man, for two years if it was a woman.
The survivors will mourn a deceased man for five months, a
deceased woman for four. But the deceased makes a long journey
to the north to the land of the dead. The time for this journey
appears to correspond with the time during which the doll is
attended to.

Specific Meaning in Rituals Illustrated in Sacrifice and Purification

It may reward us to single out for examination two rituals,
variants of which have been very widespread: (1) the sacrifice
presented as an offering to the divinity and (2) the purification
of the person. What specific message about the ideal do these
rituals convey—in addition to the general message conveyed by
repetition? Sacrifice appears in religion in the most simple and
most complex expressions. Probably the peak of complexity is in
the sacrifice the Mahayana Buddhist attributes to the Buddha
and that which the Christian attributes to Christ. The Buddha is
seen to have sacrificed the pure enjoyment of enlightenment
once he had attained it, choosing instead to make himself a
saviour by teaching other men the way. Christ is seen to have
forfeited his heavenly throne to be made man and then to have
died voluntarily to open a way to God for sinners. Yet these
teachings are the culmination of a habit of thought with very
modest beginnings.

The Zuni of Arizona, for instance, sacrifice a turtle.[16] The Ainu
of Japan sacrifice a bear which they then eat ceremonially.[17]
Some Australian aborigines kill and eat their sacred cult totem
ritually once a year.[18] The South African Baronga consider it immaterial whether an ox or a fowl is offered.[19] The Nuer sacrifice
oxen, but many substitute a sheep, goat or wild cucumber.[20] The
Dinka, likewise, will substitute a cucumber when the animal
victim is not available.[21] The Swazi have a much valued animal,
the licabi, which is ultimately sacrificed only when it is too old to
be a display animal.[22] But it dies by proxy many times before,
for animals are shepherded near it in the byre to absorb some
of its power, and are sacrificed as substitutes. Abraham was
asked to be prepared to sacrifice his son Isaac, but God provided
a ram as a substitute.[23] The Book of Leviticus lays down detailed ceremonial law for the making of sacrifices by the Israelites.[24] Cattle, sheep, goats, turtle-doves, pigeons, flour, cakes and
wafers, are all acceptable offerings in appropriate circumstances.
The Brahmin offers butter.[25] It is Vedic practice to sacrifice a
horse.[26] The Roman threw small gifts into the fire as sacrifices
to the hearth, Vesta.[27] Delegates from the towns of the Latin
League sacrificed a white steer and ate it together.[28] Roman
clansmen made common anniversary sacrifices in honour of

their gods and ancestor spirits.[29] These are but a sample of many practices of the same kind.[30]

Ritual purification also has its simple and complex expressions, and the most complex is probably Christian baptism. Whether effected by the immersion of adults or the sprinkling of infants, it signifies nothing less than spiritual rebirth of the person. It is from sin that he is cleansed. His washing is his death to sin, and the new life of righteousness to which he rises is identical with the life of Christ and the church. This baptism, indeed, is initiation into the fellowship. The baptism of John the Baptist is similar. It is a bath of purification from sin and initiation into the company of those who wait for the reign of God. Jewish proselyte baptism, in contrast, is not for forgiveness of sin. Used in conjunction with circumcision it is a purifying bath that washes away ritual defilement to make one a member of the congregation of Israel.

It is partly because such a variety of things are believed to defile that purification rituals are so varied. Preparation for admission to the mystery religions and Gnostic sects can involve numerous rites of purification: fasting, lustration, baptism and even castigation.[31] Evident in these societies is a longing for purification, born of a consciousness of a cosmic defilement having entered human nature. The Israelite's Book of Leviticus has many detailed prescriptions for distinguishing between the clean and the unclean, and for purifying oneself when unclean.[32] The animals, birds and insects are classified as one or other, and the unclean are either not to be eaten or not to be touched. Certain physiological changes can make one unclean. After giving birth to a male child, for example, a woman has to wait thirty-three days for her blood to be purified. Commonly, the prescribed method for regaining purity is to offer a sacrifice—so here the two rituals before us are drawn together. One particularly dramatic case of it is the scapegoating ritual. Once a year the priest laid all the sins of the Israelites ritually on the head of a goat who was then lead away to the wilderness to die. The Romans observed a general public cleansing at the beginning of each New Year.[33] Participants in the Indian Ghost Dance of 1870 prepared for it by a purifying bath in the lake.[34] When incest occurs in the Central Celebes the whole village is made unclean and a buffalo, pig and cock have to be slaughtered by a man standing in the river.[35] To regain purity all the inhabitants, together with the offending couple, have to bathe in the blood-suffused water.

Are not sacrifice and purification two means of facilitating the approach of the person and community to the divinity? These are conceived as starting with some handicap in the relationship. The approach is apparently not unimpeded—a door has to be opened. Both actions express a wish for a closer intimacy, and in this attitude their most general meaning as well as their common meaning is expressed. In this also, perhaps, lies their essential effectiveness. To be literal and try to press the detailed analogies between the religious significance of a gesture and the significance the action has in a utilitarian context would be gauche. The actions can be given deeper significance as religion evolves, as we saw; but this heightened significance is certainly not reached by applying analogies in greater detail. Doing that is what accounts for some of the curious doctrines of the atonement that Christian theology has devised. In contrast, the original Christian scriptures draw out the spiritual significance of the atoning sacrifice of Christ with a fine disregard for the analogy.

Reduced to its simplicity, the offering of sacrifice indicates that the worshipper is friendly and respectful in his approach and hopes this will be reciprocated. The act of cleansing, reduced also to its simplicity, indicates his desire to be acceptable by washing away whatever could give offence. To put himself in the place of receiving what the divine can give, what more could he do? It is the bond of union that is being forged or reinforced, both in gift-giving and in making oneself presentable. Both rituals show men responding to the constraint of the ideal, then. It is as if they are saying "We want to be 'in it,' we want to be strong in the greater strength." The offering of sacrifice expresses an awareness of the *costliness* of the ideal solidarity, an awareness that it is a most exacting constraint. Purification and initiation express the distance and, indeed, complete *discontinuity* between the ideal and the actual, the qualitative difference between the sacred and profane. They express the need for not only one but a succession of deaths and rebirths—of transformations—if power from the ideal is to cross to the real.

The Limitation Inherent in Ritual

The account of ritual can only be concluded on the same sober note as marked the conclusion of the accounts of myth, dogma and fellowship. Like them, ritual can be subverted by its own inherent limitation. Just because it is sublimely non-utilitarian, there is the possibility that it can be hollow—"mere ritual" as we say. Because it is pure formality it can be—"a mere formality." Presumably it is because of this possibility that ritual has been attacked time and again by the champions of ethical religion. Religion is proved by conduct not by observance, they declaim. We must assume the attack is against the abuse of ritual, not against it *per se*. For how else could we accommodate in the one system the Book of Leviticus and the renunciations of Isaiah, Jesus and Paul? Jesus says a man cannot be defiled by anything he eats but only by evil inclinations arising in the heart.[36] Paul says nothing is unclean in itself, but it is unclean to the man who considers it so.[37] Isaiah cannot forbear.[38]

> *Hear the word of the Lord . . .*
> *To what purpose is the multitude of your sacrifices unto me?*
> *saith the Lord: I am full of the burnt offerings of rams, and*
> *the fat of fed beasts; and I delight not in the blood of bull-*
> *ocks, or of lambs, or of he goats.*
> *When ye come to appear before me, who hath required*
> *this at your hand, to tread my courts?*
> *Bring no more vain oblations; incense is an abomination*
> *unto me; the new moons and sabbaths, the calling of as-*
> *semblies, I cannot away with; it is iniquity, even the solemn*
> *meeting.*
> *Your new moons and your appointed feasts my soul hateth:*
> *they are a trouble unto me; I am weary to bear them.*
> *And when ye spread forth your hands, I will hide mine*
> *eyes from you: yea, when ye make many prayers, I will not*
> *hear: your hands are full of blood.*
> *Wash you, make you clean; put away the evil of your*
> *doings from before mine eyes; cease to do evil;*
> *Learn to do well; seek judgment, relieve the oppressed,*
> *judge the fatherless, plead for the widow.*[39]

Can this self-defeat of ritual ever be averted? Is it to be done, perhaps, by giving equal attention to the other points of the star, and by remembering the conventional and instrumental character of them all? For although it should be self-evident that none of them is its own end, they are so near to that which is its own end, that it can be forgotten. Religious man's most exacting discipline is to separate his religion from his god.

The Religious Ethic as the Purposed Realization of the Ideal

It is interesting, however, that the prophet accepts conduct as the proof that a man's religion is genuine—and he seems to have the common man with him. "By their fruits you shall know them"[40] must be just about the first article of the common man's creed. Utterly scornful of hypocrisy though always expecting it, and distrustful of every kind of religious extravagance, the common man defers to good works. But what is it that compels this agreement between prophetic discernment and common sense? If a person is genuinely religious it should make a difference, and it will be in the direction of closer conformity to the ideal; that is the presupposition they share. The student of religion is compelled also to agree—although it is a separate question whether this supplies an overriding criterion. Religions have tended to enjoin an ethic of their own, which is not simply the customary or conventional morality. And at least in the ethic itself, if not in its actual carrying out, we see religion figuring the ideal society in a highly visible way. The reality of the ideal is affirmed in ethics in a way easy to understand. If some adherents realize the ethic to a degree, this affirmation is reinforced. Possibly it is this high visibility that gives ethics its advantage as a criterion. People whose conduct is exceptionally good cannot but stand out as shining lights. If people have seen that light shine, or even have only imagined it, they can find it utterly appealing. Dogma and ritual may leave them unmoved, but "I still hold to the Ten Commandments," they will say, "and if everyone lived by the Sermon on the Mount the world would be a vastly better place." Of course the religious person will reply that his religion is not just an ethic. In this he is entirely right, and a large part of the strength of the religious ethic is its anchorage in something greater.

An ethical system represents a strenuous effort towards the unification of experience in a particular aspect. I have aimed to show that doctrine tries to unify our knowledge of our total situation, while fellowship in doctrine spreads concord through our supporting group, thereby unifying our sympathies; ritual unifies our feelings about our total situation. An ethic, in turn, tries to unify our action in it, leaving us with the sense that we are acting and living to some purpose. It does this by imposing a rational order on the actions possible in the situation. It makes discriminations between ends and means and categories of means, states priorities and proposes motives, standardizes norms and stabilizes expectations. By using it we can organize our action as a system of means leading to the ends it teaches us to endorse. Weber thought evolution in religion was largely a matter of breakthroughs in which traditional ethics were rejected in favour of ethical systems exhibiting ever greater rationality and systematization.[41]

But whether an ethic is rudimentary or advanced it is a systematization of some sort. For one thing, just because it offers general rules of conduct, the person does not have to seek a particular directive for every situation. He can watch for the recurrence of the same types of situation and meet them all in the standard way. But an ethic also recognizes the many-sidedness of life and makes separate rules for all departments. Amongst primitive people it may rest at that, the ethic being simply a collection of separate taboos and enjoined practices. But more sophisticated societies begin to tie the rules together, so that in remembering any obligation one is made to remember its place among them all. Perhaps indications are given of different degrees of importance amongst the rules. Characteristically, we speak of an ethical "code," and it is precisely this arranging in order that codification means. It is this that enables the person to organize his life as a whole and live purposively. He learns to accept responsibility not for isolated actions only but for a life.

Codification moves in two directions. It can be the complete enumeration of regulations elaborated in great detail or it can be a boiling down, an attempt to state the most essential principles or some very general principles which summarize others. The Book of Leviticus is an illustration of the former, the Ten Commandments an illustration of the latter. Another illustration of the summarizing procedure are the two commandments of Jesus—to love God and to love one's neighbour. On these two commandments, Jesus taught, the whole of the law and the prophets hang. Another illustration of the summarizing procedure would be the Five Pillars of Islam. This is a reminder to the Muslim that the religious observances required of him reduce to five, namely, recital of the creed, prayer, fasting, almsgiving and—in the course of his life—a pilgrimage to Mecca. At the same time Islam has a vast enumeration of regulations in the Shari'a. There, in detail, are prescriptions for virtually every aspect of the Muslim's life. Theravada Buddhism in Ceylon has a gradation of precepts to match the religious involvement of the person. For the laymen there are five, and they define the Buddhist as such: not to kill, steal, commit adultery, lie, or drink intoxicating liquor. For the fully ordained monk 227 precepts are obligatory. For the upasaka eight or ten are obligatory. The upasaka are religiously ambitious laymen who embrace this increment of asceticism to help them progress in the Noble Eightfold Path.

But to say a religious ethic proposes something more ideal than customary or conventional morality is but to summarize a whole range of possibilities. It seems that in the particular ethic they devise, men register a decision on what they can expect regarding the discrepancy between the actualized and the ideal. Can the ideal be actualized—and, if so, how? Some believe the ideal can be actualized by their own direct action, and beginning immediately. This is utopianism—if it helps to give it a distinguishing name. Some believe it will come of itself, but at the end of the age. Present activity is not a contribution to it but simply a tarrying or waiting; or, at the most, it is a time of purification so that the indivdual can be made worthy to enter. This is millenarianism. Some believe it will come if worked for as the culmination of progressive reforms. This is progressivism. Some believe it will come of itself as the result of a natural developmental process. This is evolutionism. Some believe it will not come to us under the conditions of our present life but we will come to it elsewhere—in heaven, say, or in the new creation. This is transformism. Some believe it will not come to us under the conditions of our present life and the most we can do is learn not to desire it. This is detachment. Some believe we will know if it is to come only if and when it does come, and that we should entirely accept the actual outcome, whatever it may be. This is fatalism. It must be clear that these positions will imply different things about right conduct for life in the world. When we remember that such alternatives are available, that men are largely guessing when they opt between them, and that their implications can be drawn out with varying thoroughness and consistency in particular systems, the diversity in the ethical outlook of people is hardly surprising.

The Ethic Derived from the View of Salvation

"The thirst that from the soul doth rise/Doth ask a drink divine."[42] While many men have been satisfied with less, it seems that only a direct involvement with perfection will satisfy others. Their hearts cry out for the living God. We can call this engagement with perfection, attempted in the midst of the imperfect world, salvation. Not all religion has been salvation religion, and it is important to remember that in what immediately follows we are speaking only of that which is. The way of salvation anyone follows will depend on his view of perfection and on how he sees it relating to actuality. It may assist us to understand how it is all worked out if we compare four different cases. Let us take first the Israelite at the time from which the following part of Leviticus dates. For him, salvation is having God's presence with him in the land of the living, while his people themselves are increasing in population, victorious over their enemies, free from oppression, and enjoying prosperity and peace.

> If you conform to my statutes, if you observe my commandments and carry them out, I will give you rain at the proper time; the land shall yield its produce and the trees of the country-side their fruit. Threshing shall last till vintage and vintage till sowing; you shall eat your fill and live secure in your land. I will give peace in the land, and you shall lie down to sleep with no one to terrify you. I will rid your land of dangerous beasts and it shall not be ravaged by war. You shall put your enemies to flight and they shall fall in battle before you. Five of you shall pursue a hundred and a hundred of you ten thousand; so shall your enemies fall in battle before you. I will look upon you with favour, I will make you fruitful and increase your numbers: I will give my covenant with you its full effect. Your old harvest shall last you in store until you have to clear out the old to make room for the new. I will establish my Tabernacle among you and will not spurn you. I will walk to and fro among you; I will become your God and you shall become my people. I am the Lord your God who brought you out of Egypt and let you be their slaves no longer; I broke the bars of your yoke and enabled you to walk upright.[43]

That is salvation. And the *way* of salvation? The obedience of Israel to the law. "If you conform to my statutes. . ." The covenant is this: if Israel collectively will fulfil the conditions, the reward will be collectively given.

For the Christian at the time of the Revelation of John salvation has a different meaning. Salvation is enjoying the presence of God in the New Creation, in the company not of the whole people but of that fraction of mankind who are regenerate and alive for evermore, having won the victory over sin, suffering and death. This New Creation is the work of God who is busy all the time making all things new. It has begun already and the believer entered it with his new birth, but it will continue beyond the end of time.

> Then I saw a new heaven and a new earth, for the first heaven and the first earth had vanished, and there was no longer any sea. I saw the holy city, new Jerusalem, coming down out of heaven from God, made ready like a bride adorned for her husband. I heard a loud voice proclaiming from the throne: 'Now at last God has his dwelling among men! He will dwell among them and they shall be his people, and God himself will be with them. He will wipe every tear from their eyes; there shall be an end to death, and to mourning and crying and pain; for the old order has passed away!'
> Then he who sat on the throne said, 'Behold! I am making all things new!' (And he said to me, 'Write this down; for these words are trustworthy and true. Indeed they are already fulfilled.') 'I am the Alpha and the Omega, the beginning and the end. A draught from the water-springs of life will be my free gift to the thirsty. All this is the victor's heritage; and I will be his God and he shall be my son.'[44]

This envisages a great separation amongst mankind. Each man is judged on the record of his deeds and only those written in the Lamb's roll of the living enter the New Jerusalem.

> Happy are those who wash their robes clean! They will have the right to the tree of life and will enter by the gates of the city. Outside are dogs, sorcerers and fornicators, murderers and idolaters, and all who love and practise deceit.[45]

What is the *way* of salvation in this case? It is a way of coming out or separating from the disobedient among mankind by identifying with Jesus, the obedient man of love, and walking in obedience as he walked. "He that believeth on the Son hath everlasting life . . ."[46]

For Buddha and his first followers, salvation is attaining to nirvana. Although, literally, the term means the state of nothingness, or extinction, we completely misunderstand it unless we realize that it is the extinction of a negative condition that is envisaged. The double negative makes a positive, and it is, indeed, a state of liberation, peace, joy, insight and love. The natural condition, in which the unenlightened man is bound, is one of endless suffering. Men suffer in this condition because they set their hearts on the wrong things, they expect lasting satisfaction from selfish craving and do not find it. Buddha speaks as though, from this perspective, we can scarcely figure what the alternative good is, except that we can know it means emancipation or escape from the present profound dissatisfaction and degrading bondage.

> *When the fire of lust is extinct, that is Nirvana;*
> *When the fires of hatred and infatuation are extinct, that is Nirvana;*
> *When pride* [false belief] *and all other possessions and torments are extinct, that is Nirvana . . .*
> *There is only one thing I preach now as before—suffering, and the extinction of suffering.*[47]

These are words attributed to Buddha. Buddha's four noble truths are that (1) existence is unhappiness and (2) this is caused by selfish craving. (3) The craving can, however, be destroyed (4) by following the eightfold path. The *way* of salvation is very precisely formulated, then. It is following the eightfold path, which is essentially the practice of a discipline of moderation, through which the appetites are extinguished. It is a middle way, a path of the golden mean. Buddha thinks that indulgence and abstinence are equally unhelpful in attaining his end. It is called an eightfold path because it calls for mastery in eight separate spheres. Right understanding, right purpose, right speech, right conduct, right vocation, right effort, right alertness and right concentration—these are all necessary.

For Muhammad and the original Muslim, salvation lies in enjoying heaven in the hereafter and the presence of God now, the double reward of the righteous. In this, it is as far removed as can be from the Israelite expectation of concrete fulfilment in the present time and place. However, the obedience that is central to the Jewish and Christian positions recurs here, as well as the separation that is central to Christianity. The Muslim's faith envisages human history as a vast watershed separating the heaven-bound and hell-bound from one another. The separation of the sheep from the goats at the final judgment, the reward of heaven and the punishment of hell, are kept vividly before everyone. Allah, the one and only God, is sovereign and will accomplish his will in all things and with all people, so one must submit to Him absolutely. If this is done one is rewarded even now with a constant sense of his presence. In the Koran Muhammad warns:

> *Yet truly there are guardians over you—*
> *Illustrious recorders—*
> *Cognisant of your actions.*
> *Surely amid delights* shall *the righteous* dwell
> *But verily the wicked in Hell-fire:*
> *They shall be burned at it on the day of doom,*

And they shall not be hidden from it.
What shall teach thee what the day of Judgment is?
Once more. What shall teach thee what the day of Judgment is?
It is a day when one soul shall be powerless for another soul;
and all on that day shall be in the hands of God.[48]

The *way* of salvation *is* Islam, which literally means submission to God. One must, of course, believe in Allah as the only God, and in Muhammad as his prophet. Heeding this messenger, one will turn from sin and rebellious self-will and live a life of justice and mercy. One will express brotherhood and equality, especially to fellow Muslims, and extend compassion, particularly to those categories of people who are in special need: the poor, the orphans, the widows, the sick and the wayfarers. In showing compassion and mercy one simply imitates Allah, for he is the compassionate and merciful one.

The differences between these four ideas of salvation, with four ways of salvation to correspond, are indeed arresting. But in this book discussion of differences is mainly reserved for the second half. What I wanted to bring to attention here is the similarity in the way a religious ethic is derived, regardless of its particular content. First some state of involvement with the ideal is laid down as the salvation to be sought. Then the belief as to whether and how that can be actualized is brought in. What men may and must do as their part in the actualizing programme is the way of salvation, and the ethic of the religion is simply any ethical requirements included in the way. In terms of the alternatives that were itemized above, the early Israelite case is an instance of utopianism, the early Christian and Muslim cases instances of transformism, the early Buddhist case an instance of detachment.

Recalling the claim made in the first chapter that the divinity is the objective ideal that is a real possibility for the society's life, it might be asked whether transformism and detachment do not deny that the ideal is a real possibility. Utopianism appears to fit rather neatly, but what about these other two? One can admit that detachment and transformism are both solutions which are reached with an acute consciousness of the extreme opposition between the real and the ideal. Detachment does not expect the ideal to be realized within the existing material conditions, but it does remain agnostic regarding the conditions in which it is realizable. It does at least say that it will not be realizable for as long as men are mastered by lust, hate, infatuations, pride, possessions, and things of that kind. Transformism leans in the same direction but goes much further. It does not expect the ideal to be realized within the existing material conditions of life, but anticipates a transformation of state in which it will be realized. Yet in the Christian case the new state (the New Creation) is the work of the divinity who makes all things new, and in the Muhammadan case (Heaven) of the divinity who is sovereign over all. This is suggesting that part of their idea of the ideal society is the achievement of such a degree of mastery over its present material conditions that human life will no longer be recognizably the same. Another way of putting it might be to say that, in this type of view, ideal society is not the unhampered fulfilment of all present-day "natural" needs, longings and aspirations, but includes some radical surgery on them. The fact that both of them envision a drastic selection process would be in keeping with that. Yet another way of expressing it would be to say that, in this view, the merging of the ideal and the real might occur at a point which is closer to the original position of the ideal than to the original position of the real. But this kind of question is more meaningfully discussed in Chapter 7.

The exercise I have just engaged in, of depicting religious ethics as a function of a view of salvation, which is itself a resolution of discrepancy between the real and ideal, finds its precedent in the work of Max Weber.[49] For it was he who initiated that type of analysis. As explained in Chapter 2, he proposed that, basically, only two paths are available to one who is convinced the discrepancy requires a radical solution: escape from the consciousness of the world's imperfection, or mastery over the world so as to bring it into conformity with the ideal. The former attitude he calls mysticism, the latter asceticism. In addition, a person adopting either stance may choose to work through the existing social institutions or make a fairly complete break with them, the former being an inner-worldly strategy, the latter an other-worldly. The two pairs of alternatives in combination allow for four possible positions. These are separately exemplified in Confucianism, Hinduism, Judaism and Catholicism, in the manner shown in Figure 1. Only one of the four positions—inner-worldly asceticism—provides a leverage for evolutionary social change. The Protestant tendency in Christianity is the most extreme development of this, although Judaism and Islam, which are of the same broad tradition, also exemplify it. At the opposite extreme from Protestantism, as the extreme case of other-worldly mysticism, is early Buddhism.

	Mysticism	Asceticism
Inner-worldly strategy	e.g. Confucianism	e.g. Judaism
Other-worldly strategy	e.g. Hinduism	e.g. Catholicism

Figure 1. Weber's Four Types of Religious Programme

Weber notes that the ethic derived from salvation belief is an ethic of brotherly love.[50] Regardless of whether the strategy adopted is other-worldly or inner-worldly, this generates tension with any existing institutional order and is difficult to apply. It seems to land its exponents in a succession of predicaments, and Weber thinks it not irrelevant to ask how feasible it can ever be. Mystics think love is sufficiently expressed in senti-ments of solidarity and a fine disregard for the practical neces-sities. Ascetics endeavour to express love in work and responsi-bility, yet in coming to terms with political and economic reali-ties, and with practical necessities in general, they can be com-promised. (Judging by the common man's enthusiasm for the ethic of love, one would think its realization was an easier thing than falling off a log. Weber's analysis reminds us that its real-ization is supremely difficult, and it seems to be due to two quite different sets of reasons. (1) Motivation for it rests on a prior conviction that salvation must be sought, for only this can free men from the dog-eat-dog competitiveness of those who expect fulfilment from the natural condition. (2) Its application is handicapped unless it is reciprocated, so it is mainly within the fellowship of believers that it can be made operable.)

The Idea of a Universal Ethic

But some may question whether the foregoing does not over-emphasize the differences between the ethical traditions. For the idea has been advanced that there is only one universal ethic, a "natural law," that finds expression in the diverse tra-ditions. To have a tag for it in all its forms—Platonic, Aristotel-ian, Stoic, Christian and Oriental—Lewis calls this the *Tao*.[51] Aldous Huxley, adopting Leibniz' phrase *philosophia perennis,* says the various religious traditions are expressions of but one perennial philosophy, which includes an ethic along with a meta-physic and a psychology.[52] In an effort to support their positions both these authors assemble quotations from a wide literature. How much truth is there in this kind of idea? If it contains truth, how can it be squared with the idea that religious ethics can vary with the idea of salvation?

There are several points to be made regarding this apparent contradiction. The first is that, according to the level at which one makes generalizations, the differences between any set of things can drop out of view, so that they will all look alike. If one looks for resemblances in different ethical traditions one will find them, for similar elements are there. It is not surpris-ing, since they confront the same class of problems. Secondly, the difference that men who live under the traditions feel be-tween them, is largely due to the fact that each is a configura-tion. As I have said, each is a code, a unitary ordering of elements. If the whole set of elements and the whole arrangement of them is not the same in two systems they will be different systems, even if *most* of their elements are the same. But my third and main point is one that has been waiting in the wings for a prompter's call anyway. It is that we have to distinguish two levels of morality and it is only for the higher level that religion supplies the pull. For want of any better way of saying it, the lower level might be described as the morality of actualities, the higher level as the morality of possibilities. They are really what Bergson calls the closed and open moralities.[53] The dichotomy I mean is illustrated in the famous saying of Jesus: "Ye have heard that it hath been said, Thou shalt love thy neighbour, and hate thine enemy. But I say unto you, Love your enemies."[54] The lower level is the morality of obligation, the upper that of aspiration. We are obliged to help maintain our society as it is and that imposes a certain ethic on us, but if we aspire to see it transformed that supplies us with another.

Certain actualities of social life can be much the same everywhere, while its ideal possibilities can be conceived variously. So one would expect more agreement among precepts that apply to the lower level. The similarities Lewis points to lie on this level, and he is consequently able to make a fairly convincing case. There *has* been a fairly widespread approval of things like goodwill towards one's kith and kin, responsibility towards one's parents and children, fair dealing and honesty, courage, honour, and self-sacrifice for the group's welfare. Even the recognition that one must also give attention to a higher call than concern with actualities, can be a common feature of moralities at this level. Lewis quotes Aristotle giving voice to that recognition:

> *We must not listen to those who advise us 'being men to think human thoughts, and being mortal to think mortal thoughts,' but must put on immortality as much as is possible and strain every nerve to live according to that best part of us, which, being small in bulk, yet much more in its power and honour surpasses all else.* (Ancient Greek. Aristotle, Eth. Nic 1177B.[55])

But how that higher call is then conceived differs, and from this point on come the more radical divergences. Huxley tries to show a similarity between the traditions on this second level and, unlike Lewis, he is not convincing. For here the situation is really more like the radical cleavage Weber depicts than the unity Huxley wishes to see. At the end of his book Huxley is disingenuously recasting all religions in the mould of oriental contemplative religion in order to make them all the same. Yet, notwithstanding the cleavage that I say must be recognized, I think it is also important to emphasize a fact already mentioned. Just because of their having an orientation to salvation, different higher-level ethical systems can have something in common. They can take the ethic of brotherly love seriously because of their disengagement from actualities.

The Limitation Inherent in an Ethic

This brings us to the inherent limitation of the religious ethic and the possibility of its own subversion. The purpose of an ethic is to generate the inward and outward freedom that come from performing it, to facilitate life by creating mutual respect and acceptance. But this is soon supplemented in experience, if not eclipsed, by the consciousness that one is failing in the performance of it again and again, or performing it outwardly only. What was meant for liberation becomes a chain. It is Paul who gives fullest expression to the anguish of this plight.[56] He says no human being can be justified in the sight of God for having kept the law: the *net* effect of the law is not the consciousness of acceptance but the consciousness of sin. It is his great discovery to experience relief from this oppression, however. God has his own way of righting wrong, he claims. Even though all have sinned, all may yet be justified—by God's grace alone, and through Christ. "For God designed him to be the means of expiating sin by his sacrificial death."[57] It is not the law that men must look to for their salvation but the fulfilment of the law, he is still saying. In Christ, thanks to God's goodness, we see that accomplished. If we accept that Christ's performance of the moral law was made on our behalf, particularly his self-offering in death, it is felt as if it were made by us. We *experience* the great liberation, and not as the result of our merit but of our faith. "For our argument is that a man is justified by faith quite apart from success in keeping the law."[58]

Religious Experience as Surrender to the Ideal

The heart lit up by experience as the result of faith is what men use to affirm the reality of the ideal when their ethic seems a dead letter. In the title of the present chapter is the phrase "hearts alight." It is simply meant to designate experience, and is meant to cover the many kinds of experience of divinity that men report. The experience of justification, where one feels accepted for being as ethical as he is expected to be, is but one of a variety of religious experiences. Yet, although these vary as experiences, it is probably true to say they are all the fruit of faith. Each of them is a different engagement with the divinity and, as such, it is a specific kind of knowledge; but that it is the divinity that is present to the person is assumed by faith.

Faith as Willingness — Rather than Wishfulness

Faith, I take it, is the uninhibited willingness to make this assumption—that the divinity is present. There are some twisted ideas about faith that we would do well to be rid of. One is that it is a magical way of knowing things that can also be known by ordinary means; one is that it is being pious enough to believe something that is contrary to evidence; one is that it is being docile enough to be told what to believe instead of finding out for yourself. If people distrust "faith" because they construe it in ways like these, they do so for good reason. Yet it is a pity if that leads them to deny the place that faith, properly understood, plays in life. Faith is something that has to be set in opposition to knowledge, not because it contradicts knowledge but because it exceeds knowledge where life gives occasion to exceed knowledge—by feeling. For faith is a matter of feeling. Faith is the willingness to give way to the feeling that all things flow together into a unity, a perfection, although we cannot see it. It is the willingness to affirm perfection without waiting or asking for proof, and the willingness to give actual things meaning by viewing them against that ideal background. It is the gratuitous affirmation that the ideal is real. It is simply a fact that people sometimes exercise faith, and because of it they are able to put concrete facts of experience in a context that gives them a meaning they would never otherwise be given.

In the account above of the Pauline experience of justification, where does faith come in, if at all? It does, and it is where the "if" comes. "If we accept that Christ's performance of the moral law was made on our behalf..." Why would we accept that it was—that it could be or would be—made on our behalf? There is, strictly speaking, no reason of proof brought forward; but, so far as faith is concerned, none is needed. Faith is prepared to affirm it because it is an ideal possibility. Faith always feels that the ideal is real and is spreading its transfiguring halo around every actualized thing. There is something admittedly constructive about this way of understanding things, as though one intentionally puts the best possible construction on them—the "rose-coloured spectacles." Yet it is not the same as "wishful thinking," when we say some testable thing is the case because we want it so; for example, that we will be well for our birthday, or will outlive a wealthy uncle or, when we have fallen in love, that our love is requited. Faith is a general, unspecific sanguineness about the things beyond testing, and to give way to it is to be flooded with a blessed assurance that all manner of thing will be well.

William James' *The Varieties of Religious Experience* has not been surpassed as a penetrating treatment of its subject.[59] James views faith there in the way I have just presented it. In his "Conclusions" he makes the point that we find a great variety of thoughts represented when we survey the whole field of religion,

but that the feelings and conduct are almost always the same.
". . . Stoic, Christian, and Buddhist saints are practically indistinguishable in their lives."[60] He therefore concludes: "The
theories which Religion generates, being thus variable, are secondary; and if you wish to grasp her essence, you must look to
the feelings and the conduct as being the more constant elements."[61] Because of the importance of feelings he asks whether
it is possible to characterize the psychological order to which
religious feelings belong. His answer is this:

> *The resultant outcome of them is in any case what Kant
> calls a "sthenic" affection, an excitement of the cheerful,
> expansive, "dynamogenic" order which, like any tonic, fresh-
> ens our vital powers. In almost every lecture, but especially
> in the lectures on Conversion and on Saintliness, we have seen
> how this emotion overcomes temperamental melancholy and
> imparts endurance to the Subject, or a zest, or a meaning, or
> an enchantment and glory to the common objects of life. The
> name of "faith-state", by which Professor Leuba designates
> it, is a good one. It is a biological as well as a psychological
> condition, and Tolstoy is absolutely accurate in classing faith
> among the forces by which men live. The total absence of it,
> anhedonia, means collapse.*[62]

I think we can say that religious experiences are the satisfactions
that people generously disposed to finding, find. "Seek and ye
shall find."[63]

The Religion of the Vestibule: Saying "Yes" to the Creation

The first major differentiation we encounter in religious experience is one that corresponds to the distinction James makes between the religion of healthy-mindedness and the religion of the
sick soul.[64] It seems, also, that it is not unrelated to the distinction theologians make between natural and revealed religion.
The healthy-minded or "natural" affirmation of the divinity is
one which claims the presence of the divinity can be felt if one
will only cultivate the sense of it. Starting just where he is, the
person must think positively, use suggestion, practise mind-cure,
relax, commune with nature. A characteristic approach to evil
is taken. Evil is the fact that faith has been blocked in its natural
unfolding and the vision it gives to us veiled. It is an error, and
is dispelled by taking a different attitude.

This is the kind of religion one finds exemplified in Mary
Baker Eddy and Christian Science, in Emerson's transcendental-
ism, in Whitman's abandonment to nature and life, in Wordsworth's nature study. It is a religion premised on the assumption
of innocence. It gives one the confidence that he may be his
created self since nature and life are beautiful as created. It is
the religion of the fulfilment of all potentialities, of health and

self-realization. It is the religion of "natural law," of the balance or inexorable order imprinted in nature from the beginning, that will never suffer denial.

> *If you love and serve men, you cannot by any hiding or strata-*
> *gem escape the remuneration. Secret retributions are always*
> *restoring the level, when disturbed, of the divine justice. It*
> *is impossible to tilt the beam. All the tyrants and proprietors*
> *and monopolists of the world in vain set their shoulders to*
> *heave the bar. Settles forevermore the ponderous equator to*
> *its line, and man and mote, and star and sun, must range*
> *to it, or be pulverized by the recoil.*[65]

In this Emersonian affirmation of the unity of the divine, moral and natural orders, the unity of the unities, this type of religious consciousness is epitomized. The *Tao* of Chinese religion and the *dharma* of Indian religion express the same repose in the created order. Yet, whatever else faith brings to view by this mode of exploration, it leaves the person unshaken and undisturbed by any sense of sin. That is reserved for the religion of the sick soul; for that, by contrast, is the labouring religion of the broken and contrite heart.

James presents the two types of religious experience as though the type of personality determines which of the two any-one will undergo.[66] It is true that the life-long religion of many people has settled into one or other of the two modes, and that there has consequently been tension between them. Yet it seems better to think of them as corresponding with phases or states of the personality, so that the one person might well experience both. It is possible to think of healthy-minded religion as the vision of our innocence that faith is able to recall. While the guilt man has contracted presents him with the deeper religious prob-lems of lost innocence, the imprint of his original innocence could still be with him and it could still be something he needs to discover. His "natural" self, as designed by his maker, need not have been irremediably infected by sin: the sin could be that it has been abused and neglected. This "natural" self is scarcely the "carnal mind" or "lower nature" of the Epistle to the Ro-mans, that is said to be at enmity with God. Are theologians who make light of natural theology inclined to confuse these? However, if one adopts this generous view and gives accommo-dation to both types of religious experience, one may still grant a greater depth and importance to the sick-soul variety. The re-ligion of healthy-mindedness is simply the religion of the vesti-bule. Interestingly enough, James agrees with this relative rating.[67]

The Religion of Redemption: Triumphing over Evil

It seems that when we find men entering the second, deeper level of religious experience they are men profoundly disquieted and disturbed. The harmony and peace they eventually reach comes by facing and resolving their deep trouble, so it has a height and depth to it that "healthy-minded" harmonies never plumb. Typically, such men are profoundly dissatisfied with themselves and the course of their lives. They may formulate it as sin and feel intense guilt and a need for repentance, or may feel empty, wasted, lost, desperate, or otherwise ill at ease. Typically, after this, they undergo a conversion—by which I mean a turning. Their wills settle firmly in a new direction, bringing them a new sense of purpose, satisfaction, selfhood, and self-acceptance. The moods and feelings associated with all this can be very variable, and the consciousness of a turning can be sudden or slow. What appears to be common to all cases is a re-evaluation of the situation that originally caused unrest. The situation is not different but a point of vantage is reached from which it is viewed differently. There is the feeling now that a great harmony is being worked out and that one has been enlisted in it, so he is taken out of himself. Even the evil of the former pattern is transmuted into good in the new, and man's extremity appears as God's opportunity. The feelings associated with that realization can also be variable. They may be sober, they may reach ecstasy. The unconscious wisdom of not suppressing the voices of dissatisfaction at the beginning, of admitting the negative, is seen in the result. It forces a larger perspective.

James examines a number of such crises minutely.[68] The cases of Henry Alline, Tolstoy, M. Alphonse Ratisbonne and Bunyan can serve as illustrations for our purpose. Alline, who worked as an evangelist in Nova Scotia around 1800, was formerly much given to "carnal pleasures and carnal company."[69] He developed so strong a sense of sin because of it that he thought everyone could read his sins at sight and that the whole earth was accursed for his sake. After much "seeking, praying, reforming, laboring, reading, hearing, and meditating"[70] his salvation was no nearer, and he desperately asked God to find some new way that he himself knew nothing of. God then came, bringing redeeming love to his soul. Within half an hour he knew that he was called to the ministry, and thenceforth he lost all taste for carnal pleasures and company and forsook them.

Tolstoy's descent into melancholy was slow, as was his ascent from it.[71] After three years, when he came out of it, he recognized what it was—the quest for God. He had been tempted by suicide because the life he lived seemed to him a parody of life. It was simply the conventional, artificial, ambition-driven life of the upper, intellectual classes of nineteenth-century Russia. But it had no root in reality, and in time Tolstoy came to realize he could only live at all if he lived differently. One could not live life merely to live, one must live to be better. When life is lived in that way "to acknowledge God and to live are one and the same thing."[72] Thereafter Tolstoy resolved to renounce vanities and live simply, working with common men to fulfil their common needs, believing in God.

Ratisbonne was a free-thinking French Jew who was converted to Catholicism at Rome in 1842.[73] His case is interesting because the period of preparation for conversion was unusually short. He thought himself inured to religion till he had several conversations with a gentleman who tried to make a convert of him. He parried his persuasions with jests, but did accept from him a prayer to the Virgin. Then came a disturbed period when for some days he could not banish the prayer from his mind. At the end of this time, in a church, he had a vision of the Virgin, and accepted the faith. His whole life was changed. He gave up his plans for marriage, joined the priesthood and went to Jerusalem to found a mission of nuns for the conversion of Jews.

The Bunyan of seventeenth-century England presents us with a very different case.[74] Bunyan's was, undoubtedly, a morbidly sensitive conscience. For some years he thought he was forsaken of God because of his "original and inward pollution" that made him "more loathsome . . . than was a toad."[75] Familiar with the gospel of forgiveness long before he could entirely believe it applied to himself, he was then, again for years, up and down: "peace now and before I could go a furlong as full of guilt and fear as ever heart could hold."[76] He seemed never to become entirely stable emotionally, but there was a transformation of character. Time gave evidence of a definite turning of will that made him serviceable as a tradesman, minister of the gospel and author.

The Religion of Sanctification: Seeking Union with God

There is yet another class of religious experiences and I think we would be entitled to say they make a third level, for they seem to lie deeper than any we have considered. They are not concerned with innocence, nor with redemption, but with sanctification. They are the experiences entailed in the pursuit of holiness, as men try to be like God in order to walk more closely with him. The qualities sought are greater singleness of will, greater purity of heart, greater consistency of life. It testifies graphically to the unity of the divinity when men consider such unity within themselves to be an imitation of him. This pursuit allows scope for great deliberateness and method. Methodical exercises can be performed with a regularity that sometimes earns them the name of "ritual." Yet while rituals proper, as they were described above, may be included among the accepted methods for achieving holiness, there is a difference between them and exercises that are mainly designed for personal transformation.

It is fascinating that this passion for purity and fullness of blessing, has held such sway over the human being. Most commonly where men and women surrender to it, it is not considered necessary for salvation at all. It is an extra that is voluntarily embraced. Yet it has become the dominant life-preoccupation of millions of people. But it is also interesting that it has led to *methods* which are very diverse and, in some respects, almost diametrically opposed.

There are at least three dimensions on which a *radical* divergence of method appears. First of all, it appears that the intense desire to be a different person can beget either a great impatience or a great patience. The impatient seek to induce an ecstatic experience that will bring instant sanctification: they envisage life as a rapture. The patient embrace a life-long ascetic discipline that will bring sanctification by degrees: they envisage life as a pilgrimage. Secondly, the desire for concentration of effort can lead either to separation from society or redoubled effort within it. The third divergence is largely an entailment of this second one: it is between élitism and equality. Society is not possible if everyone separates from it in the pursuit of holiness; so, where that is the way, the necessary conditions can only be provided for a chosen few. On the other hand, if sanctification results from dedication to any calling, it is equally available to all.

Instant Sanctification and Sanctification by Degrees: Ecstasy and Asceticism

The attempt to realize instant sanctification has a long history. In a way, this can be thought of as the internalization of purification. In the early stages of religious development it could be enough to be made ritually pure, but the devotee of later religion has desired to be pure in heart. Some of the earliest association of drugs with religion was for the purpose of effecting this change. Ancient Hindus drank *soma* to attain light, immortality and fellowship with the gods.[77] The Greeks were aware that the great intensity of excitement, which they called frenzy, could carry a person out of himself.[78] It was this state that was sought, for example, through the use of wine in the Dionysian orgies. Some primitive shamans drum and dance into an ecstasy to achieve a transformation of consciousness.[79] Muslim dervishes will dance, whirl or howl to draw the divine in-filling.[80]

The Western world's familiarity with this type of phenomenon, however, is mainly through the Pentecostalist movement. It is expressed chiefly in the Christian churches having that name, but early Quakerism and early Methodism exhibited a great deal of it.[81] The Quakers took their name from the fact that they quaked and trembled when under the influence of the Spirit. Methodists were inclined to believe that sanctification was instantaneous, mainly from having so many cases to point to of instantaneous deliverance from sin. Many congregations in the more sedate and long-established churches, including the Roman Catholic and Episcopalian, have experienced waves of Pentecostalism in recent times. Pentecostalists pray for what they call the "second blessing," the first being the conversion already experienced. The second blessing is Spirit baptism and the conferral of the gifts of the Spirit. The mood of the services in Pentecostalist churches is one of intense emotional excitement as they wait for these. There is spontaneous prayer and singing, speaking in tongues and prophesying, weeping and crying out, moving about, swaying, physical contact and embracing. Thus it is they seek to have the Spirit come.

But in contrast to this is the austere sobriety of those who undertake a prolonged discipline, entailing many denials, with the same end in view. If the method just described is like an internalization of purification, this resembles an internalization of sacrifice. Yoga means union, and Hindu Yoga was an elaborate system of body and thought control that was undertaken with the aim of achieving union with Brahman, the Universal Spirit.[82] Controlled breathing, posture and diet were as much a part of it as meditation. Demanding though that could be, such a Yoga is only the preliminary discipline of the revised Hinduism of Sankara. For that, one must also practise the non-attachment extolled in the Bhagavad-Gita, and, finally, seek the knowledge that sets one free. That search entails intensive study of the scriptures, reflection on the evidence that all things make a unity in Brahman, and meditation that turns one's acquired head-knowledge into heartfelt insight. The Buddhist monks have their distinctive asceticism.[83] They pursue the Noble Eightfold Path withdrawn from the world in monasteries. Worldly possessions are surrendered and one does not work even for a living: one lives entirely on the alms that are voluntarily given. One sleeps on a hard, rough bed, becomes celibate and forgoes alcohol and afternoon meals.

Anthony was one of the third- and fourth-century pioneers of what became a tradition of asceticism in Christianity.[84] He gave away his possessions and withdrew into the desert, in the expectation that isolation, starvation and prayer would bring him spiritual purity. In the same pursuit monks subsequently collected together in monasteries, taking a vow of chastity, obedience and poverty. Benedict was one of the first to devise a discipline by which such communities might live.[85] For example, the monk's range of movement was strictly circumscribed, he ate no flesh food, dressed in the habit, observed periods of silence and periods of devotion. There was a tendency at one time for monastic disciplines to become more severe, and even punishing. There was a rigorous movement emanating from Cluny which imposed things like the wearing of a hair shirt, flagellation, repetitive genuflexion and periods of solitary confinement.[86]

The nineteenth-century Russian sects of the Khlysty and Skoptsy illustrate some of the effects of extreme asceticism.[87] An eventual pendulum-swing to ecstasy on the part of the Khlysty also lends support to the idea I shall present shortly, of an equivalence between these two methods. Originally the Khlysty practised flagellation, fasting, blood-letting and sexual continence (even though married), took cold baths and went barefoot, and avoided alcohol, tobacco, potatoes, meat, onions and garlic—all in the interests of purity. Apparently the extreme sense of purity attained left the Khlysty with the impression that they were beyond sin: old actions performed by them now could not have the old meaning. In this antinomian innocence they were particularly attracted to sexual activity. The Holy Spirit descended upon them, they came to believe, at the end of a round dance in which they worked themselves into a frenzy, a near-hypnotic trance. The dance involved flagellation, leaping and pirouetting and glossolalia. At last they sank down exhausted but utterly elated and, in their joy, celebrated the coming of the Spirit by engaging in promiscuous intercourse. It was largely as a reaction to the excesses they saw in the Khlysty that the Skoptsy developed their position. So appalled were they by the possibilities latent in sex that they named every trace of it—a glance or a touch even—evil. They came in time to preach and practise castration as the path to holiness. The common man has a profound suspicion of religious experience, and the churches say it must unfold under their restraining care. The reversal in excess shows us why. The fire that lights up the believing heart, if not controlled, can be deadly.

Separation from Society and Redoubled Effort Within It

Now let us consider the divergent directions pursued for the sake of concentrating effort. Separation from society by withdrawal into monastic orders is a method that has been devised in many traditions. It appears in Islam, Buddhism, Jainism, Taoism and Manichaeism as well as in Christianity. But it finds its greatest elaboration in Roman Catholic Christianity. The Jesuit order founded by Ignatius Loyola in 1540 illustrates the gains that are sought by adopting this strategy.[88] The stated aim of this order is the salvation and perfection of individual Jesuits and of all their fellow men, and the combating of heresy is one of its special concerns. With this intent the Jesuit undergoes an intellectual and spiritual training that may continue for something like fourteen years. Those candidates who eventually take the three solemn vows of chastity, poverty and obedience add a fourth vow of special obedience to the Pope, should he direct them to accomplish any mission. The *Spiritual Exercises,* the manual prepared by Ignatius, prescribes the type of spiritual cultivation practised. It is systematized prayer which may sometimes occupy four or five hours of the day. In it the Jesuit meditates with all possible empathy on Christ's passion and Kingdom, with the aim of discovering God's will for him as an individual. The organization of the order is highly centralized and achieves an almost military efficiency and obedience. Its members give service in society, often as teachers in schools, colleges, seminaries and universities, and as missionaries.

The Franciscan orders, the first of which was founded in 1209, are a rather different attempt to embody the same principle of separation.[89] The approach to Christian perfection pioneered by Francis of Assisi is the one followed there. A literal imitation of the life of Jesus, which is seen to imply extreme simplicity, plays a large part in this. A sense of kinship with all men and creatures is another principle, since God is viewed as the Father of men and creatures alike. The Franciscan also passionately seeks union with God in prayer. The first friars were wandering evangelists who retired periodically to secluded places to pray. In contrast to the Jesuit ideal, which is modern in that it prepares mobile individuals for individualized careers, the Franciscan ideal is stereotyped and archaic, in that it makes the career of Jesus standard for all members and for all times. The attempt to imprison that idyllic conception in organization was not highly successful and, as organization was achieved, there was a series of reform movements within the order advocating return to a stricter poverty and simplicity. The eventual result was three separate orders. Some of the reformists retreated to remote hermitages in order to have the conditions for observing the primitive Franciscan rule. It is of interest to note that this difficulty of implementing the monastic ideal even in the monastery, has been experienced elsewhere. It is reported that some Buddhist monks in Ceylon find it impossible to pursue their *arahat* ideal in the monastery.[90] They make their escape to secluded caves in the dense forest or jungle. They are on the second line of retreat from the compromising world.

There is another variation on the withdrawal theme that ought to be noticed here. This is the founding of a completely separate total community—or one that is almost so. One great difference between these and the monastic fellowships is that they incorporate families and family life, but they also incorporate employment and political problems and all the other features of ordinary life. For the spiritual discipline is simply ordinary life lived at a higher intensity. The object is to realize the ideal life directly, amongst people who conceive of it in the same way, unimpeded by error. The Oneida Community of Perfectionists of New York State was founded in 1848 to make perfect holiness a way of life.[91] The Hutterian communities in various parts of North America and elsewhere perpetuate a tradition that began in sixteenth-century Europe.[92] They pursue the service of God in a way of life. It is a way that is communistic in regard to property, and may include common dining and common child-rearing.

In contrast to all this is the notion of remaining in the world but finding one's vocation in it. Vocation has degenerated in popular usage, where it means finding the place of one's own choice. But in its original religious meaning, as expounded by the Protestant theologians Luther and Calvin, vocation (or calling) meant nothing unless it meant finding the place of God's choice.[93] In Luther it seemed to be rather more passive, in Calvin more active. Passive in the sense that the Lutherans learned a resignation to the existing social structure from believing that the status anyone had was the one he should keep; active in the sense that Calvinists believed that filling one's vocation was exploiting one's God-given opportunities. But, in either case, to fulfil one's vocation was to do the will of God as much as anyone could. To do it properly demanded discipline of life and could call for as many denials as any monastic existence. This one way was available to everyone, albeit, it may be, in a thousand different vocations. The belief gave laymen a conviction that the spiritual fulfilment available to people in religious orders was no greater than that available to them, and that such fulfilment was realizable through accepting responsibility in the world. It has shaped the attitudes and practices of Protestant Christianity to the present day.

Annihilation of Separateness the Object of all Methods of Sanctification

But, for all the diversity in the styles of spiritual exercise, there is a great unity in it. To be filled with God is the end of them all. This is the objective, both for pleasure in the feasting and for the strengthening of right inclination. There is, furthermore, basically only one way in which it is being attempted. Only by the annihilation of the individual's separateness and isolation can he be absorbed in the unitary whole. There is an almost quantitative underlying assumption. The annihilation of the fragment is the restoration of the whole: a man's nothingness is the fullness of God. But immediately there comes a division into two possible paths to annihilation—these not being exclusive of one another. One is the annihilation of separated will, one the annihilation of separated consciousness. The former is to be accomplished by the way of obedience. There are two alternative ways for accomplishing the annihilation of separated consciousness, although, again, these are not necessarily exclusive of one another: either by exhaustion from over-excitement or by denial. Whether it is done by exhausting the senses through over-stimulation or by starving them, the self of which we are normally conscious is worn thin.

Obedience may be exemplified equally well in membership of a monastic order and dedication to a secular calling. By obedience in the routines of the monastic community and any mission it may have to the world, the individual sinks into place in a larger order, which itself is laid into God's great design. It is the same in a secular calling. God has his own intricately co-ordinated but perfect strategy: he apportions the parts and it is for each man to be in his place. In both situations obedience makes each person a tile in a mosaic. Between them all together God accomplishes his work. We might note, incidentally, that many auxiliary spiritual exercises really exist to make the nice adjustments necessary to get this collective service of God accomplished. Self-examination, confession and repentance, prayers of supplication and for guidance, study and devotions to strengthen discipleship, all play a part.

The annihilation of separated consciousness, whether induced by quaking or fasting, by intoxication or meditation, is really always the same experience; there is a consciousness that God is displacing the attenuated self. The term "mysticism" is sometimes used to refer to the natural capacity for this kind of exercise or to the actual practice of it in any degree and, with that meaning, it is a part of any orthodoxy. But it can also be used to refer to the cultivation of this consciousness for its own sake, a cultic tendency that entails a neglect of the other sides of life. Mysticism is then an addiction in which the mystic concentrates on his identity with God, and it is not unknown for such a mystic to claim to be God. Were he consciousness only, or his will as perfect as his knowledge, his peers might not find his claim as ridiculous as they do. Because of the possibility of this aberration the orthodoxies are always as wary of mysticism as they are appreciative of it. But the *form* of it does illustrate with wonderful transparency the nature of both sanctification and divinity. For the mystic, union is the overwhelming theme. The merging is so complete there is no I or Thou, no in or out, no subject or object; there is only one undivided being, one unity. The mystic holds in consciousness what the man of feeling holds by faith.

The Limitation Inherent in Religious Experience

But aberrant mysticism also illustrates the self-limitation in all religious experience. If that limitation is not recognized men will take the divinity to be no larger than their experience of him and will repose their trust in that instead of in his perfection and power. They need a way to trust not in their hold on God but in his hold on them. It is faith that finds that way, feeling that the unity in which man lies must be greater than creation's order, redemption's harmony and the mystical union, separately or together.[94]

Although with the consideration of religious experience it might appear that we had moved into psychology, that was scarcely the intention. It is true that there is a psychological way to analyze this experience, and it is exemplified superbly in James. It is also true that we have made use of psychological description to characterize the different types of religious experience. But my purpose was to remind us that the pursuit even of religious experience is patterned by social expectation. Any society will provide opportunities for those types of experience it deems worthwhile and authentic, and will lead successive generations into them. Psychology takes note of how such experience functions in the mind. Sociology takes note of how it is standardized and how, in that aspect, it is enjoined by society as an instrument for orientation to life. Faith, innocence, conversion, redemption and sanctification—all these are defined and means of realizing them made available, in the religious culture. I wanted to suggest that experience in that sense, as much as ritual, ethic, doctrine and fellowship, is something that men devise collectively in order to explore more exhaustively the reality of the ideal. The recurrence of these same expressions in different systems, is what has claimed our attention up till now of course. It is very significant that such common elements can be found in systems that are otherwise diverse. But it is time for us now to turn our attention to the differences.

Notes, Chapter 4

1. G. van der Leeuw, *Religion in Essence and Manifestation*, pp. 49-50.
2. Bronislaw Malinowski, "Magic, Science and Religion," in J. Needham, editor, *Science, Religion and Reality*, New York: Macmillan, 1925.
3. A.R. Radcliffe-Brown, *Taboo* (The Frazer Lecture, 1939), Cambridge: Cambridge University Press, 1939.
4. Freud did not give attention to this difference, and consequently gives an unconvincing interpretation of religion as a "universal obsessional neurosis." See Sigmund Freud, *Collected Papers*, translated by Joan Rivière, London: Hogarth Press and the Institute of Psycho-Analysis, 1948-50, pp. 25-50.
5. For details see Van der Leeuw, *op. cit.*, pp. 23-28, and the references given there.
6. A.R. Radcliffe-Brown, *Taboo*.
7. For details see A.P. Elkin, *The Australian Aborigines: How to Understand Them*, 3rd edition, Sydney: Angus & Robertson, 1954, pp. 132-55.
8. For a detailed study see E.O. James, *Seasonal Feasts and Festivals*, London, Thames & Hudson, 1961.
9. Arnold van Gennep, *The Rites of Passage*, translated by M.B. Vizedom and G.L. Caffee, Chicago: University of Chicago Press, 1960.
10. Mircea Eliade, *Rites and Symbols of Initiation, The Mysteries of Birth and Rebirth*.
11. Erving Goffman, *On Face-Work: An Analysis of Ritual Elements in Social Interaction*. See pp. 9-10 above.
12. For details see Arnold van Gennep, *op. cit.*, pp. 42-3.
13. For details see Mircea Eliade, *op. cit.*, pp. 1-20.
14. For details see Arnold van Gennep, *op. cit.*, pp. 135-7.
15. *Ibid.*, pp. 149-51.
16. See Sir James George Frazer, *Spirits of the Corn and of the Wild*, London: Macmillan, 1925 (Part V. of *The Golden Bough*), Vol. II, pp. 175-9.
17. See Van der Leeuw, *op. cit.*, p. 357.

18. See A.P. Elkin, *op. cit.*
19. See Robert Will, *Le culte, Etude d'histoire et de philosophie religieuses.* Strasbourg: 1925-1929.
20. See E.E. Evans-Pritchard, *Nuer Religion,* Oxford University Press, 1956, pp. 146, 184.
21. See Godfrey Lienhardt, *Divinity and Experience, The Religion of the Dinka,* Oxford: The Clarendon Press, 1961, p. 257.
22. See Raymond Firth, "Offering and Sacrifice: Problems of Organization," *Journal of the Royal Anthropological Institute,* XCIII, 1963.
23. See *The Holy Bible,* Gen. 22.
24. *Ibid.,* Lev. 1 to 10 especially.
25. See Van der Leeuw, *op. cit.,* p. 350.
26. See Van der Leeuw, *op. cit.,* p. 358.
27. See W. Warde Fowler, *The Religious Experience of the Roman People from the Earliest Times to the Age of Augustus,* London: Macmillan and Co., 1911, pp. 68-86.
28. *Ibid.,* p. 172.
29. *Ibid.,* pp. 169-191.
30. For detailed studies of sacrifice see W. Robertson Smith, *Lectures on the Religion of the Semites,* New York: D. Appleton & Co., 1889; E.O. James, *Origins of Sacrifice, A Study in Comparative Religion,* London: Kennikat Press, 1933; *Sacrifice and Sacrament,* London: Thames & Hudson, 1962; Henri Hubert and Marcell Mauss, *Sacrifice: Its Nature and Function,* translated by W.D. Halls, London: Cohen & West, 1964; Royden Keith Yerkes, *Sacrifice in Greek and Roman Religions and Early Judaism,* New York: Charles Scribner's Sons, 1952.
31. For details see Rudolf Bultmann, *Primitive Christianity in Its Contemporary Setting,* pp. 159-205.
32. *The Holy Bible,* Lev. 10 to 17 especially.
33. See W. Warde Fowler, *Roman Festivals of the Period of the Republic, An Introduction to the Study of the Religion of the Romans,* New York: Kennikat Press, p. 145.
34. See James Mooney, *The Ghost Dance Religion and the Sioux Outbreak of 1890,* edited by Anthony F. Wallace, London: University of Chicago Press, 1965; Cora du Bois, *The 1870 Ghost Dance,* University of California, Anthropological Records, Vol. III (1939), No. 1.
35. See Van der Leeuw, *op. cit.,* pp. 344-5.
36. *The Holy Bible,* Matt. 15: 1-20.
37. *Ibid.,* Rom. 14.
38. *Ibid.,* Isa. 1.
39. *The Holy Bible,* Authorized Version, Oxford University Press, Isa. 1: 10-17.
40. Cf. *The Holy Bible,* Matt. 7: 20.
41. Max Weber, *The Sociology of Religion,* pp. xxxii-xxxv, 45-60.
42. From Ben Jonson, "To Celia."
43. Reprinted from *The New English Bible,* copyright 1961 and 1970 by Oxford & Cambridge University Presses, Lev. 26: 3-13.
44. *Ibid.,* Revelation 21: 1-7.
45. *Ibid.,* Revelation 22: 14-15.
46. *The Holy Bible,* Authorized Version, Oxford University Press, John 3: 36.
47. Harald Höffding, *The Philosophy of Religion,* translated from the German edition by B.E. Moyer, London: Macmillan, 1906, pp. 302-3.
48. *El-Kor'ân; or The Koran;* trans. from the Arabic, with notes and index by J.M. Rodwell, London: Bernard Quaritch, 1876, Sura 82, p. 29.
49. Max Weber, *op. cit.,* pp. 151-274.
50. *Ibid.,* pp. 211-2, 221-2, 225-6, 242.
51. C.S. Lewis, *The Abolition of Man, or Reflections on Education with Special Reference to the Teaching of English in the Upper Forms of*

Schools (Riddell Memorial Lectures: Fifteenth Series), Oxford University Press, 1943.

52. Aldous Huxley, *The Perennial Philosophy*, London, Chatto & Windus, 1946.
53. Henri Bergson, *The Two Sources of Morality and Religion*, translated by R. Ashley Audra and Cloudesley Brereton, with the assistance of W. Horsfall Carter, New York: Henry Holt & Co., 1935.
54. *The Holy Bible*, Authorized Version, Matt. 5: 43-44.
55. C.S. Lewis, *op. cit.*, p. 48.
56. See, e.g., *The New English Bible*, Rom. 3 to 8.
57. *Ibid.*, Rom. 3:25.
58. *Ibid.*, Rom. 3:28.
59. William James, *The Varieties of Religious Experience, A Study in Human Nature*, New York: Collier Books, 1961.
60. William James, *ibid.*, p. 390.
61. William James, *ibid.*, pp. 390-1.
62. William James, *ibid.*
63. *The Holy Bible*, Authorized Version, Matt. 7: 7.
64. William James, *op. cit.*, pp. 114-210.
65. Ralph Waldo Emerson, *Lectures and Biographical Sketches*, London: George Routledge and Sons, 1884, p. 186.
66. William James, *op. cit.*, pp. 78-113, 378-9.
67. *Ibid.*, pp. 139-42.
68. *Ibid.*, pp. 114-210.
69. For the detailed account see William James, *op. cit.*, pp. 137, 180, 205.
70. *Ibid.*, p. 180.
71. For the detailed account see William James, *op. cit.*, pp. 130, 151, 156.
72. *Ibid.*, p. 157.
73. For the detailed account see William James, *op. cit.*, pp. 184-209.
74. For the detailed account see William James, *op. cit.*, pp. 136-138.
75. *Ibid.*, p. 136.
76. *Ibid.*, p. 158.
77. For details see Gordon Wasson, *Soma: Divine Mushroom of Immortality*, New York: Harcourt, Brace & World, 1968, pp. 35-67.
78. See Van der Leeuw, *op. cit.*, pp. 487-492
79. See Mircea Eliade, *Shamanism, Archaic Techniques of Ecstasy*, New York, Pantheon Books, 1964.
80. For details see A.J. Arberry, *Sufism, An Account of the Mystics of Islam*, London: George Allen & Unwin, 1950, pp. 84-92; Reynold A. Nicholson, *The Mystics of Islam*, London: Routledge & Kegan Paul, 1966; J. Spencer Trimingham, *The Sufi Orders in Islam*, Oxford: The Clarendon Press, 1971, pp. 194-217.
81. For details see Thomas Clarkson, *A Portraiture of Quakerism*, London: Longman, Hurst, Rees and Orme, 1806, Vol. II. pp. 105-212; T. Edmund Harvey, *The Rise of the Quakers*, London: Headley Brothers, 1905, pp. 51-70; Richard T. Vann, *The Social Development of English Quakerism*, Cambridge, Massachusetts: Harvard University Press, 1969, pp. 1-46; Joseph Nightingale, *A Portraiture of Methodism: being an impartial view of the rise, progress, doctrines, discipline, and manners of the Wesleyan methodists in a series of letters, addressed to a lady*, London: Longman, Hurst, Rees, and Orme, 1807; Robert C. Monk, *John Wesley, His Puritan Heritage*, London: Epworth Press, 1966, pp. 67-167; Rupert E. Davies, *Methodism*, Harmondsworth: Penguin Books, 1963.
82. For details on yoga see Sri Aurobindo, *The Synthesis of Yoga*, New York: Aurobindo Library, 1950. For the Sankara system see Edwin A. Burtt, *Man Seeks the Divine, A Study in the History and Comparison of Religions*, pp. 273-289.
83. For an outline of the Theravadin monk's routine see John B. Noss, *Man's Religions*, fourth edition, New York: Macmillan, 1969, pp. 150-1.

84. For details see Peter F. Anson, *The Call of the Desert, The Solitary Life in the Christian Church*, London: S.P.C.K., 1964, pp. 13-16, 231; Charles Kingsley, *The Hermits*, London: Macmillan, pp. 21-82.

85. For details see Lowry John Daly, *Benedictine Monasticism, Its Formation and Development Through the 12th Century*, New York: Sheed & Ward, 1965; Ildephonse Cardinal Schuster, *Historical Notes on St. Benedict's "Rule for Monks,"* translated by Leonard J. Doyle, Hamden, Connecticut: The Shoestring Press, 1962.

86. For details see the article on "Asceticism" in Hasting's *Encyclopaedia of Religion and Ethics*. For the routines at Cluny itself see Noreen Hunt, *Cluny Under Saint Hugh, 1049-1109*, London: Edward Arnold, 1967; Noreen Hunt, editor, *Cluniac Monasticism in the Central Middle Ages*, London: Macmillan, 1971.

87. An extended discussion of the Khlysty and Skoptsy is to be found in Werner Stark, *The Sociology of Religion, A Study of Christendom*, Volume II, Sectarian Religion, New York: Fordham University Press, 1967. Stark leans heavily for documentation on F.C. Conybeare, *Russian Dissenters*, Cambridge, Massachusetts: Harvard University Press, 1921; and K.K. Grass, *Die russischen Sekten*, Leipzig, 1905-1914.

88. For details on the Jesuit order see J. Brodrick, *The Origin of the Jesuits*, London: 1940, and *St. Ignatius Loyola: the Pilgrim Years*, London: Burns & Oates, 1956.

89. For details on the development of the Franciscans see Rosalind B. Brooke, *Early Franciscan Government, Elias to Bonaventure*, Cambridge University Press, 1959; Cajetan Esser, *Origins of the Franciscan Order*, translated by Aedan Daly and Irina Lynch, Chicago: Franciscan Herald Press, 1970; John Moorman, *A History of the Franciscan Order from its Origins to the Year 1517*, Oxford University Press, 1968.

90. Gananath Obeyesekere, "Theodicy, Sin and Salvation in a Sociology of Buddhism," in E.R. Leach, editor, *Dialectic in Practical Religion*, Cambridge: Department of Archaeology and Anthropology, 1968, p. 37.

91. For details see R.A. Parker, *Yankee Saint: John Humphrey Noyes and the Oneida Community*, New York: Putnams, 1935.

92. For details see John W. Bennett, *Hutterian Brethren*, Stanford University Press, 1967; Victor Peters, *All Things Common: The Hutterian Way of Life*, Minneapolis: University of Minnesota Press, 1965.

93. For a discussion of this teaching see Gustaf Wingren, *Luther on Vocation*, translated by Carl C. Rasmussen, Philadelphia: Muhlenberg Press, 1957; John Calvin, *Institutes of the Christian Religion*, a new translation by Henry Beveridge, Grand Rapids, Michigan: Eerdmans, 1953, especially volume II, pp. 31-35; A. Mitchell Hunter, *The Teaching of Calvin, A Modern Interpretation*, Westwood, N.J.: Fleming H. Revell, 1950.

94. Festinger advocates what he calls "a theory of cognitive dissonance," which he considers to be well grounded in fact. This notion might possibly be invoked in support of the idea I have been developing, although it touches only on a special aspect of the unification sought in religion. For it is restricted to cognitions that are initially dissonant. Festinger says that if cognitive dissonance has occurred the person seeks to remove the dissonance or, in any case, not to let himself be burdened with more. Thus, for example, persons exposed to new information that would increase an existing dissonance, were observed to evade its impact in various ways. They misperceived it, for instance, or denied its validity. It is true that this kind of minimizing of incompatibles can be part of the synthesizing that is undertaken by religion. Yet religious synthesizing involves a great deal more than the avoidance of dissonance. It has for its goal the synthesis of all of life's elements. Many of these elements are not necessarily dissonant at all, but simply different. See Leon Festinger, *A Theory of Cognitive Dissonance*, London: Tavistock Publications, 1962.

Part Two
DIVERSITY

The Diversity in Religion Explained by a Concern for Assurance under Diverse Conditions of Life and Knowledge

Chapter 5

The Birth of Different Religion in the Sectarian Protest of the Alienated

When we survey the contemporary world and all the known past there seems to be no end to the different religions. Yet those we know of must be only a sample of the total. Wallace's crude estimate is that mankind must have produced in the order of 100,000 different religions all told.[1] He arrives at this by assuming that there was already religion everywhere about 100,000 years ago, since we know that religion existed among the Neanderthals at that time; that at all times since then there have been a thousand or more distinct human communities each with its own religion, and that these religions would have changed to something different at least every thousand years. Even if this were so, however, we should not attend exclusively to differences. The point made in the last chapter concerning ethical systems is also true of religions as a whole. Each is a configuration and it is this which can make one seem so different from another. But in any one there can be elements that are common to others.

The Two Distinct Bases of Religious Differences: Geographic Separation and Social Change

Yet account for the diversity we must. A great deal of the puzzlement begins to dissipate after a little reflection on the considerations Wallace takes into account for his estimate. As a cultural phenomenon a religion is a human creation. So it must be true of every religion that there was a time when it was not yet in existence. (This realization alone, incidentally, should correct the tendency to expect that a religion can only have truth if it has the truth for all time. What about the time before the religion? What was the truth then?) But, by the same token, we would expect that there will be a time when the religion becomes obsolete, since all man's creations *are* dated in that way. There will be a tendency here as elsewhere to displace older, less adequate inventions by new and more adequate ones. So the passage of time alone should give rise to a diversity of religions. But, in addition to this, insofar as mankind at any time has comprised a set of independent, self-contained communities, one would expect as many religions as there were communities. If they differ it is because each community has been thrown on its own resources to devise whatever religion it could. If the communities have spread from a common stock or been open to diffusion from neighbours, there may be common elements making it possible to detect families of religions. Yet insofar as a religion belongs to some independently operating community it will be uniquely the religion of that people.

It is only in comparatively recent times that communication has broken down the separation of communities, so that they could scrutinize one another's ways. And, even now, the breaking down is not much more than an exposure to outside observation, unless there has been invasion and domination. There is not yet much fusion into more inclusive communities on the basis of economic cooperation or migration—although, of course, this consolidation is on the move. A great part of the entrenched religious diversity of mankind, then, is surely traceable to the fact that the religions were devised by communities living independently of one another. For as long as they did, and could, live in this way, the diversity was scarcely a problem to them. Insofar as they are coming together and have just the beginnings of a life together, the diversity *is* a problem, since a religion is the expression of the life in common. This is a type of situation that would seem to force new religion.

Wallace has a world map, reproduced here as Figure 2, which shows thirteen religious culture areas in the year A.D. 1600. This indicates that religions have recognizable family resemblances by which they can be grouped. But the groupings themselves separate from one another by area, indicating that difference of religion is a function of independence of life. There are four major living traditions in what we might call modern religion: the Hindu-Buddhist, Chinese, Judaeo-Christian and Islamic. It is clear that each of these has a geographical zone in which it is the dominant faith and this must largely account for its survival and vitality. One zone may have more than one community, but the religions have thriven because of being community-based within them. What I am saying is in no way contradicted by what we know about "the spread of religion." I am not denying that the religion a community makes its own may come to it by diffusion from elsewhere. I am saying that if it has a different religion from that found elsewhere it may simply be because it lives an independent life. Differences that arise from an original geographic separation are scarcely problematic in the same way as other differences. They are only to be expected. It is hardly surprising that the Jews were not Hindus or the Hindus Jews. They did not have the chance to be.

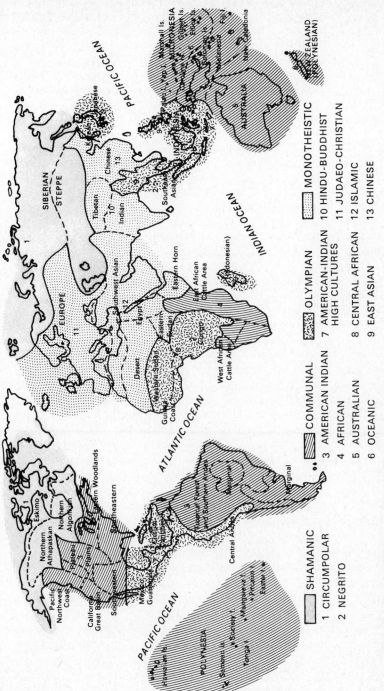

Figure 2. World Map of Religious Culture Areas, A.D. 1600.

Reproduced with permission from Anthony F. C. Wallace, *Religion, An Anthropological View*, Random House, New York, 1966, p. 98.

What *is* suprising is that at a certain time some Jews became Christians and some Hindus Buddhists. What *is* surprising is that at a certain time the Buddhism originating in India should become the new dominant religion in Ceylon, Burma, Thailand and Tibet, the Christianity originating in Palestine the new dominant religion of communities in Europe, the Islamic faith originating in Arabia the new dominant faith of communities of North Africa and Central Asia. These differences are due to social change, and it is differences of this kind rather than differences due to original separation that can be the more puzzling ones. To understand them we need to focus our attention on the circumstances surrounding the adoption of new faiths. This is what we shall be doing in the present chapter. Then in Chapter 7 we shall be looking into the different paths the religious traditions took because of their original isolation from one another.

It is imperative before we go further, however, to have a clear understanding of what we will be meaning when we speak of *a* religion. Is Presbyterianism *a* religion, or can we only use the term of "Christianity"? Is United States' Catholicism *a* religion, and Irish Catholicism *a* religion, or can we only use the term of "Catholicism"? Can third-century B.C. Indian Buddhism be called *a* religion? Is the religion of the congregation worshipping at the Blenheim United Church in Ontario, Canada, *a* religion? At first it seems the really tricky question is how far down one is entitled to come, for no one would have qualms over calling Christianity, Islam or Judaism *a* religion. Cultural forms do achieve a certain independence of the groups of whose culture they originally were a part, so we do tend to think of religions as cultural systems. And yet, properly speaking, we only have *a* religion when the culture is embodied in the actual practice of some community of people. To be sociologically meaningful *a* religion has to be something that could be observed in practice, or could have once. There is, then, more warrant for calling the religion of a particular congregation in Ontario *a* religion, than there is for calling "Christianity" *a* religion—when the latter is used for the mental construct abstracted from many historical manifestations. Because of these considerations I am inclined to come down a long way and call *a* religion the unique system of practices followed by any community whatsoever. The reader should expect this specificity and should not be surprised if I refer, for example, to the Methodist and Lutheran religions as freely as I refer to the Buddhist or Islamic.

Sundkler was exercised by the great proliferation of native sects in the Union of South Africa.[2] By the early 1950s there were more than 2,000 of these. There is a real sense in which each of them is entitled to be called *a* religion. Were we to take such an inclusive view, incidentally, Wallace's estimate of 100,000 religions for mankind would surely become very conservative.

The Dynamic for New Religion in the Upward Climb of the Alienated

How any of the religions reaching back beyond our knowledge came into being is something on which we can only speculate. On the circumstances surrounding the birth of the others there is a very variable quantity of information. Some of the gaps are being slowly filled in, but it is only recently that researchers began to realize the special importance of collecting data on the social position and aspirations of the first recruits to new religious movements. What information there is has to be interpreted carefully anyway. For one thing, while the social position of the first *thinkers* in a religious movement may well be representative of that of the first following as a whole, sometimes they will voice the aspirations of a stratum to which they do not belong but from which their following is drawn. This capacity of the intellectual for broader sympathies is well known, and it has to be allowed for in the examination of evidence I am proposing. Yet, while acknowledging the need for more data to test it, I would be prepared to venture the following hypothesis in explanation of new religion. A fairly uniform pattern does seem to be discernible.

New religions are the creation of groups of people who are alienated from the existing social order because their aspirations cannot be fulfilled within it. However, not everyone who feels thus excluded will turn to religion, so alienation alone is not enough. Being of the alienated, these groups are also on the move. They are determined not to take their disadvantage lying down but are seeking gains politically and economically that will help redress their grievance. They could be described as upwardly mobile. They take political, economic and religious initiative at one and the same time. In giving their protest a religious form they are really making the most radical of all possible forms of protest, as well as taking the most strenuous possible initiative. For, to borrow Swanson's formulation, they are rewriting the society's very constitution. They are, in effect, saying to the existing society that has denied them a place in the sun: "If our plight is one effect of implementing your constitution it cannot be true and we will not endorse it. Instead of it, we propose this other one which will legitimate an acceptable place for us."

It must be understood that I use "alienation" as meaning essentially some kind of disaffection from or lack of identification with the system. It is more a power position than an economic one. It may entail economic disadvantage, but need not. It is possible for this kind of squeeze to be felt by people who are materially comfortable and perhaps wealthy, and even by people who have a certain amount of power and influence. The point is, they lack what they aspire to, they feel relatively deprived. What they seem to lack critically is a sense of status, the respect and recognition of their fellows. Indeed, the tremendous momentum generated by religious movements is one demonstration of the profound importance this need has for man. To be humiliated—which, incidentally, is quite a different thing from learning to be humble and is certainly not the way it is done—is one of the most excruciating and unacceptable of deprivations. The religious sect is the beginning of the long climb upward of humiliated groups into the respectability that everyone craves. (No one should affect to be above a need for respectability! Yet this is, of course, very commonly done in our time. People speak as if the last thing that could matter would be to do anything for the sake of earning respectability—even while they pursue it without abatement.) Because new religion is the path to status, and because new movements are forever being born to bring it to newly awakened groups, it has possibly been the greatest of all dynamics for egalitarianism in human history. Also, if anyone claims an entitlement to rights and dignity just by virtue of his humanity, he is making a claim that can never really be given any vindication but a religious one. It is because in the ideal society everyone is an indispensable contributor, that men can dare to claim they are entitled to rights and dignity just as they stand. The ground of their inalienable worth is their root in divinity.

Richard Niebuhr suggested that sectarian religion was the religious protest of the "dispossessed," by which he meant the materially disadvantaged, the poor.[3] This does not seem to me to formulate the situation accurately, even though it contains a germ of the right idea. We obtain the greater breadth needed if we think of it as the religion of the disaffected. Besides, the extremely poor, especially if they are not beginning to be upwardly mobile, do not give much evidence of religious initiative. Niebuhr also wrote of this sort of sectarian development as a kind of aberration from the desirable course of religious growth. But I would not want to suggest that. I want to suggest, rather, that this is the way new life is being injected into religion continually and that all religious traditions are, in fact, sectarian born. It is the standard way. Why it should be so is not easy to say. There seems to be something in it of the idea that the weak are the strong, the poor the rich, the least the greatest, the last the first —which is itself a religious idea, of course. But, speaking more naturalistically, it is as though those who are furthest down cannot but look highest up—and in such a notion the reader cannot fail to detect echoes of the Marxian camera obscura. I do not see them to be down where Marx saw them to be, of course. Also, unlike Marx, I do not see this as providing people with an illusory compensation, but with a leverage for the actual climb upward.

The person dissatisfied with the conditions actually existing turns his attention more readily to the ideal. His dissatisfaction with the world shaped under the old interpretation of the ideal, leads him to interpret it afresh. Werner Stark takes a view similar to the one I am advancing.[4] He wants to locate the causes of sectarianism in alienation, and he also wants to define alienation broadly and allow many causes for it. Yet I am soon quite out of step with him, for he writes about sectarian religion as if it were second-class religion. He even seems to suggest it is not religion at all but rebellion in disguise. It might aid the acceptance of my hypothesis if it could be shown that what are now the great and altogether respectable orthodoxies had their origin in a tender new start of the kind described. I think that can indeed be done and propose that we consider in illustration the origin of four: Buddhism, Judaism, Christianty and Islam.

The Dynamic Illustrated in the Origins of Four of the Great Religions

Buddhism

Buddha (c. 563 B.C.—483 B.C.) was a wealthy prince who lived a life of luxury and ease in his city palace—but was spiritually empty.[5] Moreover, for all his wealth, he occupied a subordinate status in the four-caste system. He belonged to the Kshatriyas, the warrior ruling kings. Though influential in practical affairs, the Kshatriyas were subordinate to the priestly Brahmins, whose religious status gave them pre-eminence. Beneath the Kshatriyas were the Vaisyas, who were the agriculturalists and craftsmen, and beneath these the Sudras or serfs. Buddha inherited the Indian religious tradition and adopted its basic structure. Like any Hindu he saw his life tied into a cycle of rebirths, each new life having its entailment of suffering. Like any Hindu, too, he had learned to aspire for *moksha* or release from this. But whereas the Hindu's release was effected when he eventually identified atman (the purified individual soul) with Brahman (the divinity), Buddha devised a new way of release which short-circuited Brahman altogether. The inevitable effect of this, of course, was to undermine the status of the priests of Brahman.

Buddha devised an atheistic system that made salvation as accessible to the Kshatriyas as to anyone, and it was an intensely individualistic system since no one could take the way on behalf of anyone else. Only through his own self-discipline could any man find salvation in nirvana, the extinction of enslaving desire. Buddha had, in fact, begun his spiritual search by seeking instruction from two famous Brahmin hermits. But, having absorbed all they had to teach, he found their doctrine wanting. When he achieved Enlightenment on his own account he was tempted to keep it to himself, but resisted this to become a teacher of others. He first converted five young men, with whom he had previously practised extreme asceticism. They had proved that tradition-honoured way was not the path to release either. These men became the first recruits to the order of monks that Buddha saw fit to found. In effect, this order replaced the Brahmins as the spiritual élite. Less than three months after the first conversions the number of followers had grown to sixty, most of them wealthy young noblemen of Buddha's own caste. He commissioned them all to go out, each in a different direction, as teachers of the new way. Is there not much more than a suggestion here of an alienated group claiming equality and rewriting the constitution? Is there not a radical protest being registered against privilege and the inequalities experienced by a subordinate caste? Furthermore, at the same time as the ascribed social order and ascribed self dissolve into the multitude of achieving individuals, Brahman dissolves in the featureless nirvana. So sudden is the repudiation of the old ideal, the new ideal cannot yet be focused. All that can be known is what it is not.

Judaism

What Judaism departed from in Ur of the Chaldees is certainly not as clear to us as the continuing line from which Buddhism turned.[6] But it is clear that with Abraham, from whom Judaism dates, a totally new orientation to the future begins. The dissenting group of people we are concerned with in this instance is a kinship group. It is sometimes said it is impossible to say what entity the Jews comprised. A nation, a race, a culture—it seems they were none of these. Yet it is not such a mystery, for it is to Abraham and those descended from him that this new faith dawned. The imperative Abraham conceived was to leave the land of his fathers and acquire another land for the sole possession of his family, which was going to multiply tremendously. So he set out from Ur of the Chaldees around 1800 B.C., towards Canaan. It was not vacant land but already occupied, so the Lord who promised the land promised conquest also. In making his covenant with Abraham he said: "To your descendants I give this land from the River of Egypt to the Great River, the river Euphrates, the territory of the Kenites, Kenizzites, Kadmonites, Hittites, Perizzites, Rephaim, Amorites, Canaanites, Girgashites, Hivites, and Jebusites."[7] They themselves would be subject to none.

Abraham was not poor. In setting out from Ur he took acquired property with him and his detour into Egypt left him very rich in cattle, silver and gold. The material prosperity to be enjoyed in the new land is a large part of the meaning of the "blessing" the Lord also promised, and this was to be so exemplary that all the other families on the face of the earth would pray to be blessed in the same way. Abraham's descendants, the

Lord promised as well, would be too numerous to count. By his wealth, influence and progeny the name of Abraham would be made great. If not first in all the earth, the family of Abraham would be second to none. In return for this they were to keep the covenant by practising circumcision to show that those whom the Lord had chosen for his special favour were separate and distinguishable. Here, if ever there was one, is a protest against every possibility of subordination. Not only will God make his chosen people equal with anyone, he will make them specially privileged. Here also is a claim not only that one's grounding in the divinity gives an entitlement to dignity, but that it gives an entitlement to all the material conditions of the good life: territorial ownership, self-determination, sons, wealth. In this first self-disclosure, the profile of the God of the Israelites is simply drawn. He is a providing Father of the family who can promise to give it a home and make its name great. He will be as good as his word, and expects his faithfulness to be reciprocated by an acknowledgement of one's membership in the family and of its indebtedness to him.

Christianity

By the time of Jesus what the Jews expected from their God had changed to something more messianic, yet their hopes still centred in the land of Israel. It was to Jerusalem the Messiah would come. The protest of Christianity was against the land-locked vision of the fulfilment.[8] The Messiah would be King of a kingdom not of this world. It was also against the exclusivism in the idea that salvation was for the family of the circumcision only. The Messiah would be Saviour of the world and bring the Gentiles in. It was also the layman's protest against the idea that the worship of God must be mediated by priest or temple. Neither in Mount Gerizim nor in Jerusalem was the Father to be worshipped, but in spirit and truth. Jesus was a carpenter from Galilee of the Gentiles. Though called a rabbi because of being a lay teacher, he was no priest. He was the leader of a band of twelve, all of whom appear to have been laymen and all but one of whom were also from Galilee of the Gentiles. Judas Iscariot was the only one who was not.

"Of the Gentiles" was the term of derision applied to Galilee by the Judaeans who lived at the centre, with Jerusalem and its temple in their midst. It was the last-settled area of Palestine and bordered on the Gentile world and was, in any case, separated from Judaea by the country of the Samaritans, whom the Judaeans also despised. But the Galileans not only learned a sympathy for the Gentiles through having Phoenicians as neighbours, they had Gentiles in their midst: Phoenicians, Arabians, Syrians and Greeks had long settled there. The Judaeans found the Galileans too independent in their religious views, of inferior education, so all the less qualified to have them, and unclean because of associating with the uncircumcised. But, as for the Galileans themselves, they were steadily developing more cosmopolitan sympathies. Jesus especially dared to voice them, and indicated that it was clear to him that the family of God was wider than the family of Abraham. The group of twelve who were the first to give loyal support to these ideas may possibly have been people of modest means, but we do not meet the suggestion anywhere that they were poor and needy. Four were fishermen, and fishermen then were comparatively comfortable. Matthew, the tax-collector, appears to have been quite affluent. Nor is there any reason to think the family of Jesus was particularly poor. At least they were invited to lavish weddings and feasts and Jesus, unlike the ascetic John the Baptist, was observed to have a fondness for the pleasures of life. We do not get the impression of an economically depressed stratum. What would fit the picture better would be a set of enterprising and possibly ambitious, self-educated men with a lively interest in the widening world, and eager for responsibility in trade and public affairs.

When Jesus' own work was accomplished and the disciples were left to continue it, they were together in Jerusalem on the day of Pentecost.[9] It was fortunate they were Galileans and had learned to speak to foreigners. For there were living in Jerusalem "devout Jews drawn from every nation under heaven,"[10] and this cosomopolitan sector gathered to hear them preach. In the exhilaration of fellowship the disciples had an unaccustomed freedom of speech and they were able to make their message understood by everyone present. Even if they only spoke in Aramaic and Greek everyone might have understood, since one or other of these languages would probably be known to all the peoples represented: "Parthians, Medes, Elamites; inhabitants of Mesopotamia, of Judaea and Cappadocia, of Pontus and Asia, of Phrygia and Pamphylia, of Egypt and the districts of Libya around Cyrene; visitors from Rome, both Jews and proselytes, Cretans and Arabs."[11] As a result of the preaching some three thousand of these were converted on the one day. When they asked the disciple Peter what they must do, he told them to accept Jesus as the Messiah, not of the family of Abraham only but of the whole world. "For the promise is to you, and to your children, and to all who are far away, everyone whom the Lord our God may call."[12]

Thenceforth these motley converts lived as one family and met constantly to hear the disciples teach. They pooled all their material possessions and took meals together in one another's houses "with unaffected joy."[13] Possibly their dispersed relatives heard of it, and possibly some were prepared by it for their coming in person when persecution scattered them from Jerusalem shortly after. Then, a little later, it was to cities in Asia Minor and other parts around the Mediterranean that Paul and the other Christian missionaries went, preaching both to Jew and Gentile. This area was their recruiting field, and it was urban, socially improving, middle-class Jews of the Hellenistic world, and their similarly placed Gentile neighbours, who constituted the first substantial following of the new faith.[14]

Paul himself had been one of the foreign Jews resident in Jerusalem. With Barnabas and others he established missionary headquarters outside of Palestine, at Antioch in Syria. With them the torch of Christian initiative passed from the Gentile-sympathizing Galileans to a Gentile-sympathizing set in international Jewry. These started the systematic formulation of Christian doctrine, and it was essentially an attempt to make Jewish thought forms meaningful to the population of the Hellenistic cities. The new faith was clearly the protest of the outsider made on his behalf by the insider who was in tune with him. It was a protest against the Jews being the exclusive, privileged recipients of the promise of God. It claimed to acknowledge the same God as the Jew acknowledged, but known through a fuller self-disclosure. Hence it could perhaps be considered a sect within Judaism. Its larger view of God showed him as the one who was drawing all mankind together into a unity, and not merely the family of Abraham. When its doctrines were mature enough to be explicitly formulated, it seemed necessary to show this God as a trinity. The ideal society of men was now seen to be integral with God in a way that had hardly been guessed before. As much as the foreseeing Father of the family of Abraham was God, so was completed, united humanity, and so was the generosity that flowed between insider and outsider to bring it about. Christianity designated the former the cosmic Son of God, the latter God's Holy Spirit.

Islam

We are not altogether misled if we think of Islam as being both similar to and different from Christianity as that faith related to Judaism.[15] Like Christianity, it sought to be a continuator of the truth in Judaism while transcending its exclusiveness in universalism. But whereas the Christian way to universalism was the extension of the family of God, the Islamic way was the extension of the territory. Not the land of Canaan but the whole wide world must be the one consolidated territory of the Lord. Muhammad conceived it to be his mission to use military and political strategy to make it so. Tribal separation must be broken down and the separate tribal gods renounced. There can be only one God for all the peoples, and let it be the God of Abraham. The land of Arabia in Muhammad's time was in constant turmoil because of inter-tribal conflicts and vendettas. This instability was especially prejudicial to the interests of anyone in trade, as Muhammad and his prosperous wife were. It seemed an anachronistic system overdue for radical reform. Essentially, then, Islam was the protest against tribalism and the multitude of faiths—many of them polytheistic—that that implied. Its protest was made on behalf of those groups of people who were looking for the advantages dependent on a wider peace. It was resisted by those with vested interests in the old system, like the Meccan leaders of Muhammad's own tribe of al Quraysh. Muhammad's first following was virtually a battalion. They were the cosmopolitanized warriors who had no motivation for local feuding any more but were hoping for enlistment in an imperialist cause.

It appears that Muhammad considered that Judaism and Christianity could supply what his country needed better than any religion his own land could then offer. He was aggrieved that his own land had no comparable prophets but believed God would equalize the situation by giving revelations to him. He saw himself as an innovator introducing this greater tradition to his people, while adding a distinctively Arabian component. He was himself cosmopolitanized, for he had travelled and met Jewish and Christian traders. It was from them he learned what he knew about these faiths, and that explains why some of it was garbled. It seems a pity that he should have been thus handicapped, since he conceived himself called to restore the religion of Abraham to its purity. An illustration of the misinformation he transmitted was the idea that the Christian trinity consisted of the Father, the Virgin and their Child—a debased idea of God that he very much opposed.

Muhammad seems to have been unusually versatile for a religious leader. Besides being a prophet he was a practical man of affairs. A successful businessman, he was also adept in politics and war. It seemed only natural to him that he should take practical steps to implement in a dictatorship the vision he had conceived. The prophet of God is also the chosen king, and in Islamic communities the political and religious headships were consequently fused in the one person. It was not for nothing he was expelled from Mecca in A.D. 622 when his enemies saw his cause gathering strength. They knew he was plotting revolution. He worked through secret societies, and, after being exiled in Medina, returned to make a military conquest of Mecca, and, after this again, of the surrounding territory. He is supposed to have sent missives to all the sovereigns and potentates he knew of, in which he promised safety to any who would embrace Islam. When he died he was organizing an expedition against Syria. In the century after his death military conquest extended the Muslim Empire through Central Asia, the Levant, North Africa, Spain and Southern France. These were all kingdoms rent by internal divisions as vexing as those that had plagued Arabia. They were crying out for consolidation, and it seemed the armed conquerors of the world-wide Canaan had come in perfect time.

The Dynamic Illustrated in the Origins of Some Christian Sects

The sectarian movements within Christianity itself exhibit the same pattern that we have now recognized in the origins of some major religious traditions. We can pay attention to a selection of these. The great, sprawling Christian diversity that is subsumed under the head of Protestantism, is what we will be sampling. As we do this, we will come to appreciate how much that diversity is a function of the changing social structures of the modern world. There has been a great loosening up that has generated new groups, each of which, although alienated, has seized the opportunity to take its share of initiative. Religious initiative was taken simultaneously with other kinds of initiative as they started a climb into respectability. It is not for nothing the whole development has been named Protestantism. It is not surprising, either, that it has seemed to be a galloping ride into division, an endless splitting of splits. It is the kind of religion one would expect to proliferate where class mobility is being made possible through power structures becoming fluid.

Lutheranism

The transition from feudalism to modernism was a change from rural empire to urbanizing nation. With this new basis for collective life men had to be tied into society in a different way. They became "individuals" in a new way. For they were now burghers of the city and citizens of the nation and "political men" willy-nilly. They had to take responsibility personally. They had to take thought and make plans on their own account and on behalf of the city and nation. The persistence of the Holy Roman Empire, and of the papacy as a secular power, seemed like a dead hand on this newly stirring life. The princes and nobles of Germany, by contrast, were in a position to be nation-makers and foster the new life, even while they were being alienated from the Empire. It was to the aspirations of these influential men that Luther's religion gave a sanction, and they were quick to adopt it.[16] The peasants tried to adopt it also, and staged an uprising against the princes in its name. Yet this was abortive and Luther himself denounced their action. The Lutheran religion did not express the particular protest they had to make.

Luther (1483-1546), a miner's son, became a monk of the Catholic Church, but developed independent opinions and an independent style of spirituality that eventually excluded him from it. In this independence he was simply exemplifying the individualism the times were demanding, and it supplied a model of thought and practice for many of his contemporaries. Urbanism, intellectualism, rationalism, sophistication, decisiveness—

these were the marks of the new man now on the stage of history. For this new man the mediaeval synthesis of Catholicism had no particular status or devotional role. The new man's habit of self-cultivation extended to the desire to cultivate an inner spiritual life and critical theology of his own. Just as he cultivated his own policies and economic plans, so he desired to cultivate his own faith and intellectual rationale for it. (Stark, who virtually expresses this same view about the origin of Lutheranism, says that it fell to Ignatius and his Jesuits to contend for this same cause *within* the Catholic Church).

The distinctive features of Lutheranism are all traceable to the needs of this new man. The authority of the church and Pope is replaced by the authority of the Bible, to which the individual must make his own appeal. The individual has direct access to God and need not wait on sacrament or priest: he is justified by faith alone. He must cultivate his own inner life of faith, and seek to fulfil his own individual calling in the world. It is not unhelpful to draw a parallel between Luther and Buddha. Their intensely individualistic styles of spirituality make their appearance simultaneously with a radical challenge to a traditionally sanctioned social order. It is, moreover, as if neither of them can see far enough beyond this pressing negative mission to focus the ideal society. Just as Buddha's nirvana is featureless, Luther's God seems to have no definable will for man collectively. It has simply to be assumed that if each individual does the will of God for him and if each secular ruler is obeyed, a pattern quite beyond knowledge must surely be worked out.

Calvinism

Calvin (1509-1564), being twenty-six years younger than Luther, belonged to the second generation of the Reformation.[17] He was the son of a French notary and agent and trained as a lawyer. In time he won a wide following in his native France and elsewhere in Europe. But it was in the Swiss city of Geneva that he was first acclaimed. The Genevans had successfully rejected the spiritual authority of the Pope and were also in political revolt against the Duke of Savoy. For they were aligned with a movement to secure the self-government of the towns. When the city gained independence, the city magistrates encouraged evangelical preachers to come there, Calvin being one of these. In a general way, Calvin voiced the same protest as Luther did on behalf of the new man, and his following was drawn from a fairly wide spectrum of people. Weber claims that his teachings had a special appeal to the newly emerging class of industrial capitalists.[18] Critics of this proposition have mainly proceeded by showing that non-capitalists were also included in the following.[19] Yet the latter could be true without the former being false. It does seem probable that whereas Luther's formulation of the faith afforded a sanction mainly for some of the political restructuring that was afoot, Calvin's afforded a sanction for the economic restructuring. The industrial capitalists who were accumulating wealth to exploit the gains of the industrial revolution, were the important new class. They were pushing up but were squeezed by the advantages reserved for others under the old system.

Once again, it was partly the stress on individualism that made the theology appealing. Each man must work out his own salvation. It differed from Lutheranism in stressing action in the world as the means for doing this, rather than faith in the heart only. Weber has a way to account for this activism that I do not find particularly convincing. He notes that Calvinism stressed the doctrine of predestination whereby some are elected, by God's decision alone, to salvation, while others are consigned to damnation. Since no one knew where he stood he would work diligently at his calling to prove by outward successes that he was of the elect. But Calvin's was a theology of grace not of self-justification. What would seem to explain the Calvinist's behaviour is the great invasion of his practical life by rationality. He was seeking to make himself and his resources into instruments of maximum efficiency for the service of God in the world. For God had indeed to be served in the world, since he was working out an ideal plan in human affairs. Calvinism differs from Lutheranism in having this collective task programmed. It has had time enough to stand back from the crumbling order and envision the new. In it God is enthroned in majesty and is working out his sovereign will in every department of the *common* life, government included. This requires that the same calculated, rational planning that goes into business shall be applied to life as a whole. In the attempt to make the ideal materialize Calvin went so far as to set up a theocracy in Geneva, where he was made head of the city—but it was a short-lived venture.

Anglicanism

Anglicanism probably illustrates more transparently even than Lutheranism and Calvinism the protest of nationalism against the outmoded and declining Holy Roman Empire.[20] Its name, the Church of England, shows more openly than theirs precisely what it was—the religion of a nation. It expressed the outlook and aspirations of the new man in England. What is, of course, common knowledge is that it started with King Henry VIII breaking with the Pope because the Pope refused to grant him a divorce—which is popularly felt to be a rather scandalous way of beginning a church. But what was at stake was power. The divorce was incidental: the real question was national independence for England. As Trevelyan points out, what seemed intolerable to Henry was that the interests of England should be subjected to the will of the Emperor, through the intervening link of the papacy.[21] As a result of his break with the Pope he was able, in the second quarter of the sixteenth century, to free both church and state from Roman domination simultaneously. He was also able to curtail the activities of the monks and friars who were the representatives on the spot of the old ecclesiastical order, and, in general, to cut back the power and privilege of the clergy.

It would be a shallow reading of history if anyone put all this down to Henry's personal pride and ambition. For another thing pointed out by Trevelyan is that throughout the entire drama Henry had the support of London and the south.[22] That would be the commercial and urban part of the country. Needless to say, he also had the support of the new nobility, the men to whom he was redistributing the wealth and estates received from the monasteries. Henry's protest was not a private one then. He spoke for the new nobility and for urban England. The features that came to distinguish Anglicanism once it separated are not unlike some of those of Lutheranism. Justification by faith, the authority of the Bible and the need for the individual to make his appeal to it, are paramount. But Anglicanism also had a particular gift for making good citizens out of its members. It upheld the national secular authority and enjoined obedience to it so successfully that to be a good Anglican was virtually the same thing as being a loyal Englishman. We must not, however, lose sight of the fact that Lutheranism and Calvinism were religions *for* nations just as much as Anglicanism was. The fact that these movements each took root in more nations than one should not mislead us. Calvinism in Scotland came in time to be called, honestly enough, the Church of Scoltand. Lutheranism in Germany, Denmark, Norway and Sweden has been, in effect, the church of those countries.

Anabaptism

There was a more radical wing of the Reformation that was expressed, for example, in the Anabaptist movement to which such groups as the Mennonites and Hutterites trace their beginnings.[23] Because it had no single outstanding systematist like Luther or Calvin it was more diffuse in its thought and organization than the movements they founded. But there was a common belief in the need to be baptised again as an adult, in order to enter the church voluntarily. Commonly held, also, were beliefs that the "inner light" given to the individual was his sufficient and reliable guide to true doctrine and morality, and that there would shortly dawn a millennial reign of Christ. An attempt to implement practical communism was sometimes made. Altogether, the movement expressed an extreme rejection of the existing institutions and authorities. If Lutheranism could be considered tailored to an upper stratum, and Calvinism to a middle stratum, this was tailored to a lower stratum again. In sixteenth-century Europe the middling peasantry and craftsmen were the chief victims of economic pressure produced by a rise in population and prices. It was these who supplied the main support for the radical religious movements. Elton writes concerning them:

> The prophets and leaders of sects were usually parish priests, or laymen of some education and standing; their followers did not noticeably include the outcasts of society, the poor and destitute, but rather the yeomanry and solid peasantry of the countryside, town artisans like weavers and fullers, and especially the miners of Saxony and the Tyrol who regarded themselves as a labouring aristocracy.[24]

The Anabaptist movement proper started in Zürich in 1524 as a breakaway movement amongst some of Zwingli's followers. They claimed they were merely carrying their leader's thought to its logical conclusions. Zwingli had introduced reformation ideas to that city and had won a following amongst the same kind of people as were following Calvin—the new élite in trade and business and tradesmen whose occupations had shown definite improvement.[25] At first these felt bitterly that they were excluded from normal entitlements. But they provide the almost classical illustration of the thesis I am advancing, of an upward movement into respectability. Before long they had won status and were actually called in Zürich *die Ehrbarkeit*, which means "the respectability." Through their associations and by other means they then made their privileges exclusive to themselves. One particular group of workers who felt the impermeability of this kind of wall—and elsewhere as much as in Zürich—were the journeymen. There were rules preventing them from achieving the full tradesman status that would let them be self-employed and hence upwardly mobile. Such journeymen were particularly responsive, it seems, to Anabaptism. But, in a quite general way, it was a stratum outside the respectability who joined the movement.

Some of the first followers in Zürich were men very highly placed—Conrad Grebel being one of these—and educated men and priests. But it was for men less privileged than themselves that they were fashioning a new way. Townsmen members of whom we have knowledge were tailors, smiths, shoemakers, a shoelatchet-maker, a skinner, a baker. Yet the first stirrings of any importance were not amongst townsmen but amongst the peasants and rural artisans. It is possible that the Anabaptist successes in the Zürich countryside followed and were due to the frustration of the peasants' attempt to win material improvements. During the fifteen-twenties and -thirties the movement spread wildly amongst poor townsmen and peasants in many European countries. Frequently their religious fervour carried over into actual physical violence. At Münster in West-phalia the idea caught hold that Münster had been selected as the New Jerusalem which would alone survive the destruction of the earth at Christ's coming in a short time. The Anabaptists took control for well over a year, expelled all Protestants and Catholics, instituted communism and polygyny, and accepted one of their number as king and messiah.

Are those who are more desperate in their protest more extreme in their proposal? The Anabaptists show with diagrammatic starkness what obsession with the ideal can do to the extremely alienated. They will expect nothing for themselves from the existing order and everything from the sustaining ideal. Their actions further either their extrication from the existing order or the constitution of an alternative order in the image of the ideal. Adult baptism rejects the basis of membership in the old community and indicates that the new is open only to those who choose it. Inner-light guidance asserts their complete self-sufficiency in devising their own alternative. Hope in the millennial kingdom indicates that they expect everything from the sustaining ideal. Communism indicates the attempt to mirror it now.

The English Baptists

Stark says we may say of England, with a little harmless simplification, that each succeeding century from the sixteenth to the twentieth produced a major sectarian formation besides some minor ones. They are, in sequence, the Baptists, Quakers, Methodists, Salvation Army and Jehovah's Witnesses. While the last originated in the United States, it has found a considerable following in England, and, though founded in the late nineteenth century, it hardly made an impact before 1900. Each of these movements can be seen as a response to a clearly recognizable feature of the class structure of the time. Like Anabaptism in Europe, the Baptist reformation in England was the poor man's reformation.[26] But, whereas the rural element dominated in the European movement, the urban dominated in England. In addition to some of the occupations already listed for the European Anabaptists, we know of these among the English Baptists: joiner, furrier, upholsterer, bricklayer, cobbler, brewer, leather-seller, soap-boiler, felt-maker, glover, button-maker and tinker.

It is important to remember that we are not yet in the presence of an industrial proletariat. This class, like that we encountered in Europe, is a mediaeval employed class working for the fully qualified tradesmen. The English Baptist movement included Cambridge graduates in its leaders and spokesmen, but it was essentially the protest of this class of people it expressed. They were, very largely, people who found themselves trapped in the occupational system, barred from full occupational status and any economic improvement. Is it because they re-jected their bosses' crass advantage that their religion rejects authority in church organization? Each congregation is its own authority and the laymen legitimate the pastor. Each individual must authorize his own religion from his conversion, baptism, conscience and reading of scripture. It seems to be very much a negative position with some considerable built-in self-defeat, both as regards church and society. For how do you build com-munities from people who are individuals purely and simply and absolutely? Like the Buddhists and Lutherans, the English Bap-tists were so overwhelmed by the collective evil they were against they did not focus the collective good they were for. To atomize the old collectivity by individualizing was as far as they could go.

Quakerism

By the seventeenth century capitalism, in its first phase of do-mestic industry, had arrived, and with it came Quakerism.[27] A certain number of the recruits came, once more, from the ranks of the journeymen, but more of them were hired workers in the domestic system. George Fox, the founder, was the son of a weaver and apprentice to a shoemaker. We have the following list of occupations for some London Quakers of 1680: mariner, weaver, farmer, cordwainer, clothier, shoemaker, schoolmaster, tallow-chandler, joiner, bricklayer, rope-maker, merchant, strong-water seller, yeoman, blacksmith, labourer, salter, ironmonger, cheesemonger, cooper, fellmonger, pin-maker, wire-drawer, silk-stocking framework knitter, plasterer, baker, glazier, fruiterer, haberdasher, car man, timber merchant, dyer. These people were scarcely in abject poverty—they were thankful to have regular employment and earn money. But they were well down on the social ladder and were in a dependent and subordinate position that rankled. Their protest, consequently, was emphatically against all privilege. While they could not claim equality of wealth with the capitalists on whom they depended and who dictated their terms of employment entirely, they claimed equal-ity of worth.

They said they would doff their caps to no one and say "thee" and "thou" to anybody, use Christian names and be friends with all. Their chosen name, Society of Friends, boldly affirmed it. No man should teach another man but simply share his concerns with him. Every man would find truth for himself through the inner light. The eccelsiastical masters were as much at a discount as the industrial, and the political as much as these. To strengthen the hand of the political authority by bearing arms was some-thing the Quaker disdained to do. Here, once again, is a rather extreme individualism. Yet it is supplemented by the hope of winning support for specific group projects by sharing concerns. The concerns that arose were reformist, inspired by the ideals of equality and dignity for everyone. Slave reform and prison reform were prominent. Many modern Quakers are very well-to-do and some are even wealthy capitalists. Like "the respectability" of Zürich, these lend dramatic support to the thesis that sectarianism is a capillary force lifting people in the social structure.

Methodism

The second phase of industrialism ushered in the factory system and, with it, Methodism.[28] It was the factory system, of course, that created the great urban proletariat that crowded into the tiny dwellings in the expanding cities of northern England. Some were so disoriented they drank—and their lives lost what potentiality they had. Although many of them were skilled workers they were very poorly paid. Class lines hardened, separating them from the rest of society and causing them to feel inferior and cut off. Although eighteenth-century Methodism had intellectuals like the Wesleys to formulate its teaching, it was to the aspirations of these people that its teachings were specifically matched. There was a precise geographic pattern in the first Methodist successes. Their chapels appeared where the workers lived, conspicuously in the textile and mining districts.

Methodism's great announcement was that all were alike before God who was waiting to fill every heart with his love. It opposed the Calvinistic doctrine that only some were predestined to salvation, and championed the Arminian view that salvation was for all. High and low were equally loved of God, high and low were equally sinners in need of his grace. It asked for an experience of conversion and sanctification, and for an outward expression of them in a changed life and brotherly love. Spontaneous warmth and affection became the Methodist's mark. There was, indeed, a rare magnanimity in the Methodist protest. For men and women were protesting not against the disadvantage they suffered because of class, but against their society being divided by class. It was division itself to which they objected. They were asking that they all be brought back together since that ideal state would make life secure enough for all to fulfil their potential. In the warmth of their chapel services, class meetings and firesides the Methodists foreshadowed the unity they wanted for all England.

The Salvation Army

By the nineteenth century a third phase of industrial capitalism had produced its unskilled proletariat.[29] The extreme poverty of this class was not necessarily its worst handicap. There were the depression and hopelessness of seeing no way out of their condition; there were the monotony and insignificance of their labour; there was the insecurity of their livelihood—for they never knew how long their employment would last and they had no guarantees. If the skilled workers of the preceding phase felt cut off from society, the unskilled workers of this phase felt abandoned. Understandably, it led to many casualties of body, mind and character, alcoholism not being the least common cause of them. By now, Methodism had come into its inheritance of respectability and could not reach them. *In Darkest England and the Way Out,* written by William Booth, the founder of the Salvation Army, prescribes for their plight.[30] Booth conceived a quixotic remedy, but at least he saw that some kind of continuing community was needed to which these people might come for support.

Such a Christian community he started in London, amongst the silk-weavers of Spitalfields and Bethnal Green, and these were the first supporters of what became the Salvation Army. People with whom nobody wanted to associate associated with that community because they were made welcome. They supported one another till their resolve to extricate themselves from degradation revived. To *rescue* was the Army's essential mission, to restore to community those who were in difficulties through lack of it. The Salvation Army was the protest against a society that provided no guarantees of material security and welfare. It pioneered a place for social services that was partly filled by public agencies when society did accept responsibility for welfare. It pioneered the redistribution of wealth by its "collection" for the needy, which became an institution. Thousands of people expected to "give to the Salvation Army" who never intended to join it. It preached the same kind of conversion as Methodism preached and looked to see lives transformed in the same way. The Army wanted to see people so set their lives in order and so draw on the community's help as to fulfil their potential and make progress in respectability.

The Jehovah's Witnesses

Regarding the Jehovah's Witnesses of the twentieth century we are more dependent on our own speculations, since the sect has not yet been thoroughly studied.[31] Although the attempt has been made to obtain detailed information on the membership, I do not know of any study that succeeded. But we know that Pastor Russell, the founder, was a Pittsburgh salesman, and that there he gathered a Bible study group around him of a similar social status. Joseph Rutherford who succeeded him as leader was a run-of-the-mill Missouri lawyer. Jehovah's Witnesses are notorious, in the public stereotype that exists of them, for being "against the government." This is a feeling many of us have in the modern world, and consideration of it may provide a key to understanding the Witnesses. We feel alienated from the sources of power in the big bureaucracy. Jehovah's Witnesses are against big bureaucracy in three distinct expressions: in politics, big business and the church. Their particularly vehement attack on the Roman Catholic Church is probably very largely due to this aspect of it. Do they, then, really represent a protest against the modern bureaucratic world—the big organization—and the way in which this panders to professionalism and semi-professionalism, in that it gives jobs and promotions to people with certificate qualifications? Has the movement attracted into its ranks many people employed in this type of system, but handicapped within it by lack of formal qualifications? If this is the case, they would make a close parallel with the first Baptists. Possibly it could be as a result of this that few fully qualified professionals are members.

It could also be as a result of this that there is a quite categorical rejection of all earthly authorities on the part of the Witnesses. They are accountable to God only—hence all the strife they get themselves into with the civil authorities. However, they can make a meaningful order amidst the ruins of their rejections if they create their own system, and this they are doing. Their meeting places are called Kingdom Hall, and they believe they are now literally bringing in the Kingdom. They are sustained by some complicated millennial expectations but, prophecies of a dated visible return having failed, they now believe Christ has returned invisibly and is consolidating his Kingdom. It transcends national barriers. Just as Lutheranism and Calvinism were a protest for nationalism, this position makes a protest against it, charging that it is outmoded.

Mormonism

With our consideration of the Jehovah's Witnesses we have made a bridge to the United States of America. It will pay us to follow right across it and give some attention to Mormonism,[32] for of all the sectarian movements this is one that best illustrates the typical pattern of development. It is older than the Jehovah's Witnesses, dating from the early nineteenth century. It is, indeed, a product of the mental climate of New England and New York at that time, when farming people were beginning to be infected with the prevailing expansionism and optimism. They began to accept the idea that their life was not fixed but could, simply by their exerting initiative, be a much better life. This would occur if they let themselves be drawn into the commercial economy and be commercial rather than subsistence farmers— or even move to the towns. Mormonism is essentially the religion of that great fork in history when the people of the subsistence farming tradition divide into two cohorts each of which marches down a new road—to commercial farming or urban occupation. It has all the spirit of progress of the adventurous change.

But it also has a certain rejection of formal education and professionalism, for the generation making the change did not have the chance to acquire it; although, obviously, it would be a tremendous advantage to have had it right then. It is probably no misrepresentation to say that Mormonism was a protest against the advantage gained by better education rather than the advantage gained by greater wealth. Its was the Tom Sawyer mentality that held that the farm boy with spirit and native intelligence could make good in the commercial and urban world, without having to get a formal education. It was part of the great outburst of assertiveness, egoism if you like, of "the common man," "the self-educated man," "the self-made man." Mormonism was the religious expression of it, and was parallelled by Thomas Paine's common man's political philosophy and Walt Whitman's common man's poetry—and they came almost at the same time.

One expression of this self-assertiveness in religion was the revivalist preacher, and it was in a part of New York State virtually burned out with revivalism that Mormonism was born. Joseph Smith, its founder, came from a family saturated with Methodist, Presbyterian and Baptist revivalism. Smith rejected all their theologies, contrived as they were by professional theologians, and, with unyielding common-man logic, concluded they were all in error because they were in contradiction. The common man's competence to do religion for himself became apparent when Smith turned prophet. He received a direct revelation from God and, through it, produced the *Book of Mormon*. This book puts the common-man American into sacred history, and makes the Mormons themselves God's latter-day saints— which is to say, the present-day Israel. The *Book of Mormon* adapts the Jewish belief in the promised land to "a place of one's own in America," and it adapts the messianic deliverance to "progress." It proposes to the Mormons a definite programme of building Zion on American soil. This they made four attempts to do: first in Ohio, then in Missouri, then in Illinois, and finally in Utah, where they have now a place of their own and have, indeed, progressed without limit.

What they have succeeded in establishing in Utah is nothing less than a civilization. Mormonism *has* lifted its members to status, education, culture and distinction. With the community in Utah stabilized, it has provided a whole way of life for them. Art, drama, dance, literature, oratory, sport and athletics—all these are cultivated assiduously. College and university education are widely enjoyed. Utah has the highest rate of literacy of any state in the Union, and recently was ahead of Massachusetts as the birthplace of the greatest number of distinguished men of science and letters. Like Abraham, the common man has won great reward for his family. It is the reward he optimistically expected when he conceived a new ideal and turned his back on the subsistence farm. So intrinsic is the notion of progress to the Mormon's ideal that he believes even God progresses. He says that as we are now so was God once.

The Dynamic Illustrated in the Origins of Some Native Protest Movements

One variety of alienation that has given rise to sectarian protest time and again in the modern world is that generated by the culture contact situation. Typically, the representatives of a more advanced culture move in and dominate, the life of the native people then falling into decay. In time, the natives' reaction comes in the form of a religious movement that expresses the unacceptability of their situation. The literature on these movements is fairly extensive and much of it very colourful. But it is hampered by three shortcomings. First of all, the phenomenon is treated too much as a thing in itself. It is not put in perspective by viewing it in relation to religion in general. Secondly, because an over-specific name is used for the whole collection of movements the impression is left that they are more uniform than they are. They may, for instance, be collectively called millenarian, messianic, nativistic or revitalizing movements. But none of these is an apt characterization of every movement that is put in the class. Thirdly, there is a definite inclination, at least on the part of some writers, to analyze these movements mainly in terms of their political consequences and to suppress or even deny their religious significance. Cohn, Hobsbawm, Kaufman, Lanternari, Lawrence and Worsley, for example, all do this,[33] and, moreover, from quite different considerations. The author may approach the movement as a Marxist, convinced that the filmy religion in it is waning and the solid political action waxing strong. Alternatively, the people looking over the author's shoulder and waiting for his report may be administrators for whom the movement is a political problem. If we can extricate these movements from the triple muddle into which some accounts have brought them and accept them more for what they are, it will be to our advantage. I propose that we look at the North American Indian Ghost Dance[34] and the Melanesian Cargo Cult as illustrations.[35]

The North American Indian Ghost Dance

There were two main waves of the Ghost Dance, starting in 1870 and 1890 respectively. Both of them originated among the Paiute

Indians of Nevada and then spread to other tribes. There is no point in looking at the Ghost Dance without looking at what went before. By force of arms the white settlers had taken the Indians' plains from them. The survivors now lived in abject humiliation and despondency on reserves. Formerly they had been skilled horsemen of the plains, hunters of buffalo, and warriors. Status was earned by outstanding mastery in these pursuits, and they had striven hard to get it. It had been an exhilarating life with peaks of glory. Now, it was clear to them, there was no realistic prospect of their ever making out as a people again. Everything was over, absolutely. There can rarely have been a moment when men were ground so small without having any way out. The only ideal it might be possible for them to conceive would be in terms of what they had known, plus, perhaps, some alliance with the still thriving whites.

In the 1890 dance there are various versions of the vision given to the prophet. In one the whites are to be taken out of the way by high winds, in another they are to live on peacefully with the Indians. Either eventuality will only follow a great series of natural catastrophes marking the end of the old order and bringing back plains teeming with buffalo. The Great Spirit will return to earth and the Indian dead will be resurrected, a larger earth being built to accommodate the augmented population. Everyone will have perpetual youth—forty being the upper age limit—perfect health and immortality. In order to restore everything to where it was before and so make it better than the present, a different code of conduct should be instituted right away. Most important of all, there is to be no more fighting or any kind of unfriendliness to the whites; and no one should drink whisky, lie or steal. To hasten the arrival of the glorious dead and to enhance morale by union with them now, a dance is instituted. The dance is performed in a circle which is left partly open so that the ancestor-ghosts may enter it as observers. The dancers prepare with a purifying bath and decorate their bodies. They wear special shirts which the whites' bullets could, they believe, never penetrate. The full ritual includes singing, chanting, trance and stripping naked. It has echoes of the older Sun Dance whereby the separate nomadic bands of Indians gathered periodically to express some degree of overriding communality.

So we are seeing the ideal figured as a millennium! Strictly, a millennium is a reign of peace on the earth we know, and as this occurs on a new earth it is a nice point whether it can even be called that. Whether with whites or without them, the millennium is an ideal state of total solidarity where the strife that proved so disastrous before is expunged. This envisaged salvation generates its own ethic and ritual. It would be superficial indeed to interpret all this as mere nostalgia for the irrecoverable past or wishes for an improbable future. It would be even more inept to interpret it as a springboard to a revolutionary future. It is a vision of the new possibility, though its idiom is old. Its ritual breathes confidence. Its ethic breathes acquiesence and cooperation. If it engenders any action at all, it is in putting one's feet on the very first rungs of the ladder that leads to respectability in the society that so obviously has the future on its side.

The Melanesian Cargo Cult

Widely dispersed in time and space have been the separate manifestations of the Cargo Cult that has been ruffling Melanesia for nearly a century now. The standard pattern is the development of an expectation that a cargo of European-type goods will be arriving, say, by ship or plane. When this happens everyone will have all his material needs abundantly supplied. Since it is going to happen quite soon, tools can be laid down even now. There are, however, certain practices that have to be observed by everyone in order to ensure that everything unfolds according to plan. Sometimes work does actually stop and the community is brought to the verge of starvation and ruin. It has then to be rescued by supplies of food and equipment from the government. It is usually classified as a millenarian movement because the miraculously arriving time of plenty is a kind of millennium.

In the Tuka movement of 1885 in Fiji, one Ndungumoi, who had travelled, said it had been revealed to him that everything was to be turned upside down.[36] The Fijians would be masters of the whites, for one thing. European supplies including cloth and tinned goods would be arriving for Ndungumoi's followers, who would also have eternal life. The Bible the Europeans used originated with the Fijians, and consequently goods were being diverted to the Europeans that were originally made for the Fijians. Followers were socialized into certain European ways; for example, by drilling, and by using money with which they paid Ndungumoi their membership fee and purchased from him bottles of water from the fountain of life. The date for the arrival of supplies was named and the followers were told to give up making any further provision for themselves. Then Ndungumoi made the mistake of threatening some Europeans and was jailed for a year. As his following continued to support him nevertheless, he was banished for a longer term. On his way home after release he died, but in expectation of his return interest had revived again. Later again a lieutenant received letters from him in the sky and the cult revived once more.

In the Vailala Madness that broke out in 1919 amongst the Orokolo tribes on the Gulf of Papua, one Evara, who had much contact with Europeans, said the ancestor spirits would shortly come on a steamship.[37] They would be equipped with rifles, rice, flour and tobacco. The ancestors were now white and would be in European clothes. In his trances in which such knowledge was disclosed he had shaking fits, and these became contagious among the followers. Paraphernalia used in the old religion was burned. Tables and benches of the European type were placed in the centre of the villages. Offerings for the ancestors were placed on the tables. Frequent rumours that the ship had been sighted proved false but the expectation was slow to die. Notwithstanding, other tribes were pleased to embrace the new hope.

In what has been called the Naked Cult, which occurred in 1944 in the New Hebrides, one Tsek instructed the people to destroy European goods and give up working for Europeans, but to await the coming of the Americans whose goods were superior yet![38] Many old practices, like marriage payments and clan exogamy, were swept aside. Clothing and ornaments were to be given up. Deliberate steps were taken to promote equality and unity amongst the followers; economic differences were reduced by killing pigs. Tsek had a particular conviction that quarrelling caused illness and so must be avoided at all costs.

What I think we see in all this is an identification with superior power. It is from their own native way the natives are alienated. These people, especially their more perceptive leaders, have seen in the white settlers a vision of what, it seems to them, must be a vastly better life. How they can move into it they do not know, but they expect it involves a great leap, a discontinuity. The better life rests on totally different conditions and they are the conditions the Europeans have at their command. To realize that life, the Europeans certainly do not have to work for material provisions in the way they do—their life line reaches beyond the island and is maintained by the cargoes of ships and planes. So the natives' own economic practices, as well as other traditions, should be abandoned, and a new start awaited.

Once the grip of this superior ideal is upon the natives, it seems nothing can remove it. The attempt must be made to cross to that other way. The persistence of the same millennial expectation, when prophecy has failed, is evidence of the persistence of the constraining ideal. The spectacle of people doing this —in such numbers and again and again—is surely cause for the greatest wonderment. Have we not documentation here on the very nature of man? How can anyone think first of the foolish impracticality of these people in taking action that is damaging to themselves? How can anyone think first of the bother they create for administrations? How can anyone think first to laugh at them or chide them? Stand back and look at them: cutting the nerve of life, pulling up all its roots, because they are convinced an altogether new ideal must be attempted! They are *men*—and this is what man *is*.

The Acute Problem of Meaning of the Upwardly Aspiring

There is ample evidence, I think, in the cases we have reviewed, of an acute problem of meaning being experiencd by groups who are seeking a change of status. Not only are they compelled to reject the prevailing definition of the human situation, they are obliged to substitute another. The picture they then give of reality is one that emphasizes those aspects to which their particular situation has made them sensitive. It is to that extent selective, and must seem, from other points of view, narrow or distorted. It does indeed often seem so to later generations in the same tradition, when their wider experience has made them conscious of needs their forbears neglected. We often find that later generations of a particular tradition, like, say, the Anglican, Baptist, Quaker, Methodist or Mormon, have an ambivalent feeling toward their founders. They are grateful for what the founders saw, regretful and even perhaps resentful for what they were blind to. Insofar as they seek to give satisfaction within the fellowship by being a "good" Anglican, Baptist, Quaker, Methodist or Mormon, they can find themselves maladapted to some aspects of life, adopting postures that seem artificial to others, and even to themselves. Sometimes, then, the cry comes of a need for reforms and revisions from within.

Reforms and revisions may well come, for adaptability is a feature of cultural systems. This is why it can be so deceptive to use one general term like "Buddhism" or "Catholicism" to cover all the manifestations of a tradition at different times. Because of this it should be emphasized—if indeed that is still needed—that what we have above called by any particular name is what it was in its beginnings, for it is that phase of the movements we are concerned with. No one wants to suggest that Methodism, Calvinism or Lutheranism, for instance, has never been anything other than what it was at its beginnings. Nor does one want to suggest that they have never appealed to any save those groups for whom they had a special attraction at first. But it is particularly illuminating if we *can* recover the outlook of the first following of a movement—and the same *kind* of outlook must surely characterize those who subsequently are the first to make revisions and reforms. For while there is a wider following even at the start than the special sector whose protest a movement voices, it can fairly be claimed that to voice such a protest is why it is born. Then it is that the three-sided nature of religion-making, noted in Chapter 2, comes clearly into view. Concern with the ideal, with power and with unity, are all evidenced simultaneously in the response made. It is to the ideal society that reference is at once made for the standard by which to propose an alternative. That this is itself taken for a power is shown by the willingness with which men will forgo normal supports, and even extricate themselves totally from them, in the belief that the ideal itself will work on their behalf. Finally, it is the ideal society that provides the all-inclusive context by which to give an interpretation of life in the present imperfect state, thereby making it meaningful to strive for betterment.[39]

The consideration we have given to some actual cases allows certain points to be made now that could scarcely have been made so easily before, but which must be made if the position I am advancing is not to be seriously misunderstood. When I say that, in any religion, men will be giving expression to their concern with the ideal society, this should not be understood simplistically. It does not necessarily mean that in every religion we will see the ideal positively, focally and self-consciously set forth. It is quite likely that a particular religion will be more preoccupied with what the ideal is not, depending on where it stands in relation to what went before. I have already suggested that this more negative concern is exhibited in Buddhism, Lutheranism and Baptism, for example. As a result of it they display an individualism that could be misleading, since one might be led to suppose concern with the ideal society is absent. I would nevertheless claim that that, precisely, *is* the underlying concern. But in such cases it is latent, unconscious, assumed. These religions find their immediate mission to be more critical than reconstructive. Similarly, just as some religions are more positive than others, some are more ambitious and exhaustive in the scope of the revision they undertake. Catholicism and Calvinism were two very exhaustive systems. The Salvation Army, in contrast, centred on a narrow, though a very urgent, set of problems. All the untidiness introduced by differences of these kinds can be accommodated by the point of view I am advocating, if the flexibility I intend is allowed for it.

Notes, Chapter 5

1. Anthony F. C. Wallace, *Religion, An Anthropological View*, New York: Random House, 1966, pp. 3-4.
2. Bengt G. M. Sundkler, *Bantu Prophets in South Africa*, 2nd edition, London: Oxford University Press, 1961, p. 374.
3. Richard H. Niebuhr, *The Social Sources of Denominationalism*, Cleveland & New York: Meridian Books, 1963.
4. Werner Stark, *The Sociology of Religion, A Study of Christendom*, New York: Fordham University Press, 1967-70, Vol. II, pp. 5-29.
5. For details on the development of Buddhism see E. J. Thomas, *The Life of Buddha as Legend and History*, 3rd ed. rev., London: Routledge & Kegan Paul, 1949; *The History of Buddhist Thought*, 2nd ed., London: Routledge & Kegan Paul, 1951; E. A. Burtt, editor, *The Teachings of the Compassionate Buddha*, New York: Mentor Books, 1955.
6. For details on the development of Judaism see Louis Finkelstein, *The Jews: Their History, Culture and Religion*, New York: Harper, 1960;

Jacob Savin, *Concepts of Judaism, A Study of the Variety of Interpretations*, New York: Exposition Press, 1964.

7. *The New English Bible*, Gen. 15:18-21.
8. For details on the development of Christianity see M. Goguel, *The Life of Jesus*, translated by Olive Wyon, London: George Allen & Unwin, 1933; *The Birth of Christianity*, translated by H. C. Snape, London: George Allen & Unwin, 1953; G. B. Caird, *The Apostolic Age*, London: Duckworth & Co., 1955; L. Duchesne, *The Early History of the Christian Church*, translated from the 4th French revised edition by Claude Jenkins, London: John Murray, 1909-24; Kenneth S. Latourette, *A History of Christianity*, New York: Harper & Bros., 1953.
9. See *The New English Bible*, Acts 2.
10. *Ibid.*, verse 5.
11. *Ibid.*, verses 9-11.
12. *Ibid.*, verse 39.
13. *Ibid.*, verse 46.
14. For detailed evidence see E. A. Judge, *The Social Pattern of the Christian Groups in the First Century*, London: Tyndale Press, 1960.
15. For details on the development of Islam see Alfred Guillaume, *Life of Muhammed*, Oxford University Press, 1955; *Islam*, Harmondsworth: Penguin Books, 1954; Richard Bell, *The Origin of Islam in Its Christian Environment*, London: Macmillan, 1926.
16. For details on the development of Lutheranism see G. R. Elton, *Reformation Europe 1517-1559*, London: Collins (Fontana Library), 1963; A. G. Dickens, *Reformation and Society in Sixteenth-Century Europe*, London: Thames and Hudson, 1966; E. G. Rupp, *Luther's Progress to the Diet of Worms*, London: S.C.M. Press, 1951; *The Righteousness of God*, London: Hodder & Stoughton, 1953; H. Boehmer, *Luther and the Reformation in the Light of Modern Research*, translated by E. S. G. Potter, London: G. Bell & Sons, 1930.
17. For details on the development of Calvinism see G. R. Elton, *Reformation Europe 1517-1559*; A. G. Dickens, *Reformation and Society in Sixteenth-Century Europe*; R. N. Carew Hunt, *Calvin*, London: Centenary Press, 1933; J. T. McNeill, *History and Character of Calvinism*, New York: Oxford University Press, 1954.
18. Max Weber, *The Protestant Ethic and the Spirit of Capitalism*.
19. See, for example, G. R. Elton, *Reformation Europe 1517-1559*, London: Collins, 1963, pp. 210-38, S. N. Eisenstadt, editor, *The Protestant Ethic and Modernization, A Comparative View*, New York: Basic Books, 1968.
20. For details on the development of the Reformation in England see G. R. Elton, *England under the Tudors*, London: Methuen & Co., 1962; A. G. Dickens, *The English Reformation*, London: B. T. Batsford, 1964.
21. George Macaulay Trevelyan, *History of England*, third edition, London: Longmans, Green & Co., 1945, p. 301.
22. *Ibid.*, p. 302.
23. For detailed accounts of this movement see G. R. Elton, *Reformation Europe 1517-1559*, pp. 86-103; A. G. Dickens, *Reformation and Society in Sixteenth-Century Europe*, pp. 125-150.
24. G. R. Elton, *op. cit.*, p. 86.
25. On the class characteristics of some early Zwinglians and Anabaptists see Norman Birnbaum, "The Zwinglian Reformation in Zurich," in *Sociology and History: Theory and Research*, W. Cahnmann and A. Boskoff, eds., New York: Free Press of Glencoe, 1964; P. Peachey, *Die soziale Herkunft der Schweizer Täufer in der Reformationszeit*, Dissertation, Karlsruhe, 1954.
26. For details on the development of the English Baptists see A. C. Underwood, *A History of the English Baptists*, London: Baptist Union Publication Department, 1947.
27. For details on the development of Quakerism see Thomas Clarkson, *A*

Portraiture of Quakerism; T. Edmund Harvey, *The Rise of the Quakers;* Richard T. Vann, *The Social Development of English Quakerism, 1655-1755.*

28. For details on the development of Methodism see Joseph Nightingale, *A Portraiture of Methodism;* Robert C. Monk, *John Wesley, His Puritan Heritage;* Rupert E. Davies, *Methodism,* Harmondsworth: Penguin Books, 1963.

29. For details on the development of the Salvation Army see Robert Sandall, *The History of the Salvation Army,* Vols. I, II, III, London: Nelson, 1947, 1950, 1955, and Arch R. Wiggins, *The History of the Salvation Army,* Vols. IV & V, London: Thomas Nelson & Sons, 1964, 1968; A. M. Nicol, *General Booth and the Salvation Army,* London: Herbert and Daniel, n.d.; S. D. Clark, *Church and Sect in Canada,* Toronto: University of Toronto Press, 1948; Roland Robertson, "The Salvation Army: The Persistence of Sectarianism," in Bryan R. Wilson, editor, *Patterns of Sectarianism, Organisation and Ideology in Social and Religious Movements,* London: Heinemann, 1967, pp. 49-105.

30. General (William) Booth, *In Darkest England and the Way Out,* London: Salvation Army, n.d.

31. For the pioneering work in this field of inquiry see Herbert Hewitt Stroup, *The Jehovah's Witnesses,* New York: Columbia University Press, 1945; Royston Pike, *Jehovah's Witnesses,* London: Watts & Co., 1954; Marley Cole, *Jehovah's Witnesses, The New World Society,* with introduction to British edition by J. W. Felix, London: George Allen & Unwin, 1956; David Roger Manwaring, *Render Unto Caesar: The Flag-Salute Controversy,* Chicago: University of Chicago Press, 1962.

32. For detailed accounts of Mormonism see Thomas F. O'Dea, *The Mormons,* Chicago: University of Chicago Press, 1957; Nels Anderson, *Desert Saints, The Mormon Frontier in Utah,* Chicago: University of Chicago Press, 1966.

33. Norman Cohn, *The Pursuit of the Millennium,* second edition, New York, Harper & Row, 1961; E. J. Hobsbawm, *Primitive Rebels,* New York: W. W. Norton and Co., 1965; R. Kaufman, *Millénarisme et Acculturation,* Brussels, 1964; Vittorio Lanternari, *The Religions of the Oppressed,* translated by Lisa Sergio, New York: Mentor Books, The New American Library, 1965; Peter Lawrence, *Road Belong Cargo,* Manchester: Manchester University Press, 1964; Peter Worsley, *The Trumpet Shall Sound,* London: MacGibbon & Kee, 1957.

34. For details see James Mooney, *The Ghost Dance Religion and the Sioux Outbreak of 1890;* Kenelm Burridge, *New Heaven, New Earth: A Study of Millenarian Activities.*

35. For a review and introduction to the literature see Kenelm Burridge, *op. cit.* Annemarie de Waal Malefijt, *Religion and Culture, An Introduction to Anthropology of Religion,* New York, Macmillan, 1968, pp. 330-9.

36. For details see A. B. Brewster, *The Hill Tribes of Fiji,* London: Seeley, Service & Co., 1922.

37. For details see F. E. Williams, *The Vailala Madness and the Destruction of Native Ceremonies in the Gulf Division,* Port Moresby, 1923.

38. For details see Annemarie de Waal Malefijt, *op. cit.,* pp. 37-8.

39. Followers of Goldmann might urge that the Jansenists contradict my thesis that new religion expresses the aspirations of groups that are alienated yet striving for upward mobility. Goldmann attempted to show that Jansenism drew its main following from a set whose striking class characteristic was its downward mobility. In Marxist fashion, he then represents their religious interest as a compensation for their political impotence and deprivation. The French king had set up a new bureaucracy, a body of commissaires, to support him in his chosen

function of absolute monarch. He transferred to these commissaires many of the tasks and prerogatives of the officers, the men of legal and administrative competence—the *noblesse de robe*—by whose considerable power he had hitherto been hampered. It was from this latter group, now declining in influence, that the main supporters of Jansenism were recruited, Goldmann asserts. Yet I think this selective emphasis on downward mobility is too distorting. I allow that the challenge to their status can certainly be viewed as an added source of alienation. But it is clear that they were determined not to accept the disadvantage into which they were being thrust. It was, in any case, only a check on the long-term trend, since it was precisely because they enjoyed power at the expense of the Crown that Mazarin and Louis XIV wanted them put down. Furthermore, the Jansenites were intractable in their attitude to both church and state authorities. They were allied with the Gallicanism that wanted to free the French church from papal domination, as well as with the *parlements* that wanted to check the king. Their movement was at its height between 1637 and 1677, which was a century later than the Protestant Reformation. Yet I think the Jansenites can be viewed as an expression of the new man, just as much as the Protestants and Jesuits were. The fact that they became critics of both of these simply indicates that they saw themselves to be competitors in the same cause. Goldmann makes much of what he calls the Jansenists' "tragic vision," by which he refers to their theological notion that it is impossible for men, even with the grace made available to them, to fulfil the moral law. He sees this to be a kind of ideological reflection of their paradoxical political situation. That is, they could not openly resist the king since their privileges depended on courting his favour; they could not do what they desired to do. Yet what is more distinctive of the Jansenists' theology is their concern to see the individual transfigured by grace, since in the natural state he was believed to have no virtue. It could simply be their intense desire for this transformation that made them aware of the impossibility of doing it completely. Here we find the same individualism in spiritual cultivation that can be observed in the Lutherans and Jesuits. See Lucien Goldmann, *Le dieu caché, Etude sur la vision tragique dans les Pensées de Pascal et dans le théâtre de Racine*, Librairie Gallimard, Paris, 1955; Lucien Goldmann, *The Hidden God, A Study of Tragic Vision in the Pensées of Pascal and the Tragedies of Racine*, translated from the French by Philip Thody, London: Routledge & Kegan Paul, 1964; and Nigel Abercrombie, *The Origins of Jansenism*, Oxford University Press, 1936.

Chapter 6

The Difference Due to the Achievement of Respectability

I have been saying that sectarian movements are born when the power structure loosens and alienated groups begin to move upward. These people can be compared with amateurs, or with growing children trying their own strength. They want to do religion for themselves, even though more experienced persons might well be found who would do it better. The independence gives them a combination of advantages and disadvantages. Their religion is marked by great sincerity and vigour, since they only engage in it at all out of conviction. Its teaching is clear, definite and simple— what is called in religion "fundamentalist" —since anyone thinking afresh on his own account starts from first principles. But it can be lacking in balance, maturity and sophistication, if it rejects any tradition that may exist of theology, ethics and liturgy. Being unsophisticated about itself it can also be exclusivist. Holding its position to be the only truth it can be intolerant of all others.

The Mellowing of Sects with Social Acceptance

But there is a definite tendency for sects to mellow. Although they may spend generations getting over their distortions and one-sidedness and becoming universal once more, that does occur. This process has sometimes been called the sect's "accommodation to the world," and it is usually taken to indicate a compromise of spirituality. Yet it is better viewed, I think, as an accommodation to the change from social rejection to social acceptance. When respectability has been earned, and status and responsibility in the total society conferred on the sect's members, its nature changes radically. I know of no reason why, in and of itself, this change should be viewed negatively. That is because, as the reader will recall, I know of no reason why respectability should be disparaged.

It helps us to be reconciled to a significant part of the diversity in religion once we appreciate that the sect is but a *phase* in the development of any religious tradition. It is a time-specific phenomenon. Richard Niebuhr suggests it has no more than a one-generation life.[1] A sect is created by people coming into voluntary association. As soon as children are born to them, and the parents expect that they will automatically associate with the movement, then the movement becomes a different thing. Although this is indeed a real difference in form, it does not seem to me that sects necessarily exhibit a marked transformation in character so soon. The real difference appears to come with the attainment of the respectability that has been sought all along. This will take a variable length of time: it may take much longer for some sects than for others. In any case, the life of a sect is most meaningfully measured as the time needed to accomplish this transformation.

Since this is the case, a sociological typology of religious organization can be made in terms of the stage of development of the religious movement. As we shall see, some fairly complicated typologies in this regard have been proposed. But a simple typology comprising only two or three stages seems to me to delineate the significant differences best. The initial stage is the sectarian or protest movement. This matures into the ecclesia when it is the only influential religious movement in the society. It matures into the denomination when it is in competition with other religious movements. The ecclesia forms a terminal stage, except that sects may separate from it again, thereby providing the initial stage of a new cycle. It is also possible for an ecclesia to turn into a denomination, if sects and denominations enter the scene and turn it into a competitor. The denomination is best regarded as an intermediate stage in a line of development that may achieve its terminal stage in the union or ecumenical church, this being the equivalent of the ecclesia for this alternative line of development. (I mean at the ultimate point, of course, when all churches are merged in one. Unions actually achieved may simply incorporate some churches. This will reduce the number in competition, but all of these will remain denominations.) Multiplicity of competing denominations results from differentiations within the population, mainly those arising from the social class divisions that are important in sect development, although migrations can make another important source.

When the present whole-community identity is felt to be more compelling than that with the sectional traditions, we may witness the emergence of the union or ecumenical church. This is really the product of a class-levelling. "Since we are all respectable now there is no point in self-consciously perpetuating our differences" is what the candidates for union seem to be implying. Ecumenism is therefore best regarded as an integration effort to pool resources and maximize efficiency on the part of groups who feel their former divisions have been made redundant by the intervening social mobility. So dialogue about doctrinal differences and organizational duplication ensues. In contrast to the inspirational mood in which sectarian division is engendered, ecumenical union can be pursued in a dreary mood of intellectual debate and administrative and economic planning. Yet the ecumenical enterprise can have its share of inspiration. It may draw sustenance from the idea that true religion is the religion of united hearts, emphasizing for this phase of church life that aspect of doctrine. Concentration on such doctrines may blind the participants to the class and status aspect of their activities—and the sectarians' concentration on doctrine may of course do the same for that earlier stage. But observers can take note of it. In Figure 3, the foregoing typology based on stages of development of the religious movement is summarized diagrammatically.

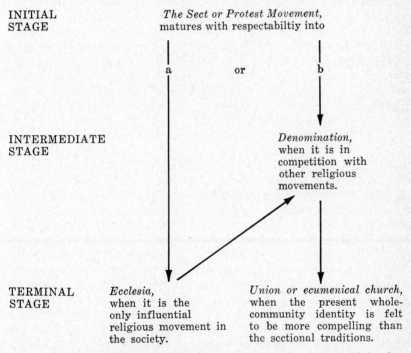

INITIAL STAGE — *The Sect or Protest Movement,* matures with respectabiltiy into

a   or   b

INTERMEDIATE STAGE — *Denomination,* when it is in competition with other religious movements.

TERMINAL STAGE — *Ecclesia,* when it is the only influential religious movement in the society.   *Union or ecumenical church,* when the present whole-community identity is felt to be more compelling than the sectional traditions.

Figure 3.   A typology of religious organization based on stages of development of the religious movement.

The typology I am suggesting is indebted to a tradition of thought on the matter. Troeltsch drew attention to the great contrast between the sect and the already dominant church.[2] He also wrote of mysticism in religion in the same connection, but that is really a classification of religion by a different principle. Since one might prefer to use the term "church" generically for religious organizations of every kind, the term "ecclesia" may be substituted for the dominant church. To the ecclesia and sect, von Wiese and Becker added the denomination and cult.[3] Yinger insists that a typology of religious organizations should be applied only to religiously differentiated societies.[1] For such societies, then, he proposes that we distinguish the following: the ecclesia (which may be of an institutional or diffused variety), the denomination (which also may be institutional or diffused), the established sect, the sect and the cult. Outside of this typology altogether, in the religiously undifferentiated societies, Yinger distinguishes the universal institutionalized church and the universal diffused church. Yet, while there is always virtue in having typologies as discriminating as possible, the significant differences may sometimes be highlighted by the simpler classification, and this is my reason for using it here. It seems to me that the all-important thing is to distinguish the sect, ecclesia, denomination and union church from one another, and to set the cult on one side as the expression of a different principle altogether. (If we adopt this typology, however, we surrender Yinger's distinction between the ecclesia and the universal institutionalized church.) It is common practice to characterize the types of a typology as ideal-types. So I shall now fill out the profiles already begun by itemizing some remaining features of the types of religious organization. (Yet the reader should remember that such types are heuristics only.)

The Ecclesia. I have depicted the sect as a phenomenon of a challenged power structure, and the simplest way to understand the contrasting ecclesia is to view it as a phenomenon of an unchallenged one. It is, in that way, historically dated, for it seems to have developed only where territorial consolidation was such an overriding consideration that men of all social strata submitted to the authority who secured it. Where the territory was an empire, allegiance went to the emperor, where it was a nation, to the king. The ecclesia as a result is the church to which all the persons born into a territory belong, regardless of their social status. It has, within the universe concerned, universal membership. It is the high tide of respectability, in that it is the church of a society of élite and retainers. Those who do not have respectability in their own right have it vicariously by identification with those who do. The Catholic Church of the Holy Roman Empire, the Church of England in the days of uniformity, Swedish Lutheranism and even perhaps the religion of Calvin's Geneva, would all be illustrative of it.

The ecclesia supports the secular authority structure and mirrors it in a way, in that its own organization is hierarchical, traditional and centralized. It may even come into competition with it, since the spiritual head and temporal head hold sway over one and the same realm. In any case, it seeks to be an influence on the secular authority, a power behind the throne, and a force in public affairs. "The world" as a religious category, is not defined as practical and political affairs as such, but these when they become autonomous and evade the guidance of religion. Its forms of worship are characterized by decorum, restraint and dignity. They do, in fact, express the good form and good taste of the social élite. To be a religious person is to be a good churchman. The church enjoins attendance at worship and the sacraments. It jealously reserves to itself the right to propagate doctrine and be the teacher of the people. It endeavours to sanction a whole way of life for the society, with a protected place for moderate pleasures. Churches of this kind that persist into the present have mainly a traditional legitimation for much of their practice. It seems unlikely that new churches of this kind will ever make their appearance again, in view of the fluid character the power structure has taken on.

The Sect. As we have seen, voluntary association distinguishes the sect—which is consequently numerically small. Authority in the sect is charismatic, leadership going to the person with spiritual gifts and natural ability. The life of the group is marked by religious and ethical fervour and there can be trends toward primitivism, in that action and belief can be legitimated by appeal to what was done at first. Discipline in the observance of religious and ethical duties can be enforced by mutual scrutiny. "The world" is defined by concrete practices and spheres of action and influence. The radical opposition to entrenched power may find part of its expression here, in that both the ecclesia and the secular authority can assume aspects of an offensive worldliness. So can the pleasures and possessions of the privileged. Sectarians may consequently be critics of the ecclesia. They may refuse to bear civil office, pay taxes, take oaths or perform military service. They may proscribe pleasures that others consider legitimate.

A simple typology of sects commonly made divides them into the militant and the withdrawing. The Anabaptists and Jehovah's Witnesses would exemplify the former, the Old Order Amish and Plymouth Brethren the latter. Wilson proposes a more elaborate typology in which seven types are distinguished, depending on the way in which the religious quest is pursued.[5] The conversionist sect is exemplified in the Herrnhuter community, the Wesleyans, Baptists, Salvation Army and Pentecostalists. The revolutionist sect—by which term Wilson designates the sect that uses prophecy to prove that God will shortly make war on the evil world and overcome it—is exemplified in the Seventh Day Adventists, Christadelphians and Jehovah's Witnesses. The introversionist sect—so named because it withdraws into both communal and personal holiness—is exemplified in the Hutterians, the Rappites, the Amana Society, the Doukhobors and the Amish Mennonites. The manipulation sect—in which this-worldly benefits are sought by supernatural manipulations—is exemplified in Christian Science, Theosophy and Scientology.

The thaumaturgical sect—in which the person expects miracles that will remedy his personal ills—is exemplified in Spiritualism, the African Aladura, and the faith-healing movements. The reformist sect is exemplified in the Quakers. The utopian sect—which founds a colony to be a perfect model for world society—is exemplified in the Oneida community and the Brotherhood of the New Life.

The Denomination. We grasp the essence of the denomination if we bear in mind that it has earned the respectability given to the ecclesia while denied its universality. It is therefore subject to a kind of status incongruence. Since it would be appropriate for a church with that status to have universality, it is in a dilemma. Will it make itself more universal by trying to expand its membership and influence, thereby intensifying the competition with other denominations, or by seeking an ultimate amalgamation with them, to be anticipated in the present by cooperation with them? Insofar as it leans in the latter direction it will move towards the ecumenical or union church. It seems that most denominations vacillate between competition and cooperation, sometimes playing up their traditional distinctiveness and sometimes playing it down. If the denomination is said to be intermediate between the sect and ecclesia, this very largely means that it is in indecision between them. In contrast to both the ecclesia and sect, the denomination breathes religious tolerance, and its being in this situation is what seems to explain the fact.

One of the most important ecclesia features of the denomination is the way in which it seeks to secure its membership by family descent. Another is the way in which it allows discipline to operate through its forms and conventions rather than through personal examination. Unlike the ecclesia, it does not expect to influence the secular authority, since it knows it has not the necessary strength; but it does uphold the secular authority. It may also seek to influence the formation of public opinion. Perhaps the most distinctive legacy that remains from the sect phase of its experience is a more democratic, elective form of church government. If it comes to the point of contemplating union with churches from an ecclesiastical tradition, one of the most agonising questions is which way the union will go. A thing that some denominations particularly regret, concerning their lack of universality, is their overwhelmingly middle-class membership. But it has, of course, been made inevitable by their history. Yet that is more typical of denominations that have reached this destination by grading up, so to speak, from the sect, than of those that have graded down from the ecclesia. For, as already indicated, the denomination is a middle ground into which one may be brought from either side. In the United States the Methodist and Baptist churches would illustrate the first dénouement, the Episcopalian, Lutheran and Roman Catholic churches the second.

These last three do become denominations in a competitive situation where they have no monopoly.

The Union or Ecumenical Church. Practical economies were largely responsible for the eventual formation of such ecumenical churches as we have seen appear. These merger churches now include the United Church of Canada (founded in 1925), the Reformed Church of France (1938), the Church of Christ in Japan (1941), the Dutch Reformed Church (1946), the Church of South India (1947) and the Evangelical Church in Germany (1948). The United Church of Canada and the Church of South India are two of the most impressive. The former was a union of Methodists, Congregationalists and a section of the Presbyterians, and in 1968 absorbed the Evangelical United Brethren as well. The latter was a merger of Anglicans and the South Indian United Church, which was itself constituted by a union of Presbyterians and Congregationalists in 1908, these then being joined by the Methodists in 1925. Although mergers, these are not churches of ultimate union, since they are surrounded by other churches still operating independently. They are therefore still strictly denominations and have the general characteristics of denominations as these have been outlined above. Until we see it, we cannot say what the true ecumenical church will be. But as these churches represent a position closer to it they may possibly suggest something about its character. Certainly they are very respectable, and moderate in every way. Their forms of worship are restrained, unemotional and orderly, their doctrine broad and undiscriminating, their conscience and social concern middle-class. Membership in the Canadian church seems to be particularly appealing to professionals and semi-professionals and clerical and other white-collar workers.[6]

Membership in the Indian church is not so overwhelmingly middle-class—for it has many impoverished adherents—but its leadership is. It is really a paternalistic development, an arrangement made by the outsider rather than a grass-roots growth. It bears the marks of its missionary origin. For it is the fruit of the decision to terminate the missionary effort and hand over the work of evangelization to Indians. To make the church indigenous it was necessary to shed the imported denominational distinctions which began to appear redundant once they were taken out of context. It is thus in this double sense—or even triple sense—that the present whole-community identity was found to be more compelling than the sectional traditions in this instance. There was a class-levelling among the foreign leaderships in the first case. Secondly, there was a levelling between these and the section of Indian society that supplied the leadership that succeeded them. Thirdly, there was a national identity uniting the main body of adherents. But its continuing dependence on élite leadership would sufficiently account for the minimal religious practice and the spiritual and intellectual indifference that are said to characterize the bulk of the membership now: ". . . the Church of South India has first-rate bishops, second-rate presbyters and third-rate lay membership. This explains much of our present difficulties and is our basic problem."[7]

The Cult. Sufficient was said in Chapter 1 to show by what principle the cult is to be distinguished from genuine religion. It is giving sacred status to something the culture defines as profane. It is regrettable that some students have given up the attempt to distinguish cults from sects, for they are quite distinct tendencies—even though they may occur as a mixture. Another regrettable thing is that we have to use a word to make a distinction which is itself used variously. For the term "cult" is also used generically to refer to religion itself, especially at its inception or development, or to its ritual as opposed to its ethical aspect. In this book I eschew that generic use of the term in order to avail myself of the other. Sects, as we have seen, adapt a whole faith to the life situation of particular groups. The discipline of the faith is expected to apply to the whole of life, for its duration, and to one's children. But, in contrast to this, the cult is a gesture made to compensate for a lack. Anyone experiencing this lack may try the proposed remedy without his life in general being made subject to scrutiny.

A cult can have a rapid membership turnover as successive waves of people "try it." There are doubtless various kinds of lack for the relief of which cults emerge. But two different kinds can be suggested. There can be a general lack of life-orientation and life-organization for which concentration on almost any interest can supply relief; and there can be some chronic block to fulfilment, like illness or a physical, emotional, intellectual or educational handicap. It seems that either condition can dispose the person to over-valuing supposed remedies. Wilson is one of those who make no attempt to distinguish cults from sects, but his manipulationist and thaumaturgical "sects" have a very cultic appearance. Faith healing, Scientology, Spiritualism and Theosophy, for example, all seem to lie in this region. What they, and all other cults, develop are occult techniques for securing utilitarian satisfactions—whereas if there *were* any method for securing the ends sought it would have to be by natural means. It is as though the consequence of giving sacred status to a profane end is to expect a sacred means for securing it. Scientology offers the technique of eliminating harmful pre-natal impressions ("engrams") in order to become a "clear." Spiritualism offers the technique of communicating with the dead in order to have the advantage of their knowledge and help. Theosophy offers clairvoyant perception of the astral plane in order to learn the truth about man's potential.

Becker suggests that the cult matures into the sect—yet I

cannot see how this could ever be so.[8] I have suggested a different outcome.

> Rather, it will undergo secularization into more effective real solutions of the problem it emerged to meet. If it was but a complication of something which was a sect from the beginning, it may slough off so that we see only the sect remaining. But the cult will be superseded by political action or by technology, science, medicine, and so on. It is a naive view which takes religious and practical action (political action especially) for alternatives, for they are directed towards different kinds of problems. It is possible the view springs from not regarding the cult as the contrary of authentic religion. For the cult may well be an alternative to political or other forms of practical action, and we may see it give way to these. Analysis yields to professional psychiatric medicine, spiritualism to psychic research, Malcolm X resorts to political action. At the same time, the cult's focus of special concern is always capable of being absorbed back into religion. There it gets recognition as being the kind of problem which is endemic in man's situation, but which has no religious solution in itself apart from the general redemption. Secular means of dealing with it are not rejected but blessed, whereas the inflation of concern into a religious one (a cult) is rejected. Thus it is that the sacred makes its deft maneuvers, not to annul the secular but to sanctify it by encirclement, meanwhile annulling the profane. The cult is an aggrieved vassal in profane rebellion. When it is appeased its claims are surrendered, the sacred and secular each taking over where they are entitled to.[9]

It is vital to appreciate that there is cause for cults in this lack of practical solutions for practical aspirations. The gestures made to find relief are of the type described already as magical ritual. That ritual standing in the place of religious ritual, is a distinguishing mark of the cult.

Making Satisfaction Secure through Institutionalization

In Chapter 3, when reference was made to the Durkheimian "church," it was pointed out that religion could be undertaken by naturally occurring groups or by groups founded with religion as their special purpose. Now, in the present chapter, we have noted Yinger's recognition of the two situations, when he says that any typology of religious organization could be applicable only to the latter. It was a large part of the burden of Chapter 1 that religion could be expressed in two modes—we adopted a colloquialism by calling them religion with and without the capital—and this is a similar kind of distinction. We shall look more closely into the difference between the two situations in Chapter 8, and try to understand why they both occur. But it is appropriate in this present chapter to give some further attention to the institutionalization of the specially founded religion. The notion of institutionalization, though fundamental to sociology, is still not very well understood. Yet we seem to have a special need of it in the study of religious organization. There is also another particular matter. During the sixties there was a popular outcry against the "institutionalization" of religion—the implication being that it would be possible to have a religion that was not institutionalized, and that it would be a better one. We need some way to evaluate this notion.

Strictly, institutionalization is a development in *culture* whereby a valued satisfaction is made secure. It is a way of *defining* it positively—and the set of practices necessary to procure it. On the one hand, this entails a sanctioning of specialization. Since the end is important, separate attention must be given to it. But, on the other hand, it entails a sanctioning of subordination to the whole social enterprise, since it is only one out of a number of important needs. This proportioning by placing a set of practices in a larger order provides a legitimation, presumably because it makes a sphere of action meaningful by bringing it under religion implicitly. Since activity must be sustained over time for satisfaction to be secured, institutionalization protects the *completion* of the productive task. In the eventuality that the task must be completed time and again because a flow of satisfactions is desired, it will also protect the *repetition* of the task. The sanctioning of a simultaneous specialization and coordination of time-taking tasks, seems to be about the heart of institutionalization. It results in a firmly structured organization of action, both within the specialized sphere and in its exchanges with society at large. With ever more unanimous endorsement of an activity by a society's influentials its definition as an institution is consolidated—and the respectability of its bearers is simultaneously enlarged. So the path of progression from the sect to the ecclesia, or to the union church, is the path of increasing institutionalization and respectability at the same time.

Specially founded religions come into being because someone experiences a new increment of religious satisfaction beyond what customary observances can yield. There is then a desire to make the flow of satisfaction continuous. The founder's is a charismatic gift, but a way has to be found to make his new insight permanent. The attempt to do this is what Weber calls the routinization of charisma.[10] For pure charisma only exists in the act of origination. The official becomes the successor to the natural leader, and with this the progression to institutionalization is launched. Office has an effectiveness that is independent of the personal effectiveness of the office-holder at the time. This is because it "stands for" something, namely, the gift, the sacred power, in the originator. With a differentiation between the office-holder and the general following we have the beginnings of organization. Auxiliary, supporting offices will probably in time appear and the organization become complex. It is clear that without institutionalization in this way the benefits of religious discovery would be confined to the first discoverers and the new light be transitory indeed.

Institutionalization Illustrated in Primitive Christianity

Since we have documentation on the course of the development of primitive Christianity, we can study institutionalization there. After the death of Jesus the founder, the first office to appear was that of the apostle. The apostles were not simply followers in the sense of having discipleship; on the contrary, they were leaders in the sense of having headship. The fact that the same persons were first disciples and then apostles should not obscure the fact that this marks a decisive change in role. To hold the office of apostle meant to be a witness to the resurrection of Christ: the apostle showed that the sacred power of the originator was not extinguished but still continuing. Officers of the Christian Church ever since have been charged with making the community realize the presence of the risen Lord. The ritual of the Lord's Supper enacted this presence with vividness, for here was the Lord as the host of his guests at table. The ritual of baptism enacted it likewise, for here was a new apostle arising with the Lord. The preaching of the Word enacted it also, for here was the Lord speaking. Officers of the Christian church were therefore perpetuators of the Word and sacraments.

The title of apostle does not seem to have been continued beyond the first witnesses, but for any particular congregation of believers the apostles appointed not one but a group of elders. By the way "apostles and elders" are grouped in New Testament references, it appears that elders were intended to be the successors to the apostles as ministers to the people of the Word and sacraments. It seems they were "elders" in a fairly literal sense of the word—older men more experienced in the faith. Apparently there was some hierarchical differentiation among them, for we also read of bishops being appointed. These appear to have been overseer elders who supervised the elders of a number of congregations. There was also differentiation in another direction. In order to leave apostles, elders and bishops undistracted in their spiritual ministry, deacons were appointed to take charge of the church's practical arrangements. But, whatever their separate functions, it was the officers of the church jointly who were the perpetuators of the Word and sacraments. If the elders ministered these directly, it was the deacons who enabled them to do so. Neither in one nor the other did any special virtue inhere, but in the risen Lord whose presence they conspired to make known.

As the later Christian Church developed, different variations on this basic differentiation have been played. Roman Catholics have emphasized ordination to office, implying that the entitlement of ministry is exclusively given to the ordained. Protestants have tended to take a view, which in modern times becomes ever more unequivocal, that every believer in the resurrection is a minister of Word and sacraments, but that elders and deacons are appointed from amongst them for reasons of practical expediency. They are appointed not in order that "these only" but that "these at least" will be busy in the task of keeping the church alive. Yet it is clear that Roman Catholic and Protestant traditions have been equally dependent on institutionalization. Neither of them could have dispensed with office, and the organization it entails, if the spiritual needs of the successive generations were to be supplied.

Institutionalized Religion as a Foundation for Civilizations

I have suggested that in the process of institutionalization the internal structuring of action is accompanied by an external sanctioning, thereby making the observed practice "official" through and through. Some have suggested that this dénouement is inevitably corrupting. They think, for instance, that when Constantine and Theodosius had succeeded in making Christianity the official religion of the Roman Empire in the fourth century, religion's death knell was sounded. They imply that the only authentic religion is that of the persecuted, struggling sect. Yet I cannot see any necessity for this. One of the most amazing things about the eventual institutionalization of a despised sect and its eventual adoption by officialdom, is that the sect has itself shaped the opinion that gives endorsement to it. It is simply a matter of its having won the recognition it claims to deserve, of being vindicated. But even if official recognition never reaches the ultimate expressed in the Theodosian laws against paganism, it can be given in the form of tacit approval and consent. The religion can be accepted as the society's rule of life. It is religion in this efflorescence that has shaped civilizations.

For we can identify a number of great civilizations that have derived their inspiration and impetus from an accepted religion. We even name the civilization by the religion. Islamic, Hindu, Mayan and Christian civilizations were civilizations of a religion. Classical and Imperial China was the China of Confucianism. It appears that each of these religions was like the charter for a whole new civilization. Their comprehensive and coherent vision of man and his situation, their formulation of the ideal, brought new life to an erstwhile exhausted and confused humanity. Once it had men in its current, that life bore them forward again for hundreds of years. Even though the religions were born as the protest of particular alienated groups, as those groups rose to respectability their ranks were augmented by the other respectable who had no particular protest to make but who were enervated by a general lack of orientation.

Such a trough of social and cultural collapse, of turmoil and ferment, can be found in the period extending from the seventh to the fifth centuries B.C. In that one era Confucianism and Taoism emerged in China, philosophical Brahmanism and Buddhism in India, Zoroastrianism in Persia, classical culture in Greece and the prophetic movement in Judaea. In a similar situation of upheaval Christianity arose. The very different Hebrew and Greek cultures were confronting one another vigorously; to their great consternation, the Jews were being absorbed into the Roman Empire; the Empire itself was on the course that brought it to decay. Similarly again, the Protestant and Catholic reformations within Christianity came at a time of disconcerting change. Feudalism was irrevocably shaken and no one could have known what would take its place. Thus the highly successful religious movement appears to rise in a vortex, and it can be likened to an ark in which a remnant takes refuge from the deluge.

The Negative Possibilities in the Institutionalization of Religion

And yet—there *can* be problems with regard to the institutionalization of religion. At least two problems—and these quite distinct—can arise: anachronism and worldliness. Since institutionalization means that forms of belief and practice are to a large extent frozen, the religion as a system can be left high and dry by widening experience and new knowledge. The religious organization can then seem a redundancy and a travesty. While any institution is open to this subversion by time, religion is especially vulnerable. Because it seeks to speak for the totality of things and give orientation for a total life, revision can only proceed slowly and the wise way to do it is often problematic. Yet if steps toward modernization are delayed, the hollowness of the outworn structure can breed cynicism and a variety of corruptions. Worldliness arises when, instead of the accepted church supplying the standards for the accepting world, the world supplies the standards for the church. As I intimated, I see no necessity for this happening, but I do acknowledge it to be a possibility where the church and society are on such good terms. The accepted church is open to a temptation here that is hardly encountered at all by the sect.

There is another cause for uneasiness about the institutionalization of religion—although it can hardly be called a problem.

There is something anti-institutional at the heart of religion, a built-in tension. It comes from religion's attachment to the ideal. Since religion is committed to that, to build any institution on this side of the ideal to make a mirror for it, is to build a halfway house that will have to be left behind. Insofar as anyone is content with anything actual he is estranged from the ideal, insofar as he is content with the ideal only he is estranged from the actual. This is Paul's anguish.

> *For to me life is Christ, and death gain; but what if my living on in the body may serve some good purpose? Which then am I to choose? I cannot tell. I am torn two ways: what I should like is to depart and be with Christ; that is better by far; but for your sake there is greater need for me to stay on in the body.*[11]

Yet we will scarcely remember that we have no continuing city here unless we have a continuing institution to remind us. Men cannot really expect to evade this tension. It does not indicate that there is anything essentially false in institutionalization but that false attachments may arise because of it. Avoiding them is all one with the art of being in the world but not of it.

Religious Traditions Unite Men and Divide the World

Yet, considering its anti-institutional proclivities, it is quite amazing what a staggering permanence religion can achieve. A religion that is successful in winning general acceptance may last not only for hundreds but for thousands of years. In the course of that time it may indeed undergo much modification, yet it can still be recognizably the same structure. This fact in itself speaks eloquently of the importance men give to a fixed set of reference points for their life—and not for the life of one generation only but for the foreseeable generations. It shows their awareness that they are engaged in long-term endeavours that span the generations. If they, their fathers and their sons are to cooperate together, they will need the same set of cues. A religion is like a foundation stone for a culture, and once one has been laboriously heaved into place, it can rest there with monumental inertia. Strange that we now impute inertia to that which we depicted in the last paragraph as anti-institutional and in the last chapter as innovating! Yet the dual characterization is true—and it involves no contradiction. It is explained by the greatness of the matter with which religion concerns itself. Once a whole foundation is thought to be tolerably well laid, men are more concerned to build on it than to shift it about. But once it is thought to be intolerably faulty, men are more concerned to tear it up than build. This is how it happens that in one of its moods religion is the great conservative and, in another, the great radical.

If we look at recent maps of the world's religions we see that the whole world divides into regions each of which is gripped by one of a small number of very old religious traditions. The youngest of them shown in the map reproduced in Figure 4 is Christian Protestantism. This is four and a half centuries old, but it is of course simply a variant of Christianity which has continued for twenty. The other variants of Christianity, Roman Catholicism and Eastern Orthodoxy, may possibly be dated from the first and fourth centuries respectively. All the other religions shown are considerably older than Christianity, except for Islam which dates from the seventh century. The map gives only the dominant religion of any region, of course. But it confronts us with the way religion brings union and division to mankind simultaneously. For amongst those whose allegiance a religion commands, it creates an internal orderliness that can facilitate many centuries of common life. We must note, however, that for the regions now under communist domination the map gives the traditional religious allegiance. It is true that much traditional religion persists there, and actually presents resistance to communism in some places. But it is just as true that it is actively discouraged by communism, especially at the inter-generational line, and that there is a marked decline. Communism itself is the one influential new religion of our time, of course. Perhaps it is too near to us to get a perspective on it. But it is already set to be the long-term foundation of a civilization. What it has accomplished in the century and a quarter since Marx and Engels issued the *Communist Manifesto* is staggering to contemplate.

The major living religious traditions have not only spread through time, they have also spread through space. If we exclude those religions that the map groups as "Primitive and Animist," the remaining ones—all founded religions—came into being on the margins of Asia. From there they have moved out until, between them, they have covered the face of the globe. These Asia-born faiths comprise three distinct families. Judaism, Christianity and Islam belong to a family of religions arising in the dry and semi-dry lands of southwest Asia. Hinduism and Buddhism (together with Jainism and Sikhism) belong to a family arising in the hot, wet Indian subcontinent. Taoism, Confucianism (and also Shinto) belong to a family arising in the Far East. These families of religion are as distinct in character as are the environments that cradled them, although their character is something mainly for consideration in the next chapter. The dry-land religions are purposive, striving and world-changing. The Indian religions are contemplative and acquiesc-

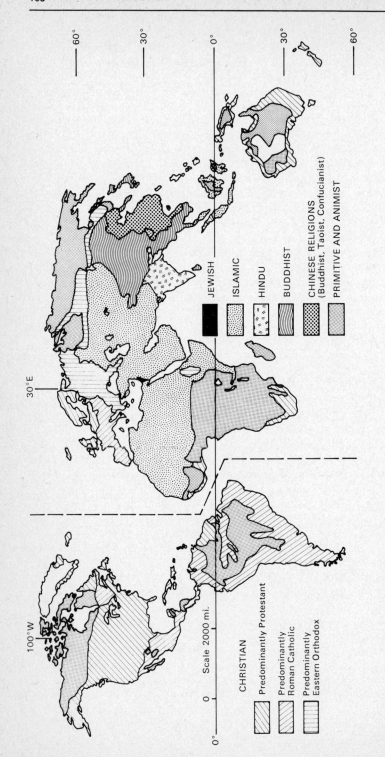

Figure 4. World Map of Dominant Religions.

Reproduced with permission from Alfred H. Meyer and John H. Strietelmeier. *Geography in World Society, A Conceptual Approach,* J. B. Lippincott, Philadelphia and New York, 1963, p. 362.

ing. The Far Eastern religions are concerned with fitting in; with stance, that is, in nature and the cosmos, and with conduct, manners and citizenship.

Judaism

Judaism, originating in Palestine, has been carried throughout the whole world, mainly by the dispersion of migrating Jews themselves.[12] They settled largely in cities, often in ghettos. They were frequently the victims of prejudice, discrimination and persecution, especially in Eastern Europe. Hope of securing relief from this led to the foundation of the modern state of Israel in Palestine in 1948. Yet in 1955 only fourteen per cent of all Jews were citizens of Israel, in 1967 seventeen per cent. They remain a widely dispersed people. Almost one-half of them live in the United States, and these are concentrated in the north-eastern cities. The Soviet Union is another country with a large Jewish population. Wherever the Jews were excluded from normal privileges in countries where they settled, they were an alienated minority who perpetuated their orthodox tradition with a sect-like separateness. But insofar as they won acceptance and status, a kind of "denomination-trend" has appeared amongst them. In the movement known in Europe as Liberal (and continuing in North America as Reformed) Judaism, successful and educated Jews have stressed the universal, ethical aspect of their faith that could be shared by non-Jews, and have played down the traditional dietary and ritual observances. Conservative Judaism in North America seems to have played the same role exactly for a different wave of upwardly mobile Jews, as they accommodated to social acceptance after migrating from Eastern Europe, but it is less radical than Reformed Judaism.

Christianity

The separation of the two older branches of Christianity came about in the fourth century following tension over the autonomy of the eastern churches whose life centred on Constantinople.[13] These churches eventually constituted the separate Eastern Orthodox Church. They were organized as self-governing patriarchates federated under the Patriarch of Constantinople. For all practical purposes they then became national churches. For centuries, much of this territory was occupied by the Turks, a situation that placed severe handicaps on church life. The clergy organized much of the opposition to Turkish rule and thereby the churches were brought further under the control of the emerging national states. It probably involves no distortion to say that this was an impeded, slower-moving growth towards national religion of the kind that Lutheranism and Calvinism exemplified in the West.

The Roman Catholic Church, in contrast, was centralized, in tune with the centralized Roman Empire whose territory it served. When the Empire disintegrated, the court of the Pope in Rome continued the work of unification to some extent, by mediating between the small sovereignties and principalities. This accustomed the church to being a power in its own right, with a mission of internationalism. The vision served very well where its European supporters were colonizing powers. Its plan of development seemed nothing but furthered as Roman Catholicism was carried to new countries. It was established as the dominant faith in Quebec by the French, in Brazil by the Portuguese, and elsewhere in the Americas by the Spanish, and it also came as a rival faith into the predominantly Protestant colonies: into North America, Australia and New Zealand, where the English had brought Protestantism, and into South Africa, made Protestant by the Dutch. But with the end of colonialism and the development of independent nationhood by the formely colonial countries the Roman Catholic crusade for internationalism had run its course.

The second half of the twentieth century has witnessed a great upheaval in Roman Catholicism, and it has largely been an assertion of greater independence by the national divisions of the church which, in any case, had been growing apart for a considerable time. It seems that now Roman Catholicism is being rather violently shaken into a recognition of the national realities that Eastern Orthodoxy and Protestantism emerged to serve. When one looks at the map one sees Europe still religiously divided: Eastern Orthodoxy in the countries of the east, Roman Catholicism in those of the southwest, Protestantism in those of the northwest. With the recognition by all of them of the national independence of the peoples, and the need for a religious expression to correspond with it, this division looks more anachronistic every day.

Islam

Islam is a religion that has experienced considerable sectarian division, there being now more than seventy sects all told.[14] Muhammad died without appointing a successor, and sectarian strife arose at once over how the appointment should be made. Muhammad's role had included that of political leader, and the question of succession at once turned into a political one, the contenders being the interested power factions. That is understandable in a situation where the original leader was attempting to bridge former divisions and had himself been driven to a religious legitimation to transcend them. The Shi'a Muslims were those who eventually held to the legitimacy of a divinely chosen Imam (or spiritual leader), but they divided amongst themselves on his divine nature and succession. Numerically, these are much the smaller of the two main divisions of Islam and are chiefly found today in Iran. The other division, the Sunni or orthodox Muslims, are more inclined to accept rather than question the tradition that did actually unfold. Most of Islam's former European territories have now been given up, although Albania remains a Muslim country. Muslim territory now is in two bands: a broad continuous one reaching from the Atlantic coast of northern Africa into Pakistan and the heart of Asia, and a narrow one reaching from the Philippines and Indonesia into Malaya and Bengal. Islam's modern missionary expansion has been by teaching instead of conquest, and by this means it has been especially successful in winning converts amongst the Negroes of trans-Saharan Africa and the United States.

Hinduism

I have called Hinduism a founded religion because it has identifiable literary sources.[15] Yet these have been accumulating for over four thousand years, and in six major instalments: the Vedas; the Brahmanas; the Upanishads; the Laws of Manu; the Bhagavad Gita; and the two epics, the Mahabharata and Ramayana. It is a tradition with a gift for eclecticism, capable of absorbing much from the outside without being compromised. The result is a religion that is indistinguishable from the way of life, and especially from the ordering of relationships by the caste system. It seems to be organic in Indian society and one could not imagine it being exported—certainly there is no interest in proselytizing. It has temples in profusion across the land. These are the habitations of gods and the Brahmins wait on them there. More than most religions, Hinduism has its sophisticated and popular levels, the latter being largely superstition. This superstition, the unyielding caste system with its exclusion of millions as untouchables, the heavy weight of tradition, and the possibility of temple worship degenerating into idolatry—these are some of the features causing a great disaffection amongst educated and progressive Hindus. They tend to reject the religion altogether or propose extremely radical reform. Gandhi's championship of the untouchables is a case of the latter.

Buddhism

The map shows Hinduism still confined to the region of its origin. But Buddhism has virtually disappeared from India, the land of its birth, only to become instead the religion of millions of people elsewhere.[16] Perhaps this is not so very difficult to understand. If I have represented the birth of Buddhism correctly, it was indeeed a radical protest against Hinduism and, moreover, against an aspect of the caste structure with which Hinduism was integral. Although it enjoyed an Indian heyday, Buddhism could scarcely have been permanently accommodated in India without that structure yielding in a way that is not likely even yet. On the other hand, societies lacking that caste system could give a ready welcome to Buddhism; especially since, as an ethical system, it could be assimilated to existing belief systems. (Christianity supplies a certain parallel, in that it turned away from the land of its origin, where it had opposed the traditional faith.) It can be deceptive to speak of "Buddhism" in general for it comprises two irreconcilable traditions. We know little of the circumstances in which the rift developed, but it appears that a few hundred years after Buddha, and in India itself, the interpretations now known as Hinayana (or the little vehicle) and Mahayana (or the great vehicle) arose.

These terms are applied from the Mahayana standpoint, for they express the judgment that Hinayana is too narrow and difficult for the mass of mankind to follow, while Mahayana is the broad and practical way. Whether this is true or not, it is a fact that three-quarters of living Buddhists follow the Mahayana way. At the present day, Hinayana is mainly found in Ceylon, Burma and Thailand, and Mahayana in China, Japan, Tibet, Mongolia, Korea and Nepal. Because of this geographical distribution, Hinayana is sometimes known as southern Buddhism and Mahayana as northern. Hinayana does seem to adhere more closely to Buddha's original formulation and the earliest teaching, and for this reason it is sometimes also called Theravada Buddhism—which means "the teaching of the elders." Mahayana introduces a Supreme Reality and makes the way of salvation not one's own pursuit of the Eightfold Path, but faith in the Buddha and Bodhisattvas. The Bodhisattvas are the compassionate ones who abstain from nirvana to assist in delivering men from error. Mahayana itself divides into many sects, three of the better known being the Zen or Meditation Sect, the Pure Land Sect and the Esoteric Sect. Zen is a way of seeking Enlightenment in this present life by a sudden realization, during meditation, of one's true nature. Pure Land, in contrast, finds the present life too defeating, and its adherents seek by faith in Amita Buddha to attain to a better world—the Pure Land—whence the passage to nirvana is much more feasible. The Esoteric Sect, which is the national religion of Tibet and Mongolia, and sometimes called Lamaism, seeks to win esoteric knowledge from the Bodhisattvas by elaborate rituals.

Jainism and Sikhism

Jainism originated contemporaneously with Buddhism and was, like it, an attempt to surpass Hinduism.[17] In its original purity it was an atheistic system which stressed asceticism and pacifism (it is, incidentally, renowned for its exceptionally beautiful temples). There are now one and a half million Indians who adhere to this religion. Yet it has always been more influential than its numbers would imply, and this is largely because most of its followers are wealthy and influential merchants. Sikhism is a quite recent outgrowth from Hinduism, making its appearance in the Punjab early in the sixteenth century.[18] It is an attempt to synthesize the religious traditions of the Indian subcontinent, especially, of course, Hinduism and Islam. There are at present about six million Sikhs, most of them farmers in the Punjab.

Chinese Religion

It is a feature of Chinese religion that it is very much a potpourri.[19] Different traditions can mingle in practice without people being conscious of the blend. Taoism was founded in China, or so tradition says, by Lao-Tze, an official of the government. He taught that virtue consists in conformity to a divine principle of order in the universe, the Tao. But it is rarely found in its original purity, having become overlaid with polytheism and magic. As we have just noted, Buddhism is also accepted in China, and has been since the first century A.D. However, it is really Confucianism that the outsider takes for the national religion of China.

Yet it must be stated that there is some difficulty in this way of looking at the situation. Confucianism was a systematization of some of the ethical ideas in China's classical tradition, and there is also a religious side to this classical tradition. If anything is to be considered the core of the Chinese religious amalgam, it should be this, a development that had already come to full flower in the thousand years before Christ. The heart of it was the worship of Heaven and its pantheon of subordinate deities, and the worship of ancestors. Rather like the Hinduism of India, the religious amalgam of China, reinforced with the ethic of Confucianism, has been overwhelmingly a conservative force. One is made to wonder whether this is why the progressively minded citizens of that country resort to revolution. China has witnessed three revolutions since the turn of the century, in 1912, 1927 and 1949. The last, the communist revolution, has evinced a particularly vehement opposition to the country's own religious and ethical traditions. In the purges of the communist regime it would appear that the number slaughtered must be counted in millions. Exponents of the higher ethical and philosophical Confucianism have figured prominently among the victims.

Shintoism

Shintoism rests on eighth-century written recordings of Japan's most ancient tradition.[20] As Shintoism supplied part of the motivation for Japanese expansionist ambitions in the Second World War, there was considerable discouragement of it afterwards. Yet, though modified, it has continued to thrive and still gives birth to new sects. It is essentially a religion of the Japanese national identity and is, for that reason, even less exportable than Hinduism. The Japanese may observe it simultaneously with Buddhism. It has three main divisions: Shrine Shinto (which includes State Shinto as a subdivision), Sect Shinto and the private Family and Neighbourhood Cults of Shinto. State Shinto is a means of inculcating patriotism, while Shrine Shinto in general is concerned with the common life. There are, for instance, doctrines concerning the special miraculous creation of the Japanese islands and the descent of the Japanese Emperor from the Sun Goddess. The government has given recognition to thirteen major sects in Sect Shinto. These represent a more congregational type of religion in which specific experiences are sought; for example, purification, ecstasy, healing. In the neighbourhood and family cults veneration is given to the neighbourhood and family patron gods and to the family ancestors.

Other Evidence of Union and Division by Religion

The map approach to the distribution of religions that we have just taken starts with the religion and asks in what countries it is found as the dominant faith. A more refined approach is to start with the country and ask what religions are found there. Unfortunately, it is not possible to pursue that line of comparative inquiry very far. For statistics on religious affiliation are notoriously uneven, of differing reliability and, in any case, unable to show strength of religious conviction. Yet the available figures can be put to considerable use. In *Principles of Political Geography* by Weigert and others, a table is given of majority and minority religions in eighty-three independent or semi-dependent countries.[21] This table is reproduced in Figure 5. The data for the table were taken mainly from the *Statesman's Yearbook* of 1953 and 1954, the sources for which, as the authors point out, are of varying accuracy and different date.[22] The main thing revealed by this table is that a majority of countries are religiously uniform—or are so for practical purposes. In fifty of them ninety per cent or more of the population belong to the same religion. This lends quantitative support to the idea that communities can be constituted as such by the like-mindedness of shared faith and that, *pari passu,* religious differences can be a simple consequence of independence of community life. The table also helps us to see that in certain countries the major religion is one that is almost unknown elsewhere. If we add to these the

NO.	COUNTRY	RELIGION OF MAJORITY	STRONG OR SIGNIFICANT RELIGIOUS MINORITIES	REMARKS
1.	Afghanistan	Sunnitic Moslems	None	
2.	Albania	Sunnitic Moslems, 68%	Greek Orthodox—21%; Roman Catholics—9%	No figures available
3.	Argentina	Predominantly Roman Catholic		
4.	Austria	Roman Catholic—90%		
5.	Australia	Protestants—82%	Among Protestants: Anglicans—36% Roman Catholics—18%	
6.	Belgium	Predominantly Roman Catholic		No figures available
7.	Bolivia	Roman Catholic		State religion
8.	Brazil	Roman Catholic—95%		
9.	Bulgaria	Orthodox—85%	Moslem—12%	Estimate of 1950, probably obsolete
10.	Burma	Buddhist—84%	Animists—5%; Moslem—4%; Hindu—4%; Christians—2%	No figures available
11.	Cambodia	Predominantly Buddhist		
12.	Canada	Protestants—54%	Roman Catholics—42%; among Protestants: United Church—19%, Anglicans—16%	
13.	Ceylon	Buddhists—64%	Hindu—20%; Moslem—6%	No reliable estimate possible
14.	Chile	Roman Catholics—95%		State religion
15.	China			State religion
16.	Colombia	Roman Catholic		No figures available
17.	Costa Rica	Roman Catholic		Estimate of 1947, probably obsolete
18.	Cuba	Predominantly Roman Catholic		
19.	Czechoslovakia	Roman Catholics—77%		State religion
20.	Denmark	Lutheran—99%		
21.	Dominican Republic	Roman Catholic		No official figures
22.	Ecuador	Predominantly Roman Catholic		
23.	Egypt	Sunnitic Moslem—91%	Christians, mainly Copts—6%	

Figure 5. Majority and Minority Religions in Independent or Semi-dependent Countries. Reproduced with permission from Hans W. Weigert and others, *Principles of Political Geography,* Appleton-Century-Crofts, New York, 1957, pp. 412-15.

Figure 5 (continued)

NO.	COUNTRY	RELIGION OF MAJORITY	STRONG OR SIGNIFICANT RELIGIOUS MINORITIES	REMARKS
24.	El Salvador	Almost exclusively Roman Catholic		No official figures
25.	England and Wales	Church of England—50-65%	Other Protestant denominations more than 20%	No estimate possible
26.	Ethiopia	Coptic Church	Moslems	
27.	Finland	Lutherans—96%		
28.	France	Roman Catholic—97%		
29.	Germany (West)	Protestants—51%	Roman Catholics—45%; most Protestants are Lutherans	No figures available
30.	Germany (East)	Prevailingly Lutheran		No figures available
31.	Greece	Greek Orthodox—98%		
32.	Guatemala	Predominantly Roman Catholic		
33.	Haiti	Predominantly Roman Catholic		
34.	Honduras	Predominantly Roman Catholic		
35.	Hungary	Roman Catholics—66%	Protestants—27%; mostly Reformed	1941 Census, largely obsolete
36.	Iceland	Lutherans—96%		
37.	India	Predominantly Hindu	Moslems, approximately 10%	
38.	Indonesia	Sunnitic Moslems more than 90%		
39.	Iran	Shia Moslem—93%	Sunnitic Moslem—6%	
40.	Iraq	Shia Moslem—57%	Sunnitic Moslem—36%	Estimate
41.	Ireland	Roman Catholics—95%		
42.	Israel	Jews—90%	Moslem—8%	November 1953
43.	Italy	Roman Catholics—99.51%		
44.	Japan	(Shinto?)		No estimates possible; state-Shinto abolished, private Shinto widespread
45.	Jordan	Predominantly Sunnitic Islam		No estimate of post-war conditions possible
46.	Korea	(Buddhism)		No figures available
47.	Laos	Buddhists		

Figure 5 (continued)

NO.	COUNTRY	RELIGION OF MAJORITY	STRONG OR SIGNIFICANT RELIGIOUS MINORITIES	REMARKS
48.	Lebanon	Christians—54%	Christians mostly Maronites; Moslem—39% mostly Sunnitic; Druzes—7%	
49.	Liberia			No reliable information
50.	Libya	Predominantly Sunnitic Moslem	Senussi sect of Islam	No figures available
51.	Mexico	Predominantly Roman Catholic		
52.	Morocco	Sunnitic Moslem—93%		Recognize the Sultan as head
53.	Netherlands	Protestants—45%	Majority of Protestants Reformed—32% Roman Catholics—36%; no church affiliation —14%	
54.	New Zealand	Protestants—88%	Among Protestants: Anglicans—40%, Presbyterians—23%; Roman Catholics—12%	
55.	North Ireland	Protestants—66%	Among Protestants: Presbyterians—30%; Anglicans—26%; Roman Catholics—34%	
56.	Norway	Lutherans—96%		
57.	Oman	Moslem	Predominantly Qadarites	
58.	Pakistan	Sunnitic Moslem—86%	Hindu—13%	
59.	Panama	Roman Catholics—93%		
60.	Paraguay	Predominantly Roman Catholics		No figures available
61.	Peru	Predominantly Roman Catholics		No figures available
62.	Philippine Islands	Roman Catholics—83%	Filipino Church—10%; Moslem—4%	
63.	Poland	Predominantly Roman Catholic		
64.	Portugal	Roman Catholics		
65.	Rumania	Orthodox, approx. 80%	Roman Catholics—8%	Figures unreliable
66.	Saudi Arabia	Wahhabitic Moslem		
67.	Scotland	Church of Scotland (Presbyterian)—60%	Roman Catholics—12%	No official figures available
68.	Spain	Roman Catholics		
69.	Sudan	Sunnitic Moslem in the majority	Pagans	
70.	Sweden	Lutherans—99%		

Figure 5 (continued)

NO.	COUNTRY	RELIGION OF MAJORITY	STRONG OR SIGNIFICANT RELIGIOUS MINORITIES	REMARKS
71.	Switzerland	Protestants, mainly Reformed—58%	Roman Catholics—40%	
72.	Syria	Sunnitic Moslem—71%	Other Moslem denominations—12%; Alawites—10%; Druzes—3%	
73.	Thailand	Buddhists—96%		
74.	Tibet	Lamaistic Buddhists		
75.	Tunisia	Sunnitic Moslem—90%		
76.	Turkey	Sunnitic Moslem—98%		
77.	U.S.S.R.			No estimate possible
78.	Union of South Africa	(whites): Dutch Reformed Church—50% (non-whites): Pagans, more than 60%	Anglicans—15%; other Protestant denominations—31% African Christian churches—14%; Anglicans—8%; Dutch Reformed—5%	
79.	United States	Many different Protestant denominations—60%	Roman Catholics—35%	Estimate
80.	Uruguay	Predominantly Roman Catholic		Last census of religion more than 50 years old
81.	Venezuela	Roman Catholic	Sunnitic Moslem	No figures available
82.	Yemen	Majority of Zaiditic Moslem		No figures available
83.	Yugoslavia	Serb Orthodox—50%	Roman Catholics—37%; Moslem—12%	

countries that share doctrine with one another but have completely separate organization, the number of countries with a religion that is virtually their own increases. This separateness of organization occurs, for instance, with the Lutherans of Germany, Sweden, Norway, Denmark, Finland, and Iceland, and with the Buddhists of Ceylon, Burma, Thailand, Laos, and Cambodia.

In a second table, the same book summarizes information from the first table to show the countries having some religious trait in common. This table is reproduced in Figure 6. From it we can read the frequency with which the same faith is found to recur as the uniform faith of the population of a country. In this respect Roman Catholicism is first by far, there being thirty Roman Catholic countries. The Sunnite Islamic states come next, but with the much smaller number of eleven.

Finally, before concluding this commentary on the distribution and relative strengths of the religions of the world, it will be worth our while to take note of some recently published estimates of their world-wide membership. The reader is, of course, cautioned that some of these estimates are necessarily cruder than others, and that "membership" can mean different things. In China and Japan, for instance, it is particularly difficult even to assign religion, since Buddhism can be followed simultaneously with other religious practices. The *Britannica Book of the Year 1971* gives the following world totals, acknowledging for its source the 1968 United Nations survey.[23]

Religion	*Estimated World Membership*
Total Christian	924,274,000
Roman Catholic	580,470,000
Eastern Orthodox	125,684,000
Protestant	218,120,000
Jewish	13,537,000
Muslim	493,012,000
Zoroastrian	138,000
Shinto	69,662,000
Taoist	54,324,000
Confucian	371,587,000
Buddhist	176,920,000
Hindu	436,745,000
Total	2,540,199,000
Population	3,369,420,000

What I have been aiming to lead up to in the second part of this chapter is some overview, however sketchy, of the way the whole globe has been supplied with stable patterns of order by the religions accepted in its different parts. By the continuity between this chapter and the one preceding, I have also wanted to make the reader aware that such stability is achieved only as the result of a process of growth that can appear anything but

RELIGIOUS CHARACTER	NUMBER	COUNTRIES
Roman-Catholic countries		
(a) generally more than 90% Roman Catholics	27	Argentina, Austria, Belgium, Bolivia, Brazil, Chile, Colombia, Costa Rica, Cuba, Dominican Republic, El Salvador, Ecuador, France, Guatemala, Haiti, Honduras, Ireland, Italy, Mexico, Panama, Paraguay, Peru, Philippines, Portugal, Spain, Uruguay and Venezuela
(b) Roman-Catholic majority, dominated by Communists	3	Czechoslovakia, Hungary, Poland
Anglican churches in the majority	3	Australia, England and Wales, North Ireland
Orthodox churches in the majority, recognizing the primate of Moscow	3	Bulgaria, Rumania, U.S.S.R.
Other Christian churches		
(a) dogmatically separate churches	4	Canada (United Church), Ethiopia (Coptic), Lebanon (Maronites), and Scotland (Presbyterian)
(b) organizationally separate national churches		
(1) Lutheran	6	Denmark, Finland, Germany, Iceland, Norway, Sweden
(2) Reformed	3	Netherlands, Switzerland, Union of South Africa
(3) Orthodox	2	Greece, Yugoslavia (Serb-Orthodox)
(c) in many churches, none having a majority	2	New Zealand, United States
Sunnitic Islamic countries	11	Afghanistan, Albania, Egypt, Indonesia, Iraq, Jordan, Pakistan, Sudan, Syria, Tunisia, and Turkey
Islamic countries, having non-Sunnitic majorities or ruling groups	6	Iran (Shiites), Libya (Senussi), Morocco (Sultan head of Moslem community), Oman (Qadarites), Saudi Arabia (Wahhabis), Yemen (Zaidites)
Buddhist countries (no common organization)	6	Burma, Cambodia, Ceylon, Laos, Thailand, Tibet (northern Lamaistic branch)
Other countries	7	China, India (Hindu), Israel (Jewish), Japan, Korea, Liberia, Viet-Nam

Figure 6. Countries Having Religious Traits in Common. Reproduced with permission from Hans W. Weigert and others, *Principles of Political Geography,* Appleton-Century-Crofts, New York, 1957, p. 418.

stable at first, when the acceptability of the religion is in question. We should always bear in mind, then, that a particular difference between two religions might well be explained by their different stage of maturation. There should also be sufficient in this chapter to indicate that a serviceable stability in religious organization is by no means the same as its being snowed under by tradition and frozen. While it is indispensable that definite organization be achieved through institutionalization, a community's widening experience can make the existing institution obsolete at any time. It can then get in the way and be a hindrance rather than a help, if it cannot change. At least three states of organization have to be recognized, then, and what we see when we look at any religious situation will largely depend on the state obtaining. There is the situation where belief and practice are sufficiently institutionalized to guarantee a stable supply of re-religious needs. Then there is the situation where this state is not yet realized but efforts toward it are under way. But there is also the situation where previously endorsed arrangements are beginning to have social acceptance withdrawn from them because they are no longer adaptive. This atrophy is really a kind of "de-institutionalization." Some are inclined to speak of it as "over-institutionalization," but that seems a rather meaningless notion and, in any case, does not accurately describe the state of affairs.

Notes, Chapter 6

1. Richard H. Niebuhr, *The Social Sources of Denominationalism.*
2. Ernst Troeltsch, *The Social Teaching of the Christian Churches*, translated by Olive Wyon, London: George Allen & Unwin, 1931.
3. Leopold von Wiese, *Systematic Sociology*, adapted and amplified by Howard Becker, New York: John Wiley & Sons, 1932; Howard Becker, *Through Values to Social Interpretation*, Durham, N.C., Duke University Press, 1950, pp. 114-18.
4. J. Milton Yinger, *The Scientific Study of Religion*, London: Macmillan, 1970, pp. 256-59.
5. Bryan Wilson, *Religious Sects, A Sociological Study*, New York: McGraw-Hill, 1970.
6. For details see Stewart Crysdale, *The Changing Church in Canada, Beliefs and Social Attitudes of United Church People*, Toronto: United Church of Canada, 1965, especially pp. 4-6; Harold Fallding, "Canada," in Hans Mol, editor, *Western Religion, A Country by Country Sociological Inquiry*, The Hague: Mouton, 1972, pp. 101-115.
7. Rajaiah D. Paul, *The First Decade, An Account of the Church of South India*, Madras: The Christian Literature Society, 1958, p. 228. For further details see also Bengt Sundkler, *Church of South India: The Movement Towards Union 1900-1947*, revised edition, London: Lutterworth Press, 1965.
8. Howard Becker, *op. cit.*, pp. 105-19.
9. Harold Fallding, "Secularization and the Sacred and Profane," p. 363.
10. H. H. Gerth and C. Wright Mills, editors, *From Max Weber: Essays in Sociology*, London: Routledge and Kegan Paul, 1948, pp. 295-301.
11. Reprinted from *The New English Bible*, copyright 1961 and 1970 by Oxford and Cambridge University Presses, Phil. 1:21-24.

12. For details on the development of Judaism see Chapter 5, footnote 6.
13. For details on the development of Christianity see Chapter 5, footnote 8.
14. For details on the development of Islam see Chapter 5, footnote 15.
15. For details on the development of Hinduism see Sir Charles Eliot, *Hinduism and Buddhism,* London: Edward Arnold, 1921; A. C. Bouquet, *Hinduism,* London: Hutchinson, 1966; Kenneth W. Morgan, editor, *The Religion of the Hindus,* New York: Ronald Press, 1953.
16. For details on the development of Buddhism see Chapter 5, footnote 5.
17. For details on the development of Jainism see Jagnanderlal Jaini, *Outlines of Jainism,* Cambridge University Press, 1940.
18. For details on the development of Sikhism see Khushwant Singh, *A History of the Sikhs,* Vol. I, 1469-1839, London: Allen & Unwin, 1963; J. C. Archer, *The Sikhs,* Princeton, N.J.: Princeton University Press, 1946.
19. For details on the development of Chinese religion see C. K. Yang, *Religion in Chinese Society, A Study of Contemporary Social Functions of Religion and Some of Their Historical Factors,* Berkeley & Los Angeles: University of California Press, 1961.
20. For details on the development of Shintoism see M. Anesaki, *The History of Japanese Religion,* London: Kegan Paul, Trench & Trubner, Ltd., 1931; Joseph M. Kitagawa, *Religion in Japanese History,* New York: Columbia University Press, 1966.
21. Hans W. Weigert, et al., *Principles of Political Geography,* New York: Appleton-Century-Crofts, 1957.
22. *The Statesman's Year-Book 1953, Statistical and Historical Annual of the States of the World for the Year 1953,* edited by S. H. Steinberg, London: Macmillan and Co., 1953; *The Stateman's Yearbook 1954, Statistical and Historical Annual of the States of the World for the Year 1954,* edited by S. H. Steinberg, London: Macmillan and Co., 1954.
23. *Britannica Book of the Year 1971,* Chicago: Encyclopaedia Britannica, Inc., William Benton Publisher, 1971.

Chapter 7

The Difference Due to the Ways of Seeking Assurance

I promised that in this chapter we would give attention to those differences in religions that are traceable to their developing in isolation. Whether the religions that have done this had some ultimate common source we cannot say, but what is significant is that they have been apart from one another throughout their growth. As I said before, it is not very surprising that differences have resulted from this isolation. Yet some would think this the biggest puzzle of all about religion. While I admit it presents a very tantalizing practical situation when the religions eventually make contact, I do not agree that it presents us with an overwhelming problem of intellectual explanation—simply because of the geographic separation involved. I suspect that what inflates it as an intellectual problem for some people is a presupposition that there can be only one religious truth for all time—so how can they be different? But it must be plain by now that I, for one, would not recommend making that presupposition. Having said all this, however, I acknowledge that we do have a problem here, even though I object to its being magnified. So I should say how I think the fact of "original" religious difference is to be accounted for.

Religious Evolution through the Transformation of Means and End

I have to insist at once on the necessity of having an evolutionary understanding of religion for solving this problem. One does have to be prepared to say that some religions are more developed than others. When I say this I do not mean that the more developed must evolve from the less along a line that is always the same. I simply mean it is possible to name criteria by which comparisons can be made and one religion be called more developed than another. I think, fundamentally, there are two such properties in regard to which religions vary, and in Figure 7 they are shown as the two axes of a graph. One has to do with the quality of the means taken in pursuit of the religious end; one has to do with the quality of the end. In regard to the means taken, religious action develops from being a sporadic, random and occasional pursuit to being a systematic and sustained pursuit. There is what Weber would call an increase in rationality.[1] Whereas at first religious action is taken in response to particular situations and necessities, it comes in time to be taken in response to the need for whole-life orientation and organization, both of the individual and the collectivity. By this enlargement of scope men strive to enhance their assurance. They seek to anchor not single needs only but their whole lives and society, present and future, in the totality. In regard to the end of religion, religion develops from conceptualizing the ideal society as one in which all natural needs are fulfilled to one where spiritual satisfaction is maximized. It is hard to draw this distinction without stumbling over words, for spiritual satisfaction is a natural need anyway. Yet I think there is a real distinction to be made. At both—or rather all—levels, I would want to maintain, the ideal society is held in view, but the ideal is differently understood. We have already encountered something of the difference I mean in Chapter 4, when we discussed the way the ideal society is envisaged in Judaism, Christianity, Buddhism and Islam.

In the most rudimentary societies the supply of man's practical necessities is the thing above all which society has to be geared to provide, so the ideal society is taken as the one where cooperation for that is achieved. The assurance then sought in religion is an assurance of providence: "The Lord is my shepherd, I shall not want." But a stage comes where society can be valued more for the exhilaration of the game than for the gain from winning it, if I may put it that way. The highest pleasure, some men begin vaguely to discern, is the pleasure of interaction itself, the delight in one another, the profound meaningfulness of mutual personal recognition, the ecstasy of being taken out of oneself in the *esprit de corps*. (As the reader will remember from Chapter 1, I have called this type of satisfaction "spiritual.") This, precisely, is what life is for, they begin to suppose, and the ideal society is the one which, while it achieves practical necessities, subordinates them so that they serve this other end. This brings in a distinctly different type of religion in which the assurance men seek is an engagement with that ideal: "God is love; and he that dwelleth in love dwelleth in God, and God in him." I would call this "salvation religion," to give it the distinguishing name it demands. Previously I depicted early Judaism, Christianity, Buddhism and Islam all as salvation religions, and this is the reason.

It is interesting that three of these religions depict the divinity in intensely personalistic terms, while original Buddhism makes no reference to a divinity. Although it is sometimes called atheistic, it might be more accurate to say it is agnostic in regard to this question. At any rate, I have already suggested why there is no reference to a divinity. Its concern was the negative one of dissolving the preceding allegiance to Brahman: it did not focus any alternative. But it is interesting to explore why salvation religions *can* focus the divinity in such intensely personalistic terms as Judaism, Christianity and Islam employ. (I might say, incidentally, that I have no sympathy with those who think this is simply a survival of anthropomorphic primitivism, and that it would have been better to conceive of their divinities impersonally. It seems there is very good reason for it being the way it is.) Is it not because personality is the product—and the highest product—of the kind of interpersonal exchange that this religion exalts as the highest good? The god that is the ideal possibility in the communion of man with man, could scarcely be less personal than the men communing. This is why the god of these religions addresses men and communicates to them his personal will for them. Of course, it is not inconsistent to represent such a divinity impersonally as well, in terms of qualities. Thus in the New Testament, for example, although the divinity is personal he is also described as light and love. In any case, he is not there represented as *a* person but *personal* in that "he" —we must in this context put the word in inverted commas— is not one person but an association of three. In Chapter 5 I suggested that this characterization was developed to convey a new awareness that divinity is the ideal society of men.

It would appear that the two different criteria of higher development—more systematic and sustained pursuit and a greater spirituality in the end pursued—could increase independently of one another. Thus there could be a highly systematic pursuit of a religion of natural-need fulfilment and a very sporadic and fitful pursuit of a religion of spiritual satisfaction. But we may consider the most developed condition to be that in which there is advancement in both these qualities. Growth on this double dimension would be represented by the forty-five-degree slope of the graph. While these qualities can presumably increase as a continuum, it seems that there might be a fairly distinct line of transition from the condition where there is no easily recognizable spiritual aspiration and also from the condition where there is no easily recognisable systematization. The area within these two transition lines would mark a type of religion distinctly different from that outside of it. This is shown in Figure 7 as the area bounded by the dotted lines.

It is surely not very surprising that we have religions at a variety of positions on this graph. The difference between them is to be explained by the different awareness of life-possibilities men have. To say that at a particular time this awareness is increased for particular persons is the naturalistic way of de-

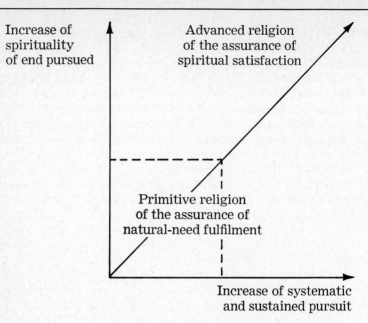

Figure 7.   The Two Major Dimensions of Religious Evolution.

scribing what the religious person may call a new revelation from God. This can simply be a direct result of a more complex life with more interaction between persons and, as a result of cultural accumulation, between persons and cultural symbols. It also demands, of course, that in the midst of this intensified interaction gifted men will let their imagination range free. Possibly there is a special stimulus to the exercise of this imagination in situations of social and cultural collapse where a pattern of life is folding because of some unprecedented challenge.

Graphing the Evolutionary Location of Religions

Although one could entertain the result only very tentatively, it may prove rewarding to try to graph the position of the religions mentioned in the preceding chapter. The following discussion gives the reasons for each location assigned: Figure 8 shows the result (see page 188). Except when attention is specifically drawn to a different period, it is to the foundation phase of the religion I shall refer.

Judaism, Christianity and Islam

Early Judaism, as summarized in the quotation from Leviticus in Chapter 4, is clearly very much taken up with natural-need fulfilment, but there is also a concern to make the presence of God secure. It therefore moves a certain distance into the sphere of advanced religion, and it illustrates the possibility of doing this while retaining a great deal of primitive content. In its written scripture, and in the observance of circumcision and the ethical and ritual law, there is a marked systematization. Christianity is a spiritual religion, being focally concerned with the divine and human fellowship made available by the New Creation. Scriptures and elaborate ritual, ethic and doctrine make all three of its major divisions markedly systematic. Protestantism is the most systematic of the three on account of its thoroughgoing rational life-ethic. Islam is a spiritual religion, being taken up with submission to and guidance from Allah, the practice of charity, the welding of brotherhood, the enjoyment of heavenly reward. It remains, at the same time, a religion of natural-need fulfilment to a certain extent. For, insofar as the spiritual head is the ruler of a territory, he makes natural satisfactions secure through religion. Islam is extremely systematized: in the Koran, Shari'a and Five Pillars there is direction for every typical situation, while whatever is idiosyncratic to the person is covered by his guidance and submission.

Hinduism, Buddhism, Jainism and Sikhism

Hinduism has been different things at different stages of its long, growing tradition. But a period is discernible over which the Brahmin priests turned away from sacrifice to meditation and the quest for mystical union. This was when the teaching of the Vedas and Brahmanas gave way to the Upanishads, from about 700 B.C. to 300 B.C. To put it schematically, this was Hinduism's discovery of God. We witness the appearance of the notions of Brahman—the objective All—and of Atman—the inner self— and of their identity with one another. I think we can say that this marks a transition within the Hindu tradition from the primitive religion of natural need to the advanced religion of spiritual satisfaction. For the priestly sacrifices of the earlier religion were essentially for assuring the supply of particular needs. The religion of that earlier time was also unsystematic. In contrast, with the introduction of philosophic reflection in the Upanishads and an accompanying asceticism, Hinduism launched on a systematization that grew ever more intense. However, as I have indicated, a popular debased Hinduism (if it is that at all) continues alongside this. That strand of Hinduism is essentially an unsystematic religion of natural need, in which the worshipper may appeal to one of the popular major deities like Shiva or Vishnu, or indeed to any of the Hindu gods which, according to the proverb, number 330 million.

Buddhism, Jainism and Sikhism have, of course, sprung from

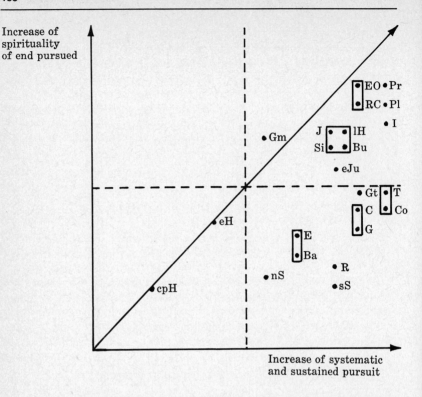

Figure 8.   Tentative Graph of the Rough Evolutionary Location of Selected Religious Positions.

Key.		
	Ba:	Babylonian
	Bu:	Buddhism
	C:	Classical Chinese
	Co:	Confucianism
	E:	Egyptian
	EO:	Eastern Orthodox Christian
	G:	Greek
	Gm:	Greek mystery religions
	Gt:	Greek tragic poets
	cpH:	Contemporary popular Hinduism
	eH:	Early Hinduism (before Upanishads)
	lH:	Later Hinduism
	I:	Islam
	J:	Jainism
	eJu:	Early Judaism
	Pr:	Protestant Christian
	Pl:	Plato
	R:	Roman
	RC:	Roman Catholic Christian
	nS:	non-Shrine Shinto
	sS:	Shrine Shinto
	Si:	Sikhism
	T:	Taoism

Note. Locations not nicely distinguishable from one another are grouped in boxes.

Hinduism after its transformation into a religion of spiritual satisfaction, and they are themselves all highly systematic religions of that kind. Like Buddhism, Jainism is what I would call a negative expression of it, in that it is more taken up with removing the obstacles to achieving the ideal than with conceiving it positively. Hence it prescribes a way to throw off Karma-matter by a discipline of detachment from the world. Sikhism, in contrast, is positive and fully taken up with the nature of God and with being absorbed into him.

Far Eastern Religions

It is the distinctive contribution to human culture of the religions of the Far East that they have brought the religion of natural-need fulfilment to a peak of development. Because of this they can dazzle the person whose culture has accustomed him to a religion of spiritual satisfaction: he is prevented from seeing their character clearly because of their peculiar lustre. As they are so highly cultivated and exquisite he is apt to approach expecting a religion of spiritual satisfaction. Since what he finds is *not* that, yet something quite entrancing anyway, he may be left delighted and disconcerted at the same time. I believe this is why Northrop says there is a particular readjustment the Westerner must make when he approaches these religions:[2]

> The Orientals are an exceedingly concrete, practical and realistic people; and their religion is best thought of by Westerners as something nearer to what the West regards as aesthetics than it is to what the West has regarded as religion . . . In short, the Oriental uses the purely aesthetic to constitute the nature of the divine.[3]

The idea that the aesthetic is made to constitute the divine helps to fill out what I mean when I say the religion of natural-need fulfilment is brought to a peak of development. The natural need for which the religion offers fulfilment is the need for a personal aesthetic repose, for poise in the world. This need may be satisfied, it says, through the realization that the mandate of Heaven completes all the activity transpiring on earth: the completeness is beautiful. The mandate of Heaven is simply the good luck or misfortune men experience, when those are understood as the just desert of their deeds, even though the justice of it may be inscrutable. It balances out what was lacking in the immediate outcome of any action. Once this complementarity of Heaven to Earth is seen, an aesthetic harmony appears. We need not, then, be distracted from the fact that it is essentially a religion of nature by the fact that Heaven looms so large. Heaven is not a figure here for that ideal society where human interaction is its own delight, but that where cooperation is consummated in practical fruitfulness. Any activities lacking this cooperativeness must eventually bring their own judgment, those having it their own reward. Heaven is scarcely above nature but the law immanent in it.

While all of this is already in the religion of the classical tradition, Taoism adds a philosophical rationale and elaborates a technique for the person to embed himself in the cosmic harmony, to yield himself to the current. I say yield himself because the Taoist Way is largely passive. It is very much a matter of giving up, of not trying, of aligning oneself with the prevailing force. Furthermore, even though the Taoists thought Confucius' formalism was unnatural, Confucius aimed for conformity with the same principle of order in social relationships. The *li* of Confucius, for instance, is essentially a matter of giving everyone the respect due to him, his *jen* a matter of creating harmony by actively seeking everyone's good. Both Taoism and Confucianism are, of course, very highly systematized, the one supplying a philosophy and mystical discipline for the whole of life, the other a code of conduct. Shinto also, in the same way as the Chinese religion just discussed, is a religion of natural-need fulfilment, but I would judge that it is not nearly so highly systematized. In the neighbourhood and family cults and the sects, much of the religious activity is unsystematic. It is in Shrine Shinto that it moves towards systematization, expressing as it does there a concern with order in the community and state.

Egyptian Religion

Having come thus far with our graph, the exercise might be made more complete if we also locate on it four of the better-known ancient religions: the Egyptian, Mesopotamian, Greek and Roman. Consideration of these additional cases should further sharpen our appreciation of the two transformations involved in religious evolution. Egyptian religion, over the stretch of time that its development can be followed, shows an increasing systematization. It corresponds, in fact, with the increasing centralization of the kingdom. First the separate village groupings, the nomes, are consolidated into larger units, these into the two kingdoms, and these eventually into one under the pharaohs, who were divine priest-kings. The gods of the united nomes might fuse and take a hyphenated name, as was the case with Amon-Re, or develop some kind of association. The short-lived attempt by Akhenaton to impose monotheism is the extreme limit of this systematizing process.

Yet Egyptian religion remains to the end a religion of natural-need fulfilment. There was a great profusion of deities, many of whom, being half animal and half man, expressed a community of man and nature. To enlist in their cooperation the principle of life in nature was the Egyptians' whole religious quest. They saw this principle embodied in the Nile, but even more ultimately in the sun. Osiris was the water of the Nile, Horus the Sun; Aton was still the Sun. The Sun was the source of the satisfaction of all needs, and Pharaoh, being able to protect the social order that secured them, was therefore like the Sun and deserved to be called the son of the Sun. Even the Egyptians' preoccupation with the dead is to be understood as part of their preoccupation with natural needs. There does not seem to have been anything very spiritual or mystical about it. For the afterlife is nothing but a continuation of this life, and elaborate arrangements had therefore to be made to see that the dead were preserved bodily and supplied with provisions. Eternal life was the reward of the virtuous who had cooperated in this life to help secure the community's needs: it was simply an endless supply of these same things.

Mesopotamian Religion

In a different way Mesopotamian religion adorns the same theme. The divinities were the sky, air and earth, moon, sun, water and fertility. It was Ishtar, the goddess of fertility, who was the one who came closest to being universally worshipped. Hence it is the natural sources of need-supply that were exalted. With the rise to power of the city of Babylon, however, Marduk, the god of that city, comes into prominence. Whether from him, Ishtar or other deities, the provision of natural needs was sought through the priests' sacrifices, incantations, ritual prayers, exorcisms and divinations. The epic of Gilgamesh explores the possibility of immortality. Contrary to the Egyptian belief, the conclusion is that this is not given to man. He should therefore enjoy this life—eat, drink and be merry. The development of Marduk demonstrates a growth in systematization, this, once again, corresponding with a growth in political centralization. Two existing gods are made his father and son, and Enlil of Nippur's lordship of the heavens is transferred to him. A number of formerly dispersed functions, in fact, are concentrated now in this one divinity. He is the god of wisdom and of power over destiny; it is he who struggled triumphantly against chaos and created the world and man.

Greek Religion

The patterns of development in the religion of the Greeks are highly instructive. This religion has a series of distinct plateaux of systematization. While for most of its course it is a religion of natural-need fulfilment, at two places, in the mystery religions and Platonism, it passes into the religion of spiritual satisfaction. In the religion of the tragic poets we see a peak of development of the religion of natural-need fulfilment which is as impressive as that in Far Eastern religion and which, as we shall see, in one way resembles it. There were expressions of systematization quite early. Invaders' gods assumed the functions of local divinities. The gods that came to be located on Olympus or in a city acropolis like that of Athens were assembled from many local traditions, rather like ensigns raised in a capital as pledges of loyalty to the federation. Homer then brought the gods under family supervision, making them largely accountable to Zeus who had fathered many of them. Hesiod tried to impose a rational order on the pantheon by showing in a theogony by what marriages and lines of descent the various divinities had been born. The tragic poets tried to resolve ambiguities in the myths concerning the gods' exercise of power over men. The philosophers made a critical review of the whole tradition to determine what parts of it, if any, had lasting worth.

That the Greeks' religion was originally one of natural-need fulfilment is very evident in the way the gods all had their sphere of influence. Indeed, they were likely to have not one but several, since there was a great tendency to load a willing horse with more work. It was their responsibility to see that any human needs within their spheres of control were well supplied. Thus Zeus, in the course of his career, was the sky-father and giver of rain, god of fertility, a guardian of certain city states, the source of genius, and parent of a vast and distinguished progeny. Apollo had interests in grazing and agriculture, youth, athletics, the arts, healing, oracular revelation, and was god of the sun. Artemis was the protectress of children, men and maidens, wild animals and vegetation, and presided at childbirth and the hunt.

But later, more reflective generations did not find it sufficient simply to lean on the gods. They wondered about the calamities that could overtake men while in the hands of these gods. Was this willed by the gods or by Fate before which even the gods were helpless? If willed by the gods, was it out of caprice or justice? The tragedians Aeschylus and Sophocles decide it is justice that moves Zeus and that he is above Fate, so that in the long run men only have their deserts. This is where the similarity with Far Eastern religion comes in. There is a balance in the cosmos, they say—a mandate of heaven indeed—that makes all things right. Thus, here again, the quest for natural-need fulfilment reaches a peak in repose in the aesthetic order. But the devotees of the mystery religions wanted something more: here the Greek adventure turns to the quest for spiritual satisfaction. By purification, sacrament, ecstasy, in the Eleusinian, Dionysiac, Orphic and other mysteries, they sought to be joined with God in this life and attain immortality. Plato was not impressed with the means they employed, but was himself also in pursuit of the same end. The soul must seek liberation from continued rebirth, he taught, by growing toward the good; until, like God, it beholds the ideal forms in their truth, beauty and goodness.

Roman Religion

If one turns to Roman religion after the Greek it is with a sense of sudden impoverishment. It has none of the adventurous, imaginative questing of Greek religion. For most of its development it clings to natural-need fulfilment at a rudimentary level. Yet it is interesting in its method of systematization, pedestrian though this is. It seems to proceed by the simple rule of finding a new god for every newly differentiated function. Different from the Greek method of adding functions to an existing god, it adds a god to an existing function. Starting with divinity as an impersonal pervasive substance, numen, it divides it up finely and precisely till there is a divinity to bring success in every minute operation. All these divinities have been reported, for instance, for the following spheres and processes: Ceres for the growth of grain; Consus for harvesting; Ops for storage of grain; Tellus for tilling of soil; Flora for blossoming; Pomona for ripening; Faunus for the woods; Lares for the sown fields; Pales for the pasture; Terminus for the boundary stone; Fons for the springs; Volturnus for the river; Vervactor for ploughing the fallow; Redarator for second ploughing; Imporcitor for making furrows; Insitor for sowing; Obarator for ploughing under; Occator for harrowing; Sarritor for hoeing; Subruncinator for weeding; Messor for reaping; Convector for carting home; Conditor for storing in the granary and Promitor for bringing out for use. In this manner every corner of the farm and home came under divine protectors.

There was a great precision and formalism in the rituals by which the aid of such divinities was invoked—sometimes it seems indistinguishable from magic. All of it was very much in keeping with the Roman leaning toward rationality, legality, organizaation, administration and military discipline. A state religion also developed, in which priests as public officials performed rituals very punctiliously on prescribed days of the calendar. This is not unlike Shrine Shintoism in its celebration of the community and its triumphs: Jupiter who became specially interested in Rome, and the war gods Mars and Quirinus, held a prominent place in this worship. Yet this style of religion proved lifeless and the Romans were pleased to welcome Etruscan, Greek and oriental innovations, including Mithraism and other mystery religions. But the resulting profusion introduced a very unsystematic phase of religious life, and the integrity of national life seemed threatened by it. The institution of emperor worship followed this in an effort to hold the empire to its centre. It was an attempted revival of state religion, but it gave way before the influx of Christianity.

In the Introduction I spoke of the importance of keeping the differences between the religions unobscured. I hope the reason for this will now be plain. It simply is not true that they have all been aiming to accomplish the same thing—and that is quite apart from the question of how successful any one has been in accomplishing its goal. The distinction between the religion of natural-need fulfilment and that of spiritual satisfaction is really fundamental. Religions in the latter category also divide into those that propose a way of engaging a positively conceived ideal and those that stop short at a negation of obstacles to it. This is the big difference we are confronted with when we set Christianity against Buddhism, for example. On the other hand, the difference we encounter when we set Christianity against the Greek mystery religions is one of systematization to a large extent. Even with such differences acknowledged, there are still differences over and above them, due to the different ways in which it is believed the end can be attained. Yet there is some very considerable gain to our understanding once we see, for instance, that Hinduism, early Judaism, the Greek mystery religions, Plato, Christianity, Islam and Sikhism can be grouped as positive religions of spiritual satisfaction, and this group set against Buddhism and Jainism as negative religions of the same kind; and all these, in a different opposition, against a group that includes classical Chinese religion, Taoism, Confucianism, the Greek tragedians, Hinduism before the Upanishads, Shintoism, Egyptian and Babylonian religion, and the main streams in Greek and Roman religion.

The Opposition of Nature and Spirit in the Religions of Spiritual Satisfaction

That men in many times and places have sought to have the fulfilment of their natural needs underwritten by following the divinity of ideal cooperation is not very surprising. The more arresting phenomenon is the development at far fewer places of religions of spiritual satisfaction. Perhaps we should dwell a little longer on what men were electing to pursue in this and how they expected to accomplish it. I think it may be helpful for making this further exploration if we consider later Hinduism, Plato and Christianity together, notwithstanding their considerable differences. While the escape from rebirth that both Hinduism and Plato seek to make is usually presented as being repugnant to Christianity, I think Christianity has a parallel concern to make an escape and that such a concern is inseparable from the religion of spiritual satisfaction. The presence of the escape theme in Christianity is proven by its eventual rejection of everything except the resurrection and New Creation. The point is that it aspires to enter into a qualitatively different experience from that which birth into nature allows. Until one is launched beyond nature one does not live. Furthermore, there is a sense of discontinuity between this second realm and the natural one, and a life of absorption in natural things is represented as a deadly threat to its realization.

As I indicated earlier in the chapter, I am prepared to see this transfer of affections stemming from a realization that solidarity with men is intrinsically satisfying, a superior and qualitatively different satisfaction from the satisfactions to be found in the practical fruits of cooperation. I am calling them "spiritual" and "natural" satisfactions to distinguish them. However, to its immense advantage, if the former is realised the latter is assured anyway. So giving attention to spiritual satisfaction entails no neglect of natural needs. These come by giving attention to the other. This, presumably, is the force of the teaching of Jesus that if men seek first the kingdom of God and its righteousness all other things will be added to them. To realize this solidarity is to know release and throw off the natural bondage. It is "freedom" in two senses of the word. It is "freedom" because natural anxieties fall away in the exhilaration of it and insurance in it. It is also "freedom" in the moral sense intended, for instance, in discussions of "Christian freedom," where it is held that natural appetites may be enjoyed without prohibitions when this transfer of affections has delivered the person from the possibility of enslavement to them. I suggest that the acute sense of an opposition of contrary attractions and of an imperative to choose between them that all three positions display—later Hinduism, Plato and Christianity—is traceable to this spiritual-natural dichotomy.

There is a considerable difference between them, though, in the way the person is expected to anchor himself with assurance in the saving solidarity, although all three clearly demand great concentration, dedication and singleness of mind. There is, in fact, a strenuousness of application here that the religions of natural-need fulfilment know nothing of. Hinduism allows the person an option from a variety of philosophies and techniques; but by practice of the ones chosen it is hoped the insight will dawn whereby he will feel and know the saving solidarity's compelling reality, and thereby hold it secure. Plato enjoins the pursuit of virtue and wisdom until, it is hoped, the person is rewarded by sharing in the divine mind, by seeing and enjoying, without possibility of losing them, the ideal forms. The notion of forms in opposition to matter is developed as a way of expressing the qualitative difference of the spiritual reality. Christianity recommends having confidence in the way taken by Jesus, and repeating the pattern of it in oneself as a consequence. This is a path *through* this decaying natural life to the incorruptible resurrection life.

Christianity makes the staggering claim that it has won the victory over death—death being, of course, the end of every natural thing. It is a way of seeming loss, seeming foolishness, seeming humiliation, seeming defeat, because it says "no" all the time to the deceptive securities of nature. But the negation of the negative makes the positive. The person is simultaneously laying foundations for widening spiritual solidarities instead, sowing the seed of the resurrection life. Through crucifixion in, to and by nature he is resurrected into eternal life, which means that he lives in the continuing and widening solidarity of those who live the resurrection life only through one another. If he once lives beyond the frontiers of decaying nature, he lives eternally and will be seen to be alive forevermore by all those who make the same crossing. Thus the Christian's "rising with Christ" in the New Testament is not seen to wait upon his death but is experienced in the present. Similarly, Jesus' having passed from death to life was appreciated by his disciples only when, after the death of his body, they realized his life had not been invested in that but in his union with them.

As I have said, for the reasons I gave, there are times when men become much more aware of life's possibilities. There has been much unevenness, for example, in the level of the religion of natural-need fufilment that different men have followed. Comparatively modern exponents are still found plumbing its possibilities, as we saw when we alluded to the religious experience of men like Emerson, Whitman and Wordsworth in Chapter 4. But to be aware at all of the possibility of a religion of spiritual satisfaction is itself a great leap forward. At a certain stage in the growth of the Hindu tradition, in Plato and in Christianity, that awareness reached an exceptionally high level. Just as the religion of China and the Greek tragic poets make peaks in the religion of natural-need fulfilment, these are peaks in the religion of spiritual satisfaction.

The Incorporation of Natural Forces and Human Power in Religion

Now that we have given some attention to the variability of content that different religions can display, we are at a point to be more explicit about the ways in which natural forces and political powers can be incorporated into religion. The reader will remember that Chapter 2 anticipated a later discussion of these questions. It is also appropriate to link with this discussion some further elaboration of the idea introduced in Chapter 1, that in religion men are orienting to a cosmos. I said in Chapter 2 that when religion takes an interest in nature it is because nature supplies stage properties for the drama enacted in the ideal society. Grasping this is fundamental, I believe, to a right understanding, and it is not clear that it is understood when people glibly say that a function of religion is to define "man's place in

nature" or to develop "a philosophy of nature" or "a cosmology."
If the political power appears in a religion I think it is for the
same kind of reason, and this does not seem to be well understood either. The presence in a society of a divine king, for instance, does not indicate anything about the natural importance
of kings but indicates the absorption of the king's function into
the divine order.

It is true that both "nature" and "the polity" eventually differentiate from the encompassing religion in the course of cultural evolution, but they are at first fully fused with it, and they
continue to be embedded in it after differentiation insofar as
religion has a regard for them. When, as students of society, we
encounter them in religion we are in danger of looking at the
undifferentiated thing from the differentiated perspective, because in our secular consciousness we know these as things in
their own right. As a result of doing this it is sometimes said that
"nature" figures prominently in the more primitive forms of religion, or that some of them are highly "political" in content.
Yet it can truthfully be said that "nature" is one of the last
categories the human intellect comes to, in the sense of a realm
that is recognized as being objective to the observer; and the
notion of "the polity" is almost as recent.

Insofar as religion depicts man in a situation, insofar as he is
shown to be surrounded by something else, it is precisely the
term "cosmos" that best describes what that surround is seen to
be. He shrugs around himself a home, autistically constructing
it for his own comfort—if it helps to say it that way. Of course,
in its most exact use "cosmos" implies a perfectly ordered harmony and unity. But I think we can adopt it for general use
without implying that that perfection is always achieved, or
even approached. Yet I do think it is likely that in making themselves a home men aim for that perfection, though they do it
largely unconsciously, and that where it is lacking they blind
themselves to the inadequacies and make that home serve for
what it is intended to be. Their religious assurance, ultimately,
is a matter of feeling at home in *that* sufficiently adequate
"world." That it can make, for them, a totality with an intrinsic
unity is traceable to the fact that the ideal society supplies them
with architectural outlines for it. To affirm the reality of that
ideal is to affirm, simultaneously, the cosmos and its unity. In
Chapter 1 I said it is the principle of unity in the cosmos that
all men are affirming in religion. Then in Chapters 3 and 4 I tried
to show that they employ the five distinct expressions of religion
to affirm the reality of the ideal society. I would want it understood that these are one and the same affirmation. *The sacred
cosmos of religion lies within the boundary of the ideal society.*
But let us look more closely at the way the natural and political
powers get assimilated to this religious cosmos.

Nature in the Religious Cosmos

That "nature" has importance by supplying the scene and resources for man's action is implicit in many myths. But creation
myths may say it very directly. By no means are these primitive
excursions into detached science: they point out a situation that
is supposed to make subsequent actions imperative. In Genesis
the earth is given to man to subdue. God asks him to name the
creatures and gives him rule over them, as well as the right
to exploit the vegetation. Woman is made for man. Eden, too, is
made for his enjoyment. But more important than the natural
creation being given into man's charge is the fact of creation
itself. Either the creation comes into being through the agency
of external personality and its action, or its parts are themselves
personal and active. It is thus arranged in accordance with purpose and design, to complement those of men. If it is hard to
find philosophical support for that kind of notion, it comes very
easily to religion. There is a Chinese myth that the first man,
P'an Ku, carved the creation from chaos with his hammer and
chisel. Then on his death, various parts of his body formed the
five sacred mountains of China. There is the Babylonian myth
that Marduk did battle with the chaos dragon Tiamat, created
the heavens and earth from her remains, and, assisted by Ea,
created man from the god Kingsu. Thus it results that both
the physical world and the creatures can appear personalized
and socialized, because of their association and interaction with
men.

We may also recall how some primitive religions think of the
natural species as living a life that is organic with man's. We
see this vividly in the practice of totemism: it is also seen in
the half-man, half-animal divinities of the Egyptians. Rather
than taking that interpenetration to mean that human society
has not yet been lifted out of nature, I think it should be taken
to mean that nature has not yet been lifted out of society. In its
lowlier expressions this organic unity with nature is nothing but
a regulation of cooperation with it to extract its resources.
The divinities appear at those points where human skill has to
be applied to some natural sphere—the situation we saw obtaining in Egypt, Mesopotamia, Greece and Rome. A much more
developed expression of the same organic unity is the one we
found in Chinese religion and the Greek tragic poets. Nature,
man and divinity are all of a piece, so that some imbalance in
one can throw the others off poise. Human misconduct can result
in famine. We noticed that there was a large element of the religion of natural-need fulfilment in early Judaism, and it shares
in this organic unity. If the commandments of the Lord are
obeyed, rain will be given at the proper time.

When we come to the religions of spiritual satisfaction the
status of "nature" becomes problematic. At this point it does

begin to be differentiated. Indeed, we may have the clue here as to why it happened. Once spiritual satisfaction displaces natural-need fulfilment as the goal of life, it is necessary to know how far and in what ways one's immersion in nature helps or hinders. Not surprisingly, a variety of answers were arrived at, some of them, like those developed in Hinduism, resting on an intricacy of subtle distinctions. But we can say that these religions are distinguished as a class by a rupture of the organic unity of man and nature and an awareness that the status to be granted nature has become problematic. Judaism and Islam keep a root in nature in a fairly literal sense, in that they hold to the holiness of a territory. From its produce they expect prosperity and the enjoyment of the senses. But the rupture is evident in Israel's transfer of attention to the presence of the Lord in special places: in the ark, then in the temple and Zion. It is evident as well in Islam's transfer of attention to Allah's supervision of our present conduct and to heaven and hell beyond. Having achieved the separation of a natural realm, Hinduism is in doubt over the way to dispose of it—hence the alternative solutions offered in the two divisions of Hindu philosophy. The Sankhya philosophy proposes a dualism of atman (the spiritual principle), and prakriti (the material principle), both of which are real. The Vedanta philosophy allows that only atman is real, everything perceived apart from it being maya or illusion. Various changes are played on this theme in Hinduism, and the same happens in Buddhism, which insists there is no ultimate reality in the sensory appearance of things. Zen Buddhism, for instance, seeks a mode of perception in which nature and spirit appear without difference.

We do not have to raise questions about the adequacy or acceptability of any of these ratings of nature. What matters is what is happening at this point. I would say it is simply that a radically new definition of the ideal society is being attempted: not one that gives us nothing but an assurance of natural-need fulfilment, but a society that gives us that, certainly, but only secondarily, as an entailment of the solidarity that gives spiritual release. By whatever means it is to be indicated and done, then, nature must be given a subordinate place. The cosmos is vaster. To depict this alternative cosmos, which is not a cosmos of the material universe but one that has swallowed it up, might understandably be difficult. Christianity ventured to do this and said, to the astonishment of many, that it was—Christ. It was, that is to say, the divine humanity, the cosmic Son of God, through whom and for whom all creation exists.

He rescued us from the domain of darkness and brought us away into the kingdom of his dear Son, in whom our release is secured and our sins forgiven. He is the image of the invisible God; his is the primacy over all created things. In him everything in heaven and on earth was created, not only things visible but also the invisible orders of thrones, sovereignties, authorities, and powers: the whole universe has been created through him and for him. And he exists before everything, and all things are held together in him. He is, moreover, the head of the body, the church. He is its origin, the first to return from the dead, to be in all things alone supreme. For in him the complete being of God, by God's own choice, came to dwell. Through him God chose to reconcile the whole universe to himself, making peace through the shedding of his blood upon the cross—to reconcile all things, whether on earth or in heaven, through him alone.[4]

Human Power in the Religious Cosmos

If political order is introduced as an ingredient of the cosmos it is for reasons parallel to those for which the natural order is introduced. Just as nature supplies some of the stage properties for the drama enacted in the ideal society, so does the power structure. It can for that reason be hallowed. The political order as much as the natural can be seen to be instrumental in supplying natural needs and spiritual satisfaction. It can thus be a mediator of the divine order and invested with some kind of borrowed or derived sacredness. When Paul wrote to the Colossians in the words just quoted, he was not endowed with modern terminology for making his distinctions. But he wanted to draw attention to the fact that both the natural and political orders are equally constitutive of the cosmos and equally creations of the creator. He called them "things visible" and "the invisible orders" respectively.

Whether a person is religious or irreligious, whether he thinks as a scholar or a citizen, he will probably be aware of a close affinity between the religious and political elements in life. What is common to them, of course, is the experience of constraining power. But to sort out their likeness, their difference and their relationship, requires considerable subtlety. I have already commented on the lack of subtlety in the Marxian approach that takes the political element as the only real one and dismisses the religious as illusory. But the same kind of prejudice in favour of the political element can be found elsewhere. Swanson quotes Rieff as saying:[5]

Men became religious when they had to approach and rationalize the chaos of powers by which they were moved and their destinies sealed. But from Hobbes to Weber there has been an insistent, ironic voice saying that religious man is really, at bottom, political man. All theologies are metaphors of politics . . .[6]

As I see it, the key to a right understanding that will keep us from confusing the two things simply because they are alike and related is this: the religious constraint issues from the power over men of the ideal society, the political constraint from the power of some men over others. Insofar as the human power holders try to implement the ideal (which is what we mean when we say they "use their power responsibly"), they are simply transmitting the pressure of the ideal constraint—and are, of course, simultaneously bound by it themselves. Insofar as they exploit their power advantage to have others serve their private interests, they are exploiters and tyrants. Human power always has both possibilities in it, and that is why men are very watchful of it. We feel the former exercise of power to be agreeable and acceptable, and from the religious perspective it is the only permissible way to use a power advantage. It may therefore be called legitimate power or authority, in order to distinguish it from the naked, wilful power of tyranny. We see now exactly why religious and political power are fated for an entanglement, why they cannot keep out of one another's way. For religion claims that no one is entitled to the exercise of power except in the service of the ideal. Natural advantages, it says, are not to be presumed upon.

Religion, then, is discriminating in regard to human power: legitimate authority it upholds, tyranny it condemns. It upholds the former as an instrument of the sacred power. On the other side, human power has an option in regard to the sacred power. If it chooses to be legitimate in its own function it can claim its power is not its own. It may rightly claim that its power is given it from the sacred and that it is the divine agent, and it will uphold religion. If it is illegitimate it will claim its power is purely its own. It will resist religion and may even try to usurp its authority. Where the exercise of human power is legitimate, then, the human and divine authorities uphold one another in an alliance that can be formidable—and this is the ultimate bulwark of social order. According to this analysis of the situation, it may finally be noted, no superior status or reality could ever be claimed for political power. On the contrary, insofar as it is legitimate and turns human advantage to the service of the ideal, it is secondary to the sacred power. Needless to say, it is power presumed legitimate that religion adopts into its cosmos. Needless to say, also, the ways in which this has been done have been various—and, of course, they have not made use of the foregoing formulation of the nature of legitimation.

History gives us a number of instances of a type of regime that can be called a theocracy, where the human ruler exercises power explicitly in the name of the sacred. This was the situation in Akhenaton's Egypt, Asoka's Buddhist empire, the Zoroastrian empire of the Sassanians, Tibetan Lamaism, the Christian empire of Constantine and Theodosius, the Arabian Caliphate, Calvin's Geneva, and the Anabaptists' Münster. But it is certainly not necessary to have that kind of setup for the political power to be built into the sacred cosmos. It occurs just as much when a democracy like the U.S.A. places itself "under God." Nor is it necessary that the power legitimized be concentrated in a single ruler, for it is really the structuring of power that is legitimized. The stratification system itself may express what is divinely ordained, which is what occurs in the case of the Hindu caste system. The differential authority given to the aged and the ancestors may express it, as in the ancestral familism of China. Patriarchal, prophetic and military leadership may express it, as was the case in Israel.

Making kings and royal chiefs sacred, either as gods or near-gods, has been quite a widespread practice. We misunderstand if we think of it as a form of self-glorification engaged in at the expense of the people. Rather, the king stands for the people, and his health and virtue are the insurance of the health and prosperity of the kingdom. Probably the fertility of its lands is invested in him. The people of the Jukun tribe of Nigeria believed this of their king and, together with his ability to control the wind and rain, it made him the guarantor of good harvest.[7] Since the king's ability depended on his continuing virtue, and the order of the kingdom on the people's allegiance, a whole system of control for the securing of needs resulted. Transparently, the divine kingship is a hallowing of the social order that complements the natural order in the processes of production. The Egyptian king, who was the son of the sun god, had the virtues of the sun, in being able to bring light and life. He was said to be food, and his mouth to be increase. The kings of Babylonia were suckled at the breast of Ishtar, the goddess of fertility. It was the exclusive prerogative of the Emperor of China, the Son of Heaven, to make the sacrifice to Heaven. Even though it was done in secret because of its sacredness, the rite was performed on behalf of all the people. The emperor was thus the only mediator between Heaven and men, and on his faithful performance of the ritual Heaven's favour in the form of good fortune depended. The Emperor of Japan, descendant of the Sun Goddess, guaranteed both the prosperity of the land and its military supremacy in the world.

It is in the religions of natural-need fulfilment that this bold equation of ruler and divinity is to be found. Just as we find a rupture in man's continuity with nature when we come to the religions of spiritual satisfaction, so we find a rupture in his continuity with political power. The problem is the same: something indispensable has to be preserved, but now it has to be subordinated. Again, there are various ways of attempting it, but it clearly becomes problematic in every case. With Islam the subordination is effected by giving the temporal authority into the hands of the spiritual head. This operation—paralleled in Calvin's Geneva and the Anabaptists' Münster—has a resemblance to the divine kingship which is quite deceptive, for it really works at a different level. Rather than elevating the political power to divine status, it is making it subordinate to that which has divine status in its own right. The Jews were at first dubious about having a king to supplement the authority given to prophet and priest. But he was required to be chosen by God and subject to the prophets. One incumbent of the office, King David, spiritualized the conception by insisting in his Psalms that it is God who is King. The notion was similarly spiritualized by transference to great David's greater son, who would be a Messiah king. This kind of king, anticipated with increasing hope from about the time of the Roman occupation of Palestine, would lead a deliverance from earthly existence into a different realm.

Christianity adopted this messianic notion and identified it with the cosmic Son of God to whom, as we saw, all earthly rulers were made subject. It did not deny them authority as earthly rulers, but allowed them a legitimation through being subject to Christ. Monarchs of Christian countries have endeavoured to conform to this conception of being rulers by the grace of God, though with varying understandings of it. The Byzantine emperor was believed to have been crowned from heaven by Christ and, after death, to share the throne of heaven. In Russia, the blessed Tsar was believed to be supreme pastor of the Christian flock. The British monarch is said to be the slave of Christ the Redeemer whose kingdom the whole world is.

In the Introduction I claimed that the scientific approach helps us to see the necessity in religious phenomena and be reconciled to the unity and diversity they display. I would hope that by now this claim has begun to seem well justified. Having treated likenesses in the first part of the book, I went on in Chapters 5 and 6 to deal with the kind of variability that depends on the stage of growth of a religious tradition. Many large and baffling religious differences are to be explained by that. Now in this chapter I have tried to account for the "original" differences of the separated traditions. I have attributed them to the degree of evolutionary advancement in the free play of imagination about life's possibilities. Life's possibilities in two distinct directions are the ones that are basic: (1) its possibilities for natural-need fulfilment and spiritual satisfaction, and (2) its possibilities for whole-life orientation and organization in these pursuits. Assurance that the particular possibility they envisage will be realized is what men then seek by the religion they practise. These religious differences are often considered the most baffling of all, and even beyond explanation altogether. But I think the acquirement of this point of view on them makes them understandable.

There is yet another class of differences in religion, however, and they are the ones I handle in the chapter to follow under the rubric of "secularization." How that term is to be defined must be considered at some length there. But to anticipate briefly, the differences in question are those induced when religion is confronted by reason. Reason and such products of it as science and philosophy, and compartmentalized and sophisticated life-organisation: these can have a marked and a differential impact on people's adherence to religious belief. We may find an *avant-garde* or "liberal" wing developing within the religion, or even abandonment by a section of religion as it has been known. At any rate, the result is a spectrum of differences of another kind from those that we have considered thus far.

Notes, Chapter 7

1. Max Weber, *The Sociology of Religion*, pp. xxxii-xxxv, 45-60.
2. F. S. C. Northrop, *The Meeting of East and West*, London: Macmillan, 1946.
3. *Ibid.*, pp. 403-4.
4. Reprinted from *The New English Bible*, copyright 1961 and 1970 by Oxford & Cambridge University Presses, Col. 1: 13-20.
5. Guy E. Swanson, *The Birth of the Gods, The Origin of Primitive Beliefs*, p. 190.
6. Philip Rieff, 'Max Weber, "Science as a Vocation," Introduction,' *Daedalus*, Winter, 1958, p. 111.
7. For details see C. K. Meek, *A Sudanese Kingdom, An Ethnographical Study of the Jukun-speaking Peoples of Nigeria*, London: Kegan Paul, Trench, Trubner & Co., 1931.

Chapter 8

The Difference Due to Secularization

In the first chapter I insisted that Durkheim's opposition between the sacred and profane is the opposition between the supernatural and natural as this is most meaningfully used by ourselves. The profane, in that understanding of it, is a neutral state. It carries no connotation of evil or unholiness, as could be the case if it were used in opposition to the sacred in its aspect of holiness. But that such an evil or diabolical principle may occur in systems of religious belief, is something Durkheim recognized.[1] He called it the "unpropitiously sacred," considering it to be properly included under the sacred and not the profane, since it is a principle of *spiritual* evil. This is, of course, sound. Yet there is something very unsatisfactory in the resulting requirement to hold "profane" to an exclusively neutral use—and Durkheim cannot be said to do it. He is just as likely to represent the profane as a contamination from which the sacred prompts men to flee. Furthermore, he has the following to say regarding the division internal to the sacred: "The good and salutary powers repel to a distance these others which deny and contradict them. Therefore the former are forbidden to the latter: any contact between them is considered the worst of profanations."[2] Here the "unpropitiously sacred" can give rise to the profane; while the profane itself is betrayed by the epithet "worst" to be a thing that exists in degrees of evil. It seems that there are really two oppositions that Durkheim may refer to under the one blanket-dichotomy of sacred and profane: the supernatural versus the natural, and the holy versus the unholy. What are we to do about this?

The Profane as Natural and as Evil

I would like to suggest that it is the unique properties of religious relationships themselves that generate this double reference. It requires a certain subtlety to sort it out. The "natural" may well be considered in its neutral aspect. But it may also be unholy—if it stands in a certain untoward relationship to the supernatural. In that situation one may speak as if there is an equivalence between the natural and the unholy: to speak of the profane then, meaning natural, is simultaneously to imply the evil. What I have called the untoward relationship, which makes the natural not only natural but unclean, may be explained as follows, although I am being more explicit than Durkheim now. The natural may place itself in subordinate relationship to the supernatural, being, so to speak, embraced by it, even though remaining qualitatively distinct. In this case it can be said to be sanctified, although not sacred. Or the natural may resist the sacred's claim of authority over it, setting itself up apart and, inevitably in consequence, opposing the sacred. In that case it is unclean or evil. Apparently it is by this progression that the "unpropitiously sacred" came into being—as the unclean profane. Figure 9 illustrates the overlap.

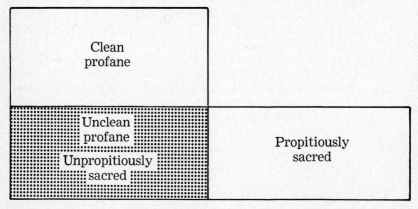

Figure 9. Identity of the Unclean Profane and Unpropitiously Sacred.

So there are really always two simultaneous relationships, the second being superimposed on the first and the second having two alternative possibilities. The natural is the opposite of the supernatural, and in this opposition the natural will be either sanctified or unclean.

In a way it is a great pity that we do not have separate terms for the "profane" as natural and the "profane" as unclean. For each of them is a very important notion in its own right. The term is used at least as often with connotations of the second kind. So we need a fuller exposition of it in that sense. For the purpose of this book we also need to have that sense of it related to the idea of the sacred as the totality; that is, the sacred as the cosmos that lies within the boundary of the ideal society. The essential thing about the profane in that sense is its *resistance* to the sacred.

> For the hallmark of it is that it resists the claim of the sacred—not merely that it exists beside it in a world apart. It goes against the sacred in the way that blasphemy and heresy do—and these, of course, are instances of it. Even so, by setting up any world apart and making it sovereign,

that resistance is implied. The essence of profanity, then, is the denial that sovereignty is the prerogative of totality. Any separate thing, any sphere made sufficient in itself, constitutes profanity. Between the sacred and the profane the war is therefore total. To make the point in Altizer's words: ". . . neither can fully become itself apart from a total negation of the other." The holy, under its own impulse, asserts an entitlement to reclaim all since it is all. (The original riddle of actuality and potentiality is confronted here.) But the profane chooses autonomy. Yet, because the sacred is forever seeking, the opportunity may remain for the profane to escape the calamity of its choice— if it will choose again, repent. To come back it must renounce its apartness, and this reincorporation is the meaning of ritual cleansing.

Profane action cannot be viewed as neutral: it is religious without being religion. It grows like that it resists, and this quasi-religious character springs directly from its arrogation of authority. The profane is what causes anything less than totality to operate as if it were the totality by denying any criteria external to itself. It is an illegitimate closure. Presumably it is to this aspect of profanity that reference is made when Satan is said to appear as an angel of light: it steals the sacred's halo of completeness. To understand it we have to see it as competing in the sphere of religious phenomena though working against cosmos-confronting religion.[3]

This daemonic principle has been on the threshold of our attention at different points in the book. The cult expresses it. Tillich recognizes it. It is against it that the religions of spiritual satisfaction watch, lest nature or human power encroach on the sacred. Indeed, one might add, it is in this type of religion that a general awareness of spiritual evil may occur, lest *anything* encroach. The possibility of the profane as natural turning into the profane as evil is explicitly acknowledged. In Mithraism, Zoroastrianism and Christianity that consciousness becomes acute; in the war of light and darkness the antagonists are portrayed. But we could also portray it in terms of the solidarity account of spiritual satisfaction proposed in the preceding chapter. It is as though this religious position fights as the archenemy the partisan's error of seeking spiritual satisfaction in the exclusive in-group (the limited good) instead of the inclusive whole.

Secularization Defined as a Phase in a Dialectical Process

As if the confusion over the profane were not enough, the term "secular" has also appeared in the discussion of religion with increasing frequency, and sometimes it has been used as an equivalent of "profane." Yet which sense of profane may be left unclear, and, in any case, "secular" itself may have a different meaning in sociological literature from the ones it has in the debate between churchmen and their opponents. Because of the looseness in those colloquial uses I try to avoid them in what follows, restricting myself to the kind of meaning that has been evolving in the sociological tradition. Also, in what now follows, I use "profane" in the sense of evil.

Redfield and Becker speak of "the secular" as a kind of rational legitimation given to practices that meet the need for adaptive change.[4] Becker states: "Briefly, societies that endow their members with a high proportion of action patterns leading to readiness to change are secular societies."[5] He cites the transformation of Chicago from a remote fur-trading post to the world's greatest railway centre as evidence of secularization. Thus the term is made to refer to the pragmatic-mindedness and present-mindedness (the "rationality") that increases with modernization. It has been expressed in diverse spheres of life—from government to the family.

> There is, indeed, the likeness of an evolutionary stage in the concurrent growth of protestantism, industrial capitalism, urban settlement, political democracy, science and technology, universal education, class mobility, and the limited and flexible family. Such a process is not unambiguous in its possibilities, Becker thinks. Within limits it is beneficial because it is adaptive; but he envisages a more extreme situation in which novelty is simply experienced as overwhelming. The individual is left without guide-posts for conduct: normlessness reigns. Hence we have to distinguish between the principled secular societies and the normless. Becker in like manner identified two closed types of society—folk and prescribed—and it is difficult to escape the impression that, of the four, the principled secular is the one that gets the best of both worlds. It combines stability with flexibility, and does so through commitment to normative standards which are highly general and so allow great variation in their application: "natural rights, national welfare, humanitarianism, free enterprise, socialism, 'rationalism,' 'greatest good of the greatest number,' 'liberty under law,' 'functional efficiency,' and so on." For this condition to be achieved a certain disjunction between the plane of principles and that of practice has to get established: they must swivel independently of each other. This looks very like the rule-guided choice of Parsons' "universalism."
>
> Becker's description of secularization makes it easy to see how a risk of profanity could arise within the process; yet the eventuality might be averted, and in any case does not authorize equating secular with profane. But the risk, as well as the case where it is not averted, must be acknowl-

edged. Although secularization and profanity are not the same, the former shows a special vulnerability to the latter. *Any novel practice, or any problem for which it is the response, is prone to become a thing of sovereign importance in itself. Differentiation and novelty both involve a risk of detachment from context because of the claim they make for special attention. It is for this reason that every concern of modern life has a tendency to take autonomy to itself: every "problem," every "cause," every technique, every field of knowledge, every occupation, every institution. Technology and science thrive, indeed, on this kind of isolation and make a methodological principle out of it. It is hard to expect otherwise when the legitimation they are seeking to give to practice is one of internal efficiency. Yet technology and science only fracture the wholeness of life when their work is left without follow-through. In one sense, they may be compared with those expert technicians who, when they do a job, leave a mess for others to clean up. Gifted specialists, they cannot be expected to take care of everything.*

If it is true, as seems may be the case, that technological, industrial, urban man is more a stranger to the sacred than was rural man, it is not because secularization is inherently inimical to religion (much less because the pavement cuts off the intimations of God in nature!). It is just that a more differentiated and differentiating life is more prone to fragmentation. What modern man would need, if he chose to hold on to religion, is not to turn away from secularization but to baptize its fruits, grafting each innovation back onto the tree of his life and consecrating them all to the service of the whole. The religious handling of physical birth itself might serve as an analogy for the religious problem inherent in all cultural differentiation. Parents are not asked to refrain from disturbing established order and unity by avoiding childbirth: the Christian church asks that children be baptized, Judaism asks for the circumcision of sons. (In this connection it is interesting to notice some religious writers giving a welcome to secularization. Tillich, Bonhoeffer, and de Rougemont have viewed it as a trend to be embraced rather than a thing to resist or evade.)

Yet the cleavage between science and religion continues to be a dominant pathology of modern society, and the hidden source, quite possibly, of many others, by virtue of the final anxiety in which it leaves every provisional certainty dangling. A society taking direction from religion can maximize morale by anchoring its members in the wholeness of being. A society having no direction except from technology and science must leave its members chronically ill at ease, and they are driven to titanic though futile efforts to disguise the fact or make up for it. Their desperation can be compounded if autonomy is made into a supreme value because of the adaptive gains coming from secular self-determination; for the religious way to unity is a way of obedience. All this purports too radical a sickness to remedy by gestures—for instance, by showing that Genesis and biology are not irreconcilable, or that certain recorded miracles are less surprising than appears. It amounts to a rift in human consciousness.[6]

The point to be made is that secularization is the analytical process that has sacralization for the complementary synthesizing process. They make a dialectic. Secularization, through the operation of reason, breaks down; sacralization, through the operation of faith, builds up.

The single overall concept which expresses this fracturing of life's unity is secularization—as Redfield and Becker used the term. It comes essentially from the invasion of our living arrangements by greater reason, for the sake of greater efficiency. Whether the closed mind is forced open by outside contact or by direct reflection, it becomes free to compare what is with what might be "better" in this sense. There is a more gratuitous kind of innovation at work here. But our aim is to substitute one means for an existing one rather than to fill a void, which is the case with the innovating response to anomie. What distinguishes secularization is a repudiation of tradition in order to tear reviewable practices out of context. Separate sides of life receive separate—and very likely unequal—attention. The result is a proliferation of disconnected specialisms that leaves men searching for the unity in their total life. Although we are inclined to celebrate the emancipating effects of secularization, we often forget that the splintering, shallowness, and sensed futility of which we complain in the same situation are traceable to the same source.

For secularization only yields a net gain if there is recovery. There has to be institutionalization of the improved practices and, ultimately, sacralization once more.[7]

From the definition I have given it and the perspective in which I have tried to place it, secularization must be seen as one of the primary social processes. To exchange that broad notion for, say, "the decline of religion," would be to forfeit the conceptual means for getting any "declines of religion" that are known to us into focus. As I understand it, secularization is a phase in a natural dialectic: it may be momentary, with an instantaneous recovery in a new synthesis, or it may take decades or centuries for a resynthesizing operation to gather momentum. Yet I think we know enough about the constancy of both reason and faith to expect that the dialectical interplay between them will continue for as long as man does. There would be no grounds, for instance, to interpret a prolonged phase of secularization— marked as it probably will be by crises of faith and widespread unbelief—as the end of religion. The secularization of the modern world has been too easily read in that way by some observers, and I think it may be because their understanding of secularization itself is lacking in depth. I shall shortly propose a different way of looking at modern secularization.

Secularization Expressed in a Spectrum of Subcultures and a Separation of Functions

The splitting process that is the work of rational, analytical thought, produces differentiation in practice and discrimination in belief. This very simple primary process of a dividing and re-dividing, is what lies behind the cultural transformations of history. The new diversity calls always for a reamalgamation of the parts, and these parts may come together in one single mass. But it is just as likely they will harden in two or more separate masses, so that in the congealing together lines of division will congeal at the same time. Possibly the division is made along a line that allows the more rational elements to segregate together. As a result of it, then, we will have the more and less "rational" divisions, the more and less "advanced," the more and less "modern," the more and less "liberal." Such expressions can simply be so many ways of expressing the emergence in a society of a spectrum of subcultures which incorporate differential degrees of rationality in their life. Then there is another line of division that can occur in this congealing process: it is one that effects a separation of function. A specialization of ends develops, and the activities serving each of them are massed together and segregated from one another. It is possible to point out instances of both kinds of divisional hardening in the field of religion.

The Spectrum of Subcultures

We can see the first kind illustrated in the superseding of magic. Some have suggested that magic is a precursor of religion and others that it is a precursor of scientific technology. I would suggest that it is a precursor of both, in the sense that they have forked out from it, each of them supplying in a more rational way a part of what it aimed to do. When religion and magic were compared in Chapter 4, it was pointed out that magical ritual is believed to be the practical cause of practical effects. But that inept gesture gives way to scientifically rational techniques which have a real effectiveness. At the same time, the ritual gives way to the ritual of religion, which does not need to be anything but non-utilitarian and expressive to accomplish its non-utilitarian end. What we call "superstition" is nothing but survivals and revivals of magic. It may exist as a tradition of practice that has persisted in its own right, and perhaps side by side with authentic religion. But it may develop as a corruption in a tradition of otherwise authentic religion, brought in by people who are not rational enough to maintain the tradition at the level at which they received it.

A differentiation within religion between its more rational and more superstitious practitioners is quite commonly found, the latter usually occurring amongst persons of less education and lower social status. Indeed, this fact makes fiction out of many textbook accounts of the world's religions. They give us the systems of thought expounded by the thinkers: almost invariably the practice of the following is something else. This wide occurrence of superstition sometimes supplies the opponents of religion with their main ammunition. Yet they are, of course, unfair to religion if they take superstition as being constitutive of religion instead of as a deviation from it. Some of them even equate religion with it, dismissing all religion as superstition. But to do that is to be undiscriminating.

Illustrations of this infiltration by superstition could be taken from any religion, but Roman Catholicism has supplied many of the instances of it occurring in Christendom. It has been especially evident in those Roman Catholic countries with illiterate and impoverished populations. As for other faiths, we have already had occasion to refer to superstition in the religious practices of India and China, and these are countries often mentioned in this connection. India is probably the country that shows the greatest contrast between a high-flying philosophical doctrine for the sophisticated person and a superstitious counterpart. Very ancient magical traditions, some of which pre-date Hinduism, have persisted under Hinduism's umbrella. The millions of untouchables who were excluded from the caste system have resorted to these traditions and others living in India as well. There has been a widespread belief in the effective powers resident in plants and animals, serpents, rivers and tools. The holiness ascribed to the cow and the Ganges River are instances of this. Prayers are also offered to a great profusion of village spirits and godlings. Rain, crops, health, safety on a journey, strength for a task, good fortune, a large progeny, thriving cattle—for each of these and every other need there is a specific provider. Many simple people have a superstitious regard for the Brahmin priests, expecting magic from them—and this illustrates exactly the acutest problem with superstition. It is not simply that extraneous beliefs are brought in to embroider the religion, but its own beliefs are given a debased interpretation.

Rather like India, China had a very ancient tradition in which a multitude of spirit powers were believed to reside in a multitude of things and places: in the planets, clouds, hills, fields, roads, rivers, and elsewhere. These powers could be invoked in magic, and the Taoism and Buddhism that became influential in China were exposed to infection by the same magical interpretation. Taoism, during a long period, was in fact little more than an elaborate magical system, so changed did it become from the original. The Tao, the principle of order in nature with which the person had sought to be conformed, came to be viewed as a magical potency of which some persons might get possession. Those who came into possession of it could defy gravity and even death, be impervious to attack by men and animals, enjoy longevity and health, walk on water, and perform a variety of other wonders. A number of disciplines were supposed to enhance one's access to Tao: breathing exercises, dietetics, alchemy to produce the liquid gold that gave immortality when drunk. Taoism in that form did not persist into recent times, but other superstition has done so. The superstition persisting in their midst became so intolerable to the educated Chinese that a drastic secularization occurred in the first half of the twentieth century.[8] From 1920 to 1930 there was a series of movements directed against superstition. In 1929 the Nationalist government issued the "Procedure for the Abolition of the Occupations of Divination, Astrology, Physiognomy and Palmistry, Magic and Geomancy." In 1930 those who sold "superstitious merchandise"—such things as incense and candles—were ordered to change their occupations.

The Separation of Functions

Now let us look at secularization being expressed in the other way; that is, in a differentiation of function. The most rudimentary expression of this is in the separation of religion itself as an institution in its own right. When we encounter religion in the most primitive societies it is indistinguishable from the society itself. It is not separately sponsored by a religious organization; there are simply religious aspects to life in general. Durkheim suggested that we look at this undifferentiated society as being *all of it* religion.[9] From that point of view religion is the womb that gives birth to everything else. So it is perhaps not surprising that when religion does separate it continues to hold everything else in its purview, prescribing for the whole of life. However, a stage of social development arrives where the work of religion (as distinct from its concern) is the work of a specialized institution. Yang calls this religion "institutional" to distinguish it from the other, which he calls "diffused." He puts the distinction to effective use in analyzing the religious situation in China.[10]

In China, Yang contends, religion was very influential, yet only because the diffused religion continued to carry great weight in the shadow of an institutional religion that was weak. The officiants of the diffused religion performed religious actions simply by virtue of their roles in practical life. It was the head of the family or clan who administered the ancestor worship for it; the officers of the guild who approached the patron god of the trade and guild; the community leaders who approached the patron gods of the community; the emperor and his government officials and local gentry who officiated in the worship of Heaven and Earth. The religion of these various spheres of life was simply the direct sanctification of the activities being performed there. "Institutional religion," on the other hand, comprised the Buddhist and Taoist priesthoods as well as the professionals of the traditional religion, such as the geomancers, diviners, sorcerers and other magicians. This emergent structure remained weak, partly because it was fragmented through decentralization but partly because it could not penetrate into layers of social life already preempted by diffused religion. Here in China, then, we see the junction of the differentiated and undifferentiated nicely illustrated.

In other situations the institutional religion has achieved a much greater separate effectiveness, in others again it scarcely emerged. Hinduism has maintained a predominant place for the undifferentiated substratum. This has allowed it to accommodate a variety of schools of thought within itself, but at the same time it has produced a tantalizing rigidity in Indian society, since the society and the religious organ are one and the same. Zoroastrianism disappeared quite suddenly from Persia after the Muslim conquest, and this is attributable to a similar identification of religious organ and whole society. A double predicament for Israel derives from the same situation. Its religion is essentially organic with society, yet the society is dispersed and only a remnant faithful.

But Islam, Buddhism and Christianity are in a different case, because of the fact that they emerged in opposition to the diffused religion. This gave them the separate institutional structure that made missionary expansion possible. Islam emerged as a military enterprise, and that made for a fusion of the religious and political authority. When religion differentiated from society government came with it. The missionary expansion of Islam was an imperialist growth in consequence. Yet world Islam has been troubled by an internal division because of this fusion. Ideally, its constituent empires and states must copy the unity of the religious community, the Ummah— but that has not occurred. Buddhism and Christianity had a greater freedom of mobility because the religious organs, the Samgha and Church respectively, were completely self-contained. They were not identical with any state nor coterminous with any society. But they were able to be an influence on state and society alike and, at the same time, a bridge between different ones.

It is Wach who has made the greatest use of the principle of differentiation in accounting for the variety in religion.[11] He shows how religion has evolved from an activity diffused through naturally occurring groups, to an activity of groups having a specifically religious purpose.* Family and kinship cults (including very frequently the veneration of ancestors) have been extremely widespread. He notes their occurrence among the Greeks and Romans, and in Polynesia, Africa, India, China, Japan, Mexico, Peru and Europe. The crises of birth, puberty, marriage and death, which are weathered jointly in the family, are the special concerns of these cults. A wide distribution of local community cults, with their local community concerns, is also found. In a similar way there have been cults based on and concerned with the needs of race and nation, sex difference and age-phase. But, Wach says, when a spiritual experience of particular quality becomes known and is shared amongst a set of persons, we have a discontinuity with this kind of religion. Then it is that religious organizations with specifically religous purposes emerge. He sees the beginnings of it in secret societies and the mystery religions, and its eventual culmination in founded religions like Buddhism, Christianity and Islam.

Doubtless because the concerns of politics and religion tangle in the ways indicated in the last chapter, their institutional differentiation within society is not always accompanied by an unambiguous differentiation from one another. It is as a result of this that we have the whole set of problems that we refer to under the rubric of "church-state relationships." Study of the ways in which those problems arise and are resolved throws much light on the secularization process. An important thing to realize at the outset is that the *separation* of church and state, a much discussed issue of recent times, belongs fairly exclusively to that period, and, in fact, makes one of the most recent expressions of secularization. That separation is really the fruit of nonconformity and the resulting religious pluralism. In the United States, the impetus for it has come from the wish to stop any religious organization being specially privileged, either through being established or through receiving government support for its educational and other programmes. Thus, to get the matter in true perspective, we could say that the state is being forced into separation by the already separated churches. It is essentially part of a process of limitation of the state. It can look like a limitation and diminution of religion, as one sees government support being withdrawn from one religious activity after another—but the shrinkage is strictly on the other side.

When United States court decisions in 1962 and 1963 ruled it unconstitutional for schoolteachers to be required to say prayers or read from the Bible in class, it might on the face of it appear that religion was being curtailed. Strictly, what was being cur-

*The reader should note that, to follow Wach here, I drop into that usage of cult which I am in general avoiding.

tailed was the right of the state to undertake for religion. A differentiation of the governing organ from the community as a whole is in process. Perhaps we do not appreciate as well as we should this difference between state and community, for the state is not the whole of the common life but simply a machinery of control. Yinger has suggested that a separation of church and state, if it is effective and not nominal, can occur only in the democratic type of situation where power is diffused.[12] I have said it occurs with nonconformity or what, up till now, I have mainly called sectarianism. I also suggested earlier that sectarianism is a phenomenon of a fluid power structure, so it would appear that the two conditions occur together. In both of the conditions, as well as in the separated state resulting from them, it is the rationality of secularization that is making its advance.

The whole reason for the appearance of nonconformist minorities becoming a problem was simply that official religion was standard in the societies where they appeared. This custom had really persisted very late. Rulers naturally expected that it was one of their prerogatives to choose the religion of their domain. When new states eventually consolidated in Europe after the dissolution of the Holy Roman Empire, it seemed only routine that each would take a religion. They made a choice from amongst the traditional faiths and the new reformation faiths. The principle followed was a time-honoured one: *Cuius regio eius religio; Une loi, une foi, un roi.* Spain and France, for instance, chose Roman Catholicism, Prussia and Sweden Lutheranism. Under that arrangement the princes were the protectors or defenders of the faith. It is a kind of relationship between rulers and religion that has been exemplified many times. The Indian King Asoka supplied an early Buddhist instance of this, the Roman Emperor Justinian an early Christian one.

The other two major alternatives were for the religious authority to exercise supervision over the temporal administration and for it to undertake that administration itself. The former is exemplified in Gregory the Great, the latter in Tibetan Lamaism, the Papal States and Calvin's Geneva. While they do differ, what we have in all are simply three ways of maintaining a mutual supervision between religion and the state. Nor is the first so much out of keeping with the other two simply because the state is, as it were, "on top" there. The defender of the faith relationship does not necessarily imply that a superior attitude is taken to religion; it can mean the service of it. Yet it seems that, in some places, a greater flexibility of operation for both state and religion has been sought by their separation.

It is interesting to compare the United States and Turkey in this regard, since they exemplify secularization in the Christian and Islamic traditions respectively. In the United States the principle of separation was incorporated in the Constitution: it was there from the beginning. In Turkey it was contrary to and, in fact, a complete negation of the tradition. There the temporal power of the Sultanate was traditionally merged with the Caliphate, the spiritual headship of Islam. There, too, the Ulema saw to it that the ruler's legislation, administration and justice conformed with the Seriat, the sacred law of Islam. Starting with the separation of church and state as given, the United States can be observed drawing them back into mutual supervision. Its history since foundation really illustrates the sacralizing phase of the dialectic. Opportunity has been taken on public occasions to stress the fact that, while the government is not religious, the community *is*. The Supreme Court has taken the position that the United States is a Christian nation, in the sense that Christian principles must be assumed to underlie its laws and values. "Under God" modifies the pledge of allegiance to the flag, and this same God is constantly invoked by the nation's leaders, particularly for help in crises. But in the case of Turkey it is the contrasting phase of secularization that we see illustrated. Islam had long exhibited sectarian division, so that particular condition was already present. It had also long been democratic in spirit, yet state machinery to express the democratic diffusion of power came late. The trend towards it began in the early nineteenth century under Mahmud II. He generated a new independent sphere of law-making and insisted that justice meant equality of everyone before the law. The new centre of government, the Porte, became ascendant over the court, and new legal codes were issued and government departments created. Then, eventually, after the revolution of 1908, it was possible to get acts passed abolishing both the Sultanate and Caliphate.

The Spectrum of Belief and Unbelief in Advanced Modern Societies

Having illustrated what I mean by the two different expressions of differentiation—subcultures and specialized functions—I would like to return to the former by giving consideration now to its peak development. I refer to the characteristic spectrum of belief that advanced modern societies exhibit. Here, superstition does persist, even though it is often a kind of perversity amongst educated people who know better. Yet it may reach a quite systematic expression in beliefs about good luck and bad luck, a reliance on horoscopes, and so on. However, it is the cultism to which I have already referred, that is really the modern-world superstition. But in those more rational reaches above superstition, a range of postures is typically found to exist, all of them being different responses to the impact of reason. At one extreme we have those people who feel that the modern advances from reason demand a militant opposition to religion—we may call them the anti-religionists—and at the other extreme those who face these rational advances but who are convinced they can be reconciled with the traditional faith—and these we may call the religious conservatives. Between them are two other equally distinct positions. Abutting on the religious conservatives are the religious liberals. These are attempting the same reconciliation as the conservatives, but they are willing to concede more changes. Adjoining the anti-religionists are the unbelievers. These feel they cannot hold to religious beliefs any longer, since they cannot square them with new knowledge, but they experience no need to oppose religion actively.

It is possible that such a range of responses to the impact of reason on received beliefs has always obtained. Certainly sceptics are found in the most primitive societies. But reason has so flowered in the modern world that its compatibility with religion becomes an issue for almost everyone, and educated people consequently adopt one of the available postures with a certain self-consciousness. From the Renaissance and through the seventeenth-century blossoming of science and the eighteenth-century French Enlightenment, a tide of increasing momentum has come to us. It is a tide of confidence in the gains that must accrue from stretching the critical faculties of the mind. By now, everyone is so patently in the debt of science, technology and critical philosophy, that no one would care to deny them their claims. In eighteenth-century France, in the vocal phase of this movement, voices like Rousseau's and Voltaire's were saying that to concede these claims was to refute the claims of religion. The modern anti-religionists found their fount of inspiration here. In the nineteenth and twentieth centuries in England and America a variety of anti-religious movements appeared, all aggrieved because religion seemed to be denying the rightful claims of reason. In England, Holyoake fused French rationalism with an English reformist rationalism he inherited from Owen, to found— *Secularism.*[13]

> The word 'secular' had first appeared in Holyoake's paper 'Reasoner' in 1851 and shortly afterwards Holyoake issued a statement of 'Principles and Aims' of a body he called the Central Secular Society. In this he set down the framework of a philosophical position which he was to modify but little over the next half-century. The principle was to be the 'recognition of the Secular sphere as the province of man' and the aims were:
>
> (1) To explain that science is the sole Providence of man ...
> (2) To establish the proposition that Morals are independent of Christianity ...
> (3) To encourage men to trust Reason throughout, and to trust nothing that Reason does not establish ...
> (4) To teach men that the universal fair and open discussion of opinion is the highest guarantee of public truth ...
> (5) To claim for every man the fullest liberty of thought and

> *action compatible with possession of like liberty by every other person.*
> *(6) To maintain that, from the uncertainty as to whether the inequalities of human condition will be compensated for in another life—it is the business of intelligence to rectify them in this world; and consequently, that instead of indulging in speculative worship of supposed superior beings, a generous man will devote himself to the patient service of known inferior natures, and the mitigation of harsh destiny so that the ignorant may be enlightened and the low elevated.[14]*

The formation of the Rationalist Press Association in 1899 was one of the fruits of this movement. In the U.S.A. a parallel secularism developed in the first part of the nineteenth century, stirred up by the founding of various free-thought societies, especially in Boston and New York. (Incidentally, the introduction here of the word *secularism,* provides us with the opportunity to draw an important distinction. The suffix *-ism* is commonly used to indicate the exaltation of some attitude into a complete system of life-orientation and -organization. This is the situation in which it assumes a cultic religiosity. The term *secularism* is very appropriately reserved for that kind of development, and it can be used to distinguish it from the process of secularization, which is conceived as neutral. It was always possible for a championship of things secular to turn into *de facto* secularism, thus becoming a religion of irreligion.)

Less extreme than active opposition to religion, in which, we know, only small numbers have ever engaged, is the simple loss of religious conviction and interest—unbelief. Wilson claims it can be shown that this has become increasingly common in Europe and Britain.[15] His sketch suggests that it was overwhelmingly the most prevalent condition in 1966. For example, average Sunday attendance was less than three per cent of population in Norway and between ten and fifteen per cent in England. He adds that fewer than twenty-five per cent of the adult population of England and Wales had any real claim to "membership" in any religious denomination. To support his views on trends in religious involvement in England, he considers statistics on membership enrolments, baptisms, confirmations, Sunday school attendance of children and teachers, attendance at communion and solemnization of marriages. Most of the tables reach from the late nineteenth century to around 1960. From the evidence he draws the conclusion: "In general, there can be little doubt about the decline in church-going, church-membership, sustained religious commitment, and the general standing of the Church in society."[16] If Luckmann's idea of an invisible religion has any substance, one could not infer a general secularization from declining church life. But Wilson's evidence at least points to the erosion of a traditional approach to the sacred.

Stark and Glock, in summing up the American findings they report in *American Piety* in 1968, state a conclusion which on the face of it seems very much in keeping with Wilson's.[17]

> What then are the main features of the changing character of American Christianity? The evidence leads us to two conclusions: the religious beliefs which have been the bedrocks of Christian faith for nearly two millennia are on their way out; this may very well be the dawn of a post-Christian era.[18]

It should be pointed out, however, that Stark and Glock's data are different from Wilson's. It is the changing belief of people who are actually church members that they examined. What they are really pointing to is a transformation or liberalization of religious belief, rather than an abandonment of religious observance. One finding that arrests them, for instance, is that interdenominational switching is commoner from the conservative to the liberal churches than in the reverse direction. Furthermore, since the liberal churches are less successful than the others in generating commitment in their members, they wonder whether there might not be a continuous passage towards greater liberalism that eventually leads out of the church altogether.[19]

We are brought now to the two remaining positions on the spectrum: the liberalism and conservatism of those who hold to belief. Probably it is no great oversimplification to distinguish between them by saying that whereas they both admit reason in addition to revelation as a criterion of belief, where these seem to be in contradiction the liberal follows reason and the conservative revelation. Revelation, of course, can be variously understood; but it usually means the Bible, the church traditions or the personal tutelage of the Holy Spirit, or any combination of these. What is admitted to modern Christianity through reason is criticism of its own sources and traditions and a vast amount of relevant new knowledge about the universe, nature and man. Current knowledge about such things as the solar system, biological evolution, cultural relativism, and the unconscious mind, has simply to be accepted and built into the system of religious belief, according to the liberal. He says that if one finds internal inconsistencies in the sources of revelation, or inconsistencies between these and modern knowledge, one is obliged to do a sorting out. Because of this, liberals tend to be very discriminating about what parts of the tradition they are prepared to "keep." The beliefs that seem to go are those in miracles, the resurrection and after-life, the return of Christ, the virgin birth, the devil and eternal damnation, the infallibility of the Bible, the authority of the clergy.

The conservative, for his part, feels that religion forgoes everything if it forgoes dogmatic closure. New knowledge can indeed be grafted onto what is revealed, but if it seems to contradict that, there must be doubt about its own validity. It must be fairly obvious that the religious liberal and conservative are, respectively, the instruments of the secularizing and sacralizing imperatives in the dialectical process. The first speaks for the new information that must be coded, the second for the code that must not be fragmented. Then if we bracket these two groups, both of whom hold to religion, and set them against the other two also bracketed together—that is, the anti-religious and unbelieving—we discern the same dialectic at a different level. It is now the former pair who champion the sacralizing imperative, the latter pair the secularizing.

Before leaving this discussion of the spectrum of religious subcultures, I should add a final word on modern superstition. I said that it is mainly in cultism that this is expressed, and also that it can be a kind of perversity practised by those who know better. But this cultism is not necessarily expressed in extravagant and esoteric practices—like witches' spells, soothsaying and telepathy, for example. More often it is simply the investment of a normal interest with transcendent significance. Rotary, golf, ethical culture, mental health, a profession, home and garden, diet, philosophy, science, freemasonry, property—these and an infinite variety of things can be made into a religion. In Chapter 6 I said that one reason why cults may develop is a general lack of life-orientation and -organization. Amongst the unbelieving in phases of extreme or prolonged secularization, that lack is very prevalent. This can account, then, for the inflated significance that can be given to normal activities at such times, as much as for the perversity in trumped-up esoterics. It is as though life lived in the exclusively secular is intolerably barren, and people assuage their spiritual thirst by giving closure to anything that captivates. Their religiosity has not been extinguished, but simply dissociated from the conventional religion that secular change has now made repugnant to them.

The New Modern Religions of Natural - Need Fulfilment

Beyond the cultic reaction of a spurious closure, is the sacralizing reaction of genuine closure—the formation of a new religion. This also has occurred in the modern world as a result of the cumulative and wide-ranging secularization that has taken place. If we take a look at the general character of five of these religions—the Positivists' Religion of Humanity, Humanism, Nazism, Communism and what I shall call "Hippieism"—I think we shall begin to see what the eventual consequences of secularization are. The new information secured by reason is built into a new dogmatic system. The vision of the ideal society incorporates the new knowledge. All five of these religions stop short, in that they are religions of need fulfilment only, yet they contrast with the earlier religions shown in Figure 8 as being of that kind. The difference is that they work with a vastly more modern and scientific understanding of what man's needs are. As a consequence, they have a double difference from our traditional religions of spiritual satisfaction. One difference makes them seem superior to those religions and one makes them seem inferior. They have a strange tantalization for adherents of the traditional religions of spiritual satisfaction, and I believe that this is what accounts for it. They seem better because they are more realistic, modern and informed about man and his world; they seem inferior because they stop at natural-need fulfilment and do not penetrate to the level of spiritual satisfaction—which is what adherents of the traditional faiths have now come to expect from religion. It is because they are religions at this level that we can get the divine king theme in the divinized dictator, he being the keystone of the social order through which need fulfilment is secured.

If anyone is inclined to look on these developments as a reversal and retrogression in the modern world, since we already had spiritual religions, he should remember two things. First, this religion was espoused by sectors of the world for whom need fulfilment was still far from assured. Secondly, modern knowledge has thrust on these religions a programme of need fulfilment that earlier religions never envisioned. There have been those two pressures making the new religion necessary, then. It would seem that if we are to have a religion of spiritual satisfaction with this enlarged kind of need-satisfaction at its base the contemporary religion of spiritual satisfaction would have to be enlarged to incorporate all modern knowledge concerning nature and man. But that is the kind of question to be taken up in the Postscript. For the present we may note that to trace the roots of these new religions we have only to draw a direct line back through the Enlightenment, the scientific revolution, and the Renaissance. In contrast, all the great religions considered in the previous chapter belong to traditions originating before any of these.

The Positivists' Religion of Humanity

This legacy of modern rational thought was displayed through clear glass in the Positivists' Religion of Humanity. In nineteenth-century France, Comte prepared the complete blueprint for this religion single-handed. In finished form, as a *tour de force* of rational planning, he produced its doctrine, ethics, ritual and church organization. The only thing lacking was a capacity to light up the heart with experience—but this deficiency was crippling. It was doubtless because Comte's system was so artificial a creation of the rational man that it proved ineffective, notwithstanding its great comprehensiveness. It seems not to have had more than a few thousand followers at any time. However, it was deliberately offered as a substitute for traditional religion. Humanity, to be known as "the Great Being," was to be substituted for God as the object of worship and service. In all his actions the follower was to further the advancement of Humanity, particularly by applying the results of science. It was not expected that these or any other benefits would be applied to the service of man unless religion required it, so all areas of life were to be brought under its control. Insofar as this religion did find a following, it was from amongst educated, middle-class people, particularly professionals. Presumably, it appealed because it mediated between science and religion rather than setting them in opposition. It breathed the spirit of contemporary science and philosophy, in that it saw man evolving towards perfection, and saw it to be in his power to forward that end by applying reason to his own condition.

Under his other hat, when not officiating as high priest of the Religion of Humanity, Comte was a sociologist. This looks very much like a sociologist's religion and, in fact, part of it so resembles the modified Durkheimian view adopted in this book that I am obliged to set them side by side. How far is this "Humanity" the objective, ideal society which, I have claimed, is the eventual object of all religious veneration? If the reader applies a distinction stressed in Chapter 1, he will see first of all that it is *not* the same because this "Humanity" is simply a doctrine of it. Even as a doctrine, however, it seems to be entangled in the same unresolved ambiguity that we saw Durkheim's "society" entangled in. That is, "Humanity" is viewed in its imperfect concreteness as much as in its ideality. This is a direct implication of Comte's deliberate attempt to represent "Humanity" purely in its human quality, and shorn of every trace of the divine. Being therefore no better than the men who are called to worship it, it can hardly constrain devotion. Thus Comte cannot have it both ways. If it is "Humanity" in its concrete human character it cannot be the object of religion; if it is the object of religion, it is "Humanity" in its ideal character and therefore supernatural. Yet it is nevertheless very interesting, of course, that Comte reaches this approximation to the true idea, discerning that "Humanity" *in some way* is integral with the divine.

Humanism

Unlike the Religion of Humanity, the movement we call Humanism has no single, clear-cut system.[20] There has been a humanist philosophy abroad for some time, but in organized form it is quite a recent development, and its adherents have only an attitude in common. It is very like the Secularism of the nineteenth century in that it wants to transfer attention from God to man and from the other world to this world. The ideal for which it strives is man's complete fulfilment in this life, since it is sceptical about any other. In the U.S.A. in the 1920s a Humanist Association was formed in Chicago, its founders being mainly Unitarian theologians. This was the precursor of what eventually became the American Humanist Association, which had seventy-five local branches in 1962 and a membership of around 4,500. The British Humanist Association was founded in 1963, absorbing town and university humanist societies already in existence. It was largely a merger of the Ethical Union and Rationalist Press Association, both of which found their traditional functions displaced by a more positive concern with human fulfilment.

The followers of this movement are largely professionals, those serving people being particularly well represented: teachers, doctors, welfare workers. The evolutionary humanism of Julian Huxley has influenced the movement and some of the followers would give general endorsement to his views. In any case, the world view adopted is that made known by science, and central to it is this idea of man's evolution within nature and an anticipation of further improvement for the species. The motivation to seek the welfare of man is grounded in this. The possible means of doing it, however, are considered to be various. It is thought equally important, for example, to aid individuals' development and to remove political impediments to it. Humanists may therefore be found championing civil liberties, extending help to one another, dispensing welfare, engaging in political action, preaching humanism.

Nazism

Already in Chapter 1 Nazism, Communism and Hippieism were introduced as instances of religion. It remains for us to notice how they arose as sacralizing responses to secularization, incorporating new knowledge into a new, dogmatic closure. It has already been pointed out, in fact, that all three of them take a Darwinian view of man, anticipating that the superior strain will survive in the struggle for existence. They differ in where they see this superiority: Nazism locates it in the superior race, Communism in the superior class, Hippieism in the superior, beautiful, uninhibited people. Nazism and Communism expect to prevail by sheer physical force; Hippieism, much shrewder, by a kind of passive resistance, leading the common life where it wants it taken by ignoring contrary cues. Yet the passivity of Hippieism's resistance should not blind us to the fact that it is resistance. It has declared war, and there is as much terror in its undercutting of normal expectations as there is in Nazism and Communism.

Nazism was born in Germany from a compounded depriva-tion.[21] The sacrifices imposed by the First World War were re-warded by nothing save defeat and humiliation at the front and injustice, disorder and want at home. The Weimar Republic, which took over from the collapsed monarchy after the revolu-tion of 1918, in turn proved traitor to the people. It violated their traditional values, and it accepted the crushing terms of the Treaty of Versailles. As an alternative, National Socialism seemed like a promise of redemption. The socialism in it prom-ised an end to class inequities, the nationalism promised a new community based on nation—nation being understood as blood ties of "race" and common habitation of the land. It was pos-sible for citizens to identify with that community and give serv-ice to it, thereby transcending self. For all its ignominious end, Nazism had that radiant beginning. Millions of people drew new hope from it. It appealed to a definite majority. Most of the workers and lower middle class were for it. These were respon-sive to nationalism, but they refused it their support unless the question of social inequality was faced. They favoured socialism, but refused to give their allegiance to Marxist internationalism. Moreover, the Germans were accustomed to having their loyalty to community expressed through loyalty to the community authority. The charismatic leadership of Hitler, the peace-time working man and wartime corporal, consequently seemed to be inspired. For he gave himself so unstintingly, so utterly, to his people's need. Hear the witnesses speak:

> *What impressed me most about Hitler was the courage with which the wartime corporal attacked all evil. I felt the urge once more to be a soldier.*[22]

> *The German soul spoke to German manhood in his words. From that day on I could never violate my allegiance to Hitler. I saw his illimitable faith in his people and the desire to set them free. His conviction upheld us, whenever we weakened amidst our trials; we leaned upon him in our weari-ness.*[23]

> *We, oldtime National Socialists, did not join the S.A. for reasons of self-interest. Our feelings led us to Hitler. There was a tremendous surge in our hearts, a something that said: "Hitler, you are our man. You speak as a soldier of the front and as a man; you know the grind, you have yourself been a working man. You have lain in the mud, even as we—no big shot, but an unknown soldier. You have given your whole being, all your warm heart, to German manhood, for the well-being of Germany rather than your personal ad-vancement or self-seeking. For your innermost being will not let you do otherwise.*[24]

> *No one who has ever looked Hitler in the eye and heard him speak can ever break away from him.*[25]

Here, unequivocally expressed, is the faith that subordination to the community and its leader will secure the common need.

Communism

There has been one persistent discrepancy between Marxist theory and communist practice all along.[26] On theoretical grounds, Marx expected the industrial proletariat to be the exclusive bearers of the communist revolution and to be, following that, the new ruling class. As things transpired, in Russia, China and the other countries that turned to communism, the rural peasantry and the question of land ownership have been just as deeply involved. Indeed, the modern revolutions made in the name of communism were really celebrating the passing of feudalism more than capitalism, and they occurred where capitalism was not particularly advanced. One could say that the Marxist vision was quickly generalized beyond Marx's specific terms, and embedded once more in a very ancient tradition. It was the *general* complaint of the exploited, oppressed and underprivileged that it was heard to voice. The three distinctively Marxian themes that were left grafted on were the calls for class solidarity, class struggle and the communal ownership of property. Marx was read as saying that the exploited—whoever they are—will never be freed from oppression until they wrest the controlling power from their exploiters. But their only chance of doing it is to organize amongst themselves and, after seizing control, to keep in their joint possession forever the ownership of profit-producing property. This rallying cry for reliance on self-help *alone* set communism off from all those utopian notions of the ideal society that had preceded it. For these had left it to the propertied and intellectual élites to apply, paternalistically, whatever reason and responsibility they could in implementing reform.

In France, England and America a whole galaxy of utopian thinkers preceded the communist thinkers. Babeuf, Cabet, Saint-Simon, Fourier, Godwin, Owen, Brisbane, Greeley and Channing: there were these and many others besides.[27] But in formulating the communist ideology of self-help, Marx and Engels claimed to tap a power that utopianism never opened up. Marxists, in surveying Europe for a readiness for revolution, were clearly led on by Marx's instinct for this rising power, and were quite willing to sacrifice his theory that leadership must come from the proletariat of the countries of advanced capitalism. That class did not have to supply the necessary class dynamic, but *some* class would. The communist revolution might never have come in Russia had the Mensheviks had their way. It was they who were the classical Marxists, and they waited to see a bourgeois republic follow the czardom and, only after that, the socialist revolution. Lenin's leadership was largely directed to persuading the organized Bolsheviks that the bourgeois phase could be short-circuited. Because they were politically organized and believed him, they were able to step in and take control when Kerensky's government collapsed in anarchy in November 1917. This discrepancy between communist practice and Marxist theory is not incidental, but a matter of central importance. For it enables us to understand what communism, as practised, really is. It is a universal religion of solidarity among the materially dispossessed, whoever they be. By cooperation amongst themselves alone and by their appropriation of property communally, they truly believe, their needs will be supplied: through their achievement mankind will be relieved of material want for all time.

Hippieism

Hippieism, in contrast, is born amongst technocracy's children, deprived by it as they are of psychological rather than material needs.[28] In the very efficiency by which it works on behalf of their material need, it does violence to these other needs. Society must be structured radically differently if these needs are to be met through human cooperation—this is what they seem to be saying. Their literary spokesmen voice the protest in a number of themes, and sometimes they are more negative than constructive. Besides the Zen theme of Ginsberg, Kerouac and Watts and the expansion theme of Leary, both of which were noted in the first chapter, there is the Rousseauan-Freudian theme of Marcuse and Norman Brown, who stress freedom from cultural repressions, and the utopian theme of Paul Goodman, who stresses the need to build up one's own community of support.[29]

The following of the Hippie movement is often drawn from amongst the affluent and, as the location of leadership in the universities shows, from amongst the educated. In their communal living the Hippies try to exemplify the cooperation they approve. But so much is the material aspect of life at a discount with them, that their communes can be set up with a crass disregard for the material basis of life and consequently they are frequently short-lived. It is interesting, in fact, to compare the practical effectiveness of Communism, Nazism and Hippieism. The first two have both supplied the dynamic for whole societies. Hippieism has not done that and seems inherently incapable of it. Nor does it have any mechanism for transmission to new generations. If it outlasts one generation it will be because another generation takes it up anew. Nazism was a successful movement for less than a quarter of a century, spanning no more than two generations. The influence of Communism, on the other hand, has grown continuously for over a century.

The Incorporation of Modern Knowledge in the New Religions

The modern knowledge that is built into Nazism is partly biological and medical, partly sociological and economic. It exploits the ideas of *Gemeinschaft* (community) before self, charismatic leadership, the abolition of classes, the purity and superiority of race. This is augmented by machine technology, especially in weaponry, which is the extension of man's biological powers of survival. The knowledge built into Communism is predominantly economic, but there is also sociological knowledge regarding class structure and class dynamics, and psychological knowledge concerning the authentic and alienated self. The knowledge built into Hippieism is largely psychological. The importance of emotional relief through uninhibited expression is quite fundamental to the attitude taken. This subculture, indeed, is very much an extension into adulthood of permissive child-rearing theory. The freedom to give way to physical attractions and express sex, to enjoy sensory experience and explore the unconscious through drugs, is all part of this.

What is arresting about all three of these positions is the attempt to build a totalitarian view of man and his world at the level of the needs which the new knowledge in each case expounded. In all cases it is a low level—biology, psychology, economics, sociology, engineering. There is nothing here about the man who needs intellectual activity to satisfy curiosity, order to give him aesthetic repose, creation to satisfy creativeness or civilization to give him dignity—and certainly nothing about his need for spiritual release. This is what gives these movements such an aspect of primitivism, and even of barbarousness, to observers used to these refinements. Yet the attempt to build a totalitarian system exclusive of those benefits was nevertheless made, and it seems that the only way to explain it is that new knowledge so fired men's imaginations with a vision of life's possibilities—even at this level—that religions emerged as the attempt to realise them without delay.

Without delay? The course of events does suggest that there is some kind of limit to how much secularization can be tolerated at a time. The open mind must at that point be closed. One has to tie into a bundle all the loose threads now in hand; one cannot afford to wait till they are all in. If we bring in the Religion of Humanity and Humanism again, and set those two religions beside the three we have just considered, the former two would appear to take greater account of man's higher needs. They view man more in his full stature. They also view him more in his collective completeness, since they do not divide mankind into warring parts. But what is of overwhelming importance is the centrality of the evolutionary vision in all five of them. Man's needs and possibilities are suddenly seen in a new light because of this way of viewing him. While the conservatives and liberals in the traditional faiths were debating whether evolution could possibly be accepted, "unbelievers" on every side were envisioning what could be expected in view of its presumed truth.

Notes, Chapter 8

1. Emile Durkheim, *The Elementary Forms of the Religious Life*, pp. 389-414.
2. *Ibid.*, p. 409.
3. Harold Fallding, "Secularization and the Sacred and Profane," p. 355.
4. Robert Redfield, *The Folk Culture of Yucatan*, Chicago: University of Chicago Press, 1941; Howard Becker, *Through Values to Social Interpretation, Essays on Social Contexts, Actions, Types, and Prospects*.
5. *Ibid.*, p. 68.
6. Harold Fallding, "Secularization and the Sacred and Profane," pp. 358-360.
7. Harold Fallding, *The Sociological Task*, p. 96.
8. Yang gives an account of several waves of secularization occurring in pre-communist China. See C. K. Yang, *Religion in Chinese Society, A Study of Contemporary Social Functions of Religion and Some of Their Historical Factors*, pp. 341-77.
9. Emile Durkheim, *The Elementary Forms of the Religious Life*.
10. C. K. Yang, *op. cit.*, pp. 294-340.
11. Joachim Wach, *Sociology of Religion*, Phoenix edition, Chicago: University of Chicago Press, 1962.
12. J. Milton Yinger, *The Scientific Study of Religion*, pp. 408-56.
13. For a detailed account see Colin Campbell, *Toward a Sociology of Irreligion*, Macmillan; London, 1971.
14. *Ibid.*, pp. 48-49.
15. Bryan R. Wilson, *Religion in Secular Society, A Sociological Comment*, London: C. A. Watts & Co. Ltd., 1966, pp. ix-xix, 1-18.
16. *Ibid.*, p. 18.
17. Rodney Stark and Charles Y. Glock, *American Piety: The Nature of Religious Commitment*, Berkeley and Los Angeles: University of California Press, 1968.
18. *Ibid.*, p. 205
19. *Ibid.*, p. 203
20. For details see Colin Campbell, *op. cit.*, pp. 89-96; Susan Budd, "The Humanist Societies: the Consequences of a Diffuse Belief System," in *Patterns of Sectarianism, Organisation and Ideology in Social and Religious Movements*, edited by Bryan R. Wilson, London: Heinemann, 1967, pp. 377-405.
21. For details on the rise of nazism see Theodore Abel, *The Nazi Movement, Why Hitler Came to Power*, New York: Atherton Press, 1966.
22. *Ibid.*, p. 152.
23. *Ibid.*, pp. 152-3.
24. *Ibid.*, p. 153.
25. *Ibid.*, p. 153.
26. For a detailed account of the development of communism see Harry W. Laidler, *History of Socialism, A Comparative Survey of Socialism, Communism, Trade Unionism, Cooperation, Utopianism, and Other Systems of Reform and Reconstruction*, London: Routledge & Kegan Paul, 1968.
27. See Harry W. Laidler, *op. cit.*
28. For detailed accounts of the Hippie culture see Theodore Roszak, *op. cit.*; Michel Lancelot, *Je Veux Regarder Dieu en face, Vie, mort et resurrection des Hippies*, Paris: Editions Albin Michel, 1968; Delbert L.

Earisman, *Hippies in Our Midst, The Rebellion Beyond Rebellion,* Philadelphia: Fortress Press, 1968; Kenneth Westhues, *Society's Shadow: Studies in the Sociology of Countercultures,* Toronto: McGraw-Hill Ryerson, 1972.

29. Herbert Marcuse, *Reason and Revolution: Hegel and the Rise of Social Theory,* Oxford: Oxford University Press, 1941; *Soviet Marxism: A Critical Analysis,* London: Routledge & Kegan Paul, 1958; *Eros and Civilization, A Philosophical Inquiry into Freud,* New York: Vintage Books, 1962; *One-Dimensional Man,* Boston: Beacon Press, 1964; Norman O. Brown, *Life Against Death: The Psychoanalytical Meaning of History,* Middletown, Conn.: Wesleyan University Press, 1959; *Love's Body,* New York: Random House, 1966; Frederick S. Perls, Ralph E. Hefferline and Paul Goodman, *Gestalt Therapy,* New York: Dell (a Delta Book), 1951; *Growing up Absurd,* New York: Random House, 1960; *The Empire City,* New York: Macmillan, 1964.

The Religion of the Future

To ask whether ideals or the material conditions of life are the primary determinants of action is hardly a clever question. Yet an unconscionable amount of time and attention has been given to it in sociology. Moreover, it has been made to appear that different answers must divide their proponents as irreconcilably as God and the Devil. Since Marx and Engels showed that change in material conditions changed the organization of work and the class structure, and since Max Weber subsequently showed that the Calvinist ideal of life changed these very same things, there have been people who wondered which was right and some, even, who made it a matter of honour to take sides. Yet a moment's reflection on the nature of human action shows how false an opposition this is. In the first place, it is not to the actual conditions of his life but to his definition of them that man's action is a response. His understanding of his circumstances will provide a set of constraints that restrict his choices. Yet there is still no inevitable response that any and every man must then make.

For, given the restraints imposed by their material conditions, men allow themselves to ask what are the ideal possibilities in their situation as given. This is how it could happen that, given the material conditions making a capitalist economy possible, men could conceive a life-ethic as an ideal that would maximize the possibilities of satisfaction under those conditions: first, things like new wealth and technology calling for a new work organization, then a new ethic to help secure the requisite work organization. Is there anything either strange, or unworthy, or contradictory, in the dénouement? The two sources of change, each of them effecting modifications in the structure of human action, are equally real. Men may act differently because they begin to perceive that material conditions have changed; they may act differently because they begin to conceive a different ideal for taking full advantage of the material conditions existing. Throughout this book I have been saying that the imperative for these guiding ideals is what supplies the dynamic of religion. The religions that mankind has seen emerge thus far can all be viewed as so many steering mechanisms that guided men under differing material conditions of life. It is a curious evidence of the indispensability of ideal factors that Marx, who stressed the sufficiency of material factors for inducing social change, was actually instrumental in formulating the communist ideal. It is as though he was better than his principles, unconsciously perceiving that the material merely poses the question of how we are to act if it is to be pressed into the service of an ideal life.

Can it be doubted that communism is the significant religious development of modern times? The challenge it throws to contemporary spiritual religion is that the latter should be equally "modern" in its base. That is to say, it should give recognition to the current material conditions of life, to modern economic production and to modern knowledge concerning man's needs and the means of securing them. Only a religion that says Yes to these things as facts, even while it says No to their being sufficient in themselves, is likely to compel the allegiance of populations of highly educated people. As traditions, all the spiritual religions we know pre-dated modern science and the modern technology and economy. To remain viable they have had to enter a scrambling race to plug into these new resources that are now available for human betterment. To say it in another way, they are having to graft an enlarging natural good onto the spiritual good they espouse. If they succeed, the secularization now upon us could prove to be a passing wave, and radiantly new religion come again.

But, even if they adopt the whole secular warehouse into their cosmos, will they survive intact? Or will they be so transformed as not to be the same thing at all? Either eventuality is possible, yet it seems it would hardly matter which prevailed. While those with a vested interest in the distinctive traditions might make it an overwhelming consideration to be, say, "a true Christian," "a true Jew," "a true Buddhist," or "a true Moslem," this scarcely seems to be the obligation that the divinity has ever required. What has been required is that men should be faithful to the light that was given them, and thereby live in faith and humility as "true men." Like Wilfred Cantwell Smith, I would consider the question of truth in religion never to have been "Which religion is true?," but "Which way of practising religion is the authentic way?"[1] Those who are faithful to the light that is given them are open to more light—and at critical times that new light has come.

To be thus open, instead of being set as the stout defender of a received tradition, has probably never been more necessary than now. At least in the West, where Christianity has been the dominant faith, it does appear that we are in a trough like the one between the Old and New Testaments, when one tradition was exhausted and men were tarrying for another to be born. The early Christians claimed that fellow Jews who closed their minds to new revelation were cutting themselves off from refreshing and renewal. No one more than Christians, then, should be aware of the benefits of keeping religion open-ended. Yet so many contemporary Christians feel threatened by the very idea that their faith might possibly be transcended by a new faith. To them, historic Christianity has to be defended as the final and ultimate truth. But do they not thereby place themselves in the shoes of the Jews who resisted the Christian revelation?

What was added by Christianity was the decisive and categorical call to spiritual satisfaction—epitomized in crucifixion to the world, resurrection and new creation. One might well wonder how this could be exceeded, or why it would ever need to be. I think it is simply because it bequeathes its inheritors the obligation to work out the implications that are in it for a later day. If Christianity is succeeded by a faith that leads beyond it, that faith would not have to deny the Christian affirmation but could underline and enlarge it. One would expect it to make announcements in relation to Christianity that are comparable to those Christianity made in relation to Judaism. That is, it would give a new, fairly precise and in some ways unexpected meaning to some ambiguities in the earlier tradition. One would venture the opinion that it is around the eschatological hope that most of the lingering ambiguity in Christianity centres. Will the new religion give a clarification of this, making plainer than before what is meant by the cosmic Christ who will assimilate all things to himself?

Presumably, that clarification will include a statement on evolution and the material factors that communism has taken into account. When I say this, I do not mean that I would anticipate any kind of simplistic summing of the two—the popular idea that man needs material goods as well as spiritual satisfaction. This much Christianity has always known—and, as we saw, was wise enough to know as well the second will never be secured unless the first is subordinated to it. New spiritual religion might well be found insisting as much as communism that no man's property is his own and that a condition of spiritual solidarity is a just distribution of rewards. Yet, when each man has his just share of this world's goods, what good will it do him in and of itself? There is, then, the possibility of spiritual starvation in material saturation. To obviate that is the demanding task of the religion of the future. The material good—or that more inclusive thing which I have called above "the natural good"—might indeed be made secure for every man once and for all. But when that has happened it will have to be cast in an expressive role. By this I mean that, if men are to take advantage of the release from sin and death that Christianity was able to secure, their natural world—which dies—will have to be made to dance and sing in worship. Men will have to learn how to make an offering out of it and let it go. They will have to experience health and well-being, possessions, love, learning and cultivation, leisure and pleasure as worship.

Notes, Postscript

1. Wilfred Cantwell Smith, *Questions of Religious Truth*, New York: Charles Scribner's Sons, 1967.

Name Index

Subject Index